Credible
Christianity

Credible Christianity

The Gospel in Contemporary Society

Hugh Montefiore

WILLIAM B. EERDMANS PUBLISHING COMPANY
GRAND RAPIDS, MICHIGAN

© 1993 Hugh Montefiore
First published 1993 by
Mowbray
A Cassell imprint
Villiers House, 41/47 Strand, London WC2N 5JE
387 Park Avenue South, New York NY 10016

This edition published 1994
through special arrangement with Mowbray by
Wm. B. Eerdmans Publishing Co.
255 Jefferson Ave. S.E., Grand Rapids, Michigan 49503

Printed in the United States of America

00 99 98 97 96 95 94   7 6 5 4 3 2 1

Library of Congress Cataloging-in-Publication Data

Montefiore, Hugh.
  Credible Christianity: the Gospel in contemporary society /Hugh Montefiore.
    p.   cm.
  Includes bibliographical references and indexes.
  ISBN 0-8028-3768-9 (cloth)
  1. Theology. 2. Apologetics — 20th century. I. Title.
  BR118.M574   1994
  230 — dc20   94-16689
                                                    CIP

CONJUGI CONJUNX CARISSIMAE

OLIM ADJUVATRICI

NUNC ADJUVAMENTUM REQUIRENTI

A.G.P.

Contents

formulation – post-Enlightenment thinking – a different category of interpretation – grace and spirit – the sinlessness of Jesus – Jesus the revelation of God – the risen Christ – Mary, the mother of Jesus – Jesus the Son of God who brings us to the Father

– rigorism – baptism and confirmation – the meaning of baptism for today – the eucharist – the Last Supper – the eucharistic action – the presence of Christ in the eucharist – the president of the eucharist – other sacraments – the need for sacraments

The beginnings of the ministry – the apostolic ministry today – apostolic succession – the theology of episcopacy – the theology of the priesthood and the diaconate – the gender of a priest

New Testament expectations of the Last Things – the end of the world – death – resurrection – resurrection, not survival or immortality – purgatory – reincarnation? – prayer for the dead and the invocation of saints – salvation outside the Church – hell – heaven

Ethics and the Gospel – personal behaviour – personal morality – the criteria of Christian morality – moral philosophy – moral theology – objective and subjective criteria – behaviour of corporate groups and states – the duty of government – Liberation theology – reasons for Christian political involvement – ethical criteria of the Kingdom of God

Faith and belief – worship – the eucharist – the eucharist and symbolism – charismatic worship – prayer – meditation – the sacrament of the present moment – providence, miracle and vocation – spirituality

The provisional nature of theology

Preface

This book is an attempt to give an honest account of the Christian faith which is soundly based academically but readable by a non-expert. For this reason I have kept the names of almost all theologians out of the main text of the book, although I have given references to the more important in the notes to each chapter. I have also included references to my earlier books, where particular subjects have been discussed more fully than can be done within the confines of this book.

I hope that the book will be perceived as standing within the mainstream of Christian tradition, yet at the same time interpreting that tradition in the light of contemporary understanding without discarding anything essential. It seems to me inevitable that, nearly two thousand years after Christ, the way in which we express Christian doctrine today must be different from the way it was expressed in the early days of the Christian Church. In 1992 I edited a book entitled *The Gospel and Contemporary Culture* in which the presuppositions of important academic disciplines were examined (and in many respects found wanting), when analysed in the light of the Christian Gospel. This was necessarily a somewhat negative undertaking, in as much as it showed up contemporary failings. At the same time I affirmed that the Gospel needs fresh inculturation in every age. This is my attempt to do this as the Church approaches the second millennium after Christ. Readers will find more references to the natural and human sciences than are usual in works of systematic theology. This is because I believe that theology today tends to be divorced from today's world, where we think in contemporary categories. If Christianity is to be credible today, it must be expressed in the images and thought forms of today as well as in contemporary language. I have quoted from the Scriptures from a variety of translations as suits each context, but mostly from the New English Bible and the Revised Standard Version, and occasionally in my own translation.

This book is not written for a particular church, but I am an Anglican, which may partly account for my theological method. I dislike labels, whether catholic or evangelical or liberal. I feel free to choose from the riches offered by all schools of churchmanship. I hope that members of particular churches will not be offended by my frankness when I have had, on occasion, to dissent from their doctrines. Ecumenical *politesse* today tends to prevent theologians from speaking their minds. By this reserve, they actually hinder rather than help the ecumenical process.

Systematic theology is hardly an indigenous Anglican product! But if Christianity is to be credible today, it has to be attempted. I hope that those who do not find my version credible will give us the benefit of theirs. Meanwhile, I put forward this volume with due modesty, 'lest nothing be said'.

I am grateful to all who have helped me in this undertaking, and especially those who have inspired my thinking over the years. I would like to thank Provost David Edwards for suggesting that I write the book, and Ruth McCurry of Mowbray for encouraging me. I am especially grateful to Professor Russell Stannard, who has read through the chapter on Creation, and to Fr John Coventry SJ and Dr David Edwards, who have read through the entire manuscript and have made many helpful criticisms and suggestions. But of course I remain responsible for all I have written.

Authors commonly in their prefaces thank their wives for their support during the writing of a book. Unfortunately my wife's increasing incapacity does not allow me to do this here, but I would like to pay a heartfelt tribute to Elisabeth for her wonderful support and loving forbearance ever since I started to read theology nearly half a century ago, without which this book could never have been written.

Hugh Montefiore

Feast of the Conversion of St Paul 1993

chapter 1

Introduction

Faith and belief

Faith in God is the response of the whole person (or as much of the whole person as can be made available) to the mysterious Being who created and renews and sustains us as we journey through life in a world which is strange and perplexing and yet also wonderful and fascinating. Faith as such is not confined to religious people. Marriage, for example, is built on the personal faith which a couple have in each other. Friends have faith in one another. Life becomes quite impossible if we cannot have faith in anyone. Those who commit themselves to any system, whether religious or non-religious, must have faith in it. The personal faith of a Christian only differs from the personal faith that one person may have in another in as much as it is directed towards God and Christ.

Belief is the attempt to understand that faith,[1] and to express it in a reasoned and rounded manner which is internally coherent (or as internally coherent as can be achieved), which corresponds to experience and which also takes into account a contemporary understanding of our world. Faith is personal to an individual, but at the same time it is upheld by and shared with others both past and present, without whom an individual's personal faith would be impossible. Belief is a statement of that faith which is also dependent on others. It draws on thinking which others have developed, it shares in the religious tradition to which a person belongs and which has moulded and modified the beliefs of that individual.[2]

It is necessary to begin this book by mentioning personal faith, because a statement of Christian belief which is so systematized that it omits the personal element is second-hand and defective.[3] In any case, the way we think about God and about Christ is affected by our prayers and the way in which we live the Christian life. The immediacy of the 'I–Thou relationship', which is the stuff of personal faith, comes before the more objective approach of the 'I–It relationship', which is the language of Christian belief.[4] (In fact, statements which we intend to be regarded as objective often contain some personal element hidden within them.) Every person is unique, with her or his own personal history and experiences and set of attitudes, and so each one of us will express our beliefs somewhat differently. All churches make allowances for such differences, although the Anglican tradition to which I belong has, I believe, been particularly generous in this respect.

Belief and culture

In many parts of the world the energies of Christians (and others) are taken up almost wholly with gaining sufficient sustenance to keep themselves and their families alive; and the function of their faith is to liberate them in some measure from the oppression with which their lives are burdened.[5] The very fact that the present writer now has sufficient leisure to attempt a rounded statement of belief is indicative of the culture to which he belongs. To this extent this book is conditioned by Western culture in the last decade of the twentieth century. However it is not to be dismissed on that account. All writing is conditioned by the culture in which its author has lived.[6] No one can write a statement of belief which is valid for all time and in all places. Different cultures produce differing climates of thought as well as different insights into truth and different symbolic imagery. The criterion by which a statement of belief should be judged is not only its adequacy to the authentic Gospel but also its adequacy for the culture in which it is produced.[7]

Our thinking is also to some extent conditioned by our own personal situation within the culture in which we live. The present writer's theology has been affected by his Jewishness within a predominantly Gentile Church. He is a married man with children, and this is bound to colour his presentation of the Christian faith, if only by the analogies that can be made between marriage and the Christian life. Again, he served during the 1939–45 war, and the memory of its horrors and of the generosity of fellow soldiers cannot but colour his presentation of human nature. Lecturing and teaching in an academic setting has sharpened both his search for truth and his realization that many extraneous factors often distort that search. Constant attendance on a loved one with Alzheimer's forces him to confront the theological issues of sickness and suffering. Having served as a bishop, especially in a church with a broad spectrum of belief and practice, is likely to influence his views about theological pluralism. One of the important roles of a bishop is to 'guard the faith'. How can search for the truth be combined with guardianship of the faith? Pastoral experience points to the need to speak to the condition and needs of people as they live in today's world, and so to seek contemporary ways of expressing the faith. That faith is not a fossilized body of doctrine. Exploration is needed to deepen the understanding of our faith in the light of contemporary knowledge, without jettisoning any of its essentials. These matters are mentioned here not for their intrinsic interest, but as illustrations of the ways in which real life affects theology.

Revelation

There can be no genuine belief in God unless he discloses himself: otherwise, all would be mere speculation. There can be no actual revelation unless God opens our eyes to the truth of his self-disclosure. The mode by which God reveals himself has been a matter of sharp disagreement. Nonetheless, questions about revelation are so primary that the subject must be tackled at the outset of this enquiry. (I refer to God here and throughout this book as 'he' not because God is male, but because tradition prescribes the masculine pronoun in a reference to the Divine. See pp. 130f.)

It used to be thought that some truths, such as the existence of God, could be apprehended by the light of reason, while other truths, such as the Blessed Trinity, required to be revealed in a different manner.[8] This distinction between 'natural' and 'revealed' theology is no longer generally acceptable, for two reasons. In the first place, the argument that truths about God can be discerned by the light of reason has very properly been contested. Agnostics and atheists may be thought to be lacking in judgement, but they are not lacking in reason compared with those who believe in God. They are often more intelligent, but they employ their reason with different presuppositions and assumptions, and so they arrive at different conclusions from those of theists.[9] The famous Five Ways by which St Thomas Aquinas thought he had proved the existence of God are not proofs at all, for it is a requirement of any proof that it cannot be flawed on logical grounds. At best they point to probabilities. They should be understood as arguments for those who are already believers (or crypto-believers) by which their implicit or actual belief can be strengthened.[10] It is still possible to build 'revealed theology' on the basis of 'natural theology' but the latter can only point to probabilities rather than certainties.

There are those who deny the possibility of finding out truths of God by the light of reason, because humanity in its natural state is 'fallen', and as a result they believe that there is no point of contact (or *Anknüpfungspunkt*, as the German theologians put it) between God and man. 'Fallen humanity' is no longer in the image of God (see p. 151). According to this view, only through the saving grace of Christ can God reveal himself.[11] The Word of God comes vertically down, as it were, and contains within itself its own authenticity and authority. This speaks to a person in a way which enables a response.

There are several difficulties about this viewpoint. In the first place, modern knowledge of primitive humanity provides no evidence of mankind living in 'original righteousness' before the 'Fall'. And 'fallen' people do seem to find a real disclosure of God in the natural world, through beauty or goodness, through the experience of human love and through spiritual experiences in which they become conscious of the divine. Nor can it be plausibly maintained that this God of whom they seem to be aware has nothing in common with the Father of our Lord Jesus Christ. It may be an inchoate and undeveloped experience of God, and it may be in some respects mistaken and erroneous; but nonetheless it is a real experience which can develop into the fullness of Christian faith. There is another difficulty in holding this very limited view of revelation. If the Word of God speaks to a person only through Christ in a way which carries within itself its own authenticity and authority, then there is no means of distinguishing this from other truth-claims made on behalf of other faiths, religious or non-religious, which are also said to contain within themselves their own authority and authenticity. Claims of this kind may be totally convincing to the person concerned, and totally unconvincing to others.

According to the old view of 'revealed theology' God's self-disclosure to man was made through written propositional statements which are to be found in the Scriptures. However, the rise of modern criticism of the Bible has stimulated a different theology of revelation, usually described as 'general' and 'special' revelation. On such a view, God does not offer truths about himself: he offers himself. It follows that there is no such thing as revealed truth. There are truths of revelation, that is to say, propositions which express the results of correct thinking concerning revelation; but these are not themselves directly revealed.[12] Such a view, however attractive, also has its difficulties, not least in deciding the boundaries which divide general from special revelation; but it is an improvement on the earlier concept. God reveals himself generally through his world. He is present within his whole universe, and he mediates that presence in many ways: through the beauty of the natural world and its elegance uncovered by physics and chemistry, a beauty of which poets, sculptors, composers and painters have caught a vision, and also through people and through events. Christians and Jews both believe that he specially revealed himself through his dealings with the Jews whom he had chosen for a special purpose, and Christians see the culmination of this self-disclosure in the life of Jesus and the work of the Holy Spirit and the creation of the Church. Revelation to be apprehended requires not just the occurrence of special events, but the coincidence of both special events and their inspired interpretation. We find these in the pages of Holy Scripture.

The Bible

In all Christian traditions (except for the most radical) the Bible plays a very large part. Most religions have their own corpus of sacred literature which their adherents regard in a special light, and Christianity is no exception. For some the Bible, both Old and New Testaments, is regarded as literally the Word of God, dictated by the Holy Spirit in the same kind of way as Muslims believe that the Qur'an was written by God. Only a very few Christians believe that all its injunctions must be kept, but many more consider that the two Testaments are absolutely true. Often this belief used to extend to the translation of the King James English version, although such a view properly relates to the words of the language in which the Scriptures were originally written. 'Fundamentalist' is a word originally applied to people who hold fast to what they believe are fundamental Christian beliefs, and among these is the 'inerrancy' of the Bible (i.e. the inability of its authors to make mistakes) or its 'infallibility' (the absence in it of any error).

The doctrine of biblical inerrancy seems inherently improbable, for two reasons. Firstly, the Scriptures contain what seem to be evident errors and contradictions (although great ingenuity has been applied to explain these away). Secondly, the books of the Old and New Testaments did not all gain their place within the 'canon', or list of approved books, as soon as they were written. The Old Testament canon was not closed until late in the Apostolic Age, and the New Testament canon was not finally closed until the fourth century. If all the Bible's contents were inerrant, one would have thought that this would have become apparent within a much shorter period. People who hold views of biblical inerrancy tend to mistrust church tradition, because they believe that they have all that they need in the Bible. But in fact no claim for the inerrancy of the canon of Scripture is ever made within the Bible itself. That belief actually belongs to church tradition, and a minority tradition at that, which is no longer part of the official beliefs of the mainstream churches.

At the opposite extreme to the doctrine of biblical inerrancy, the Scriptures are regarded as inspired only in so far as they are inspiring. This is a purely subjective and therefore unsatisfactory point of view and, as individuals differ greatly in what they regard as inspiring, it only leads to confusion.

The Old Testament, as its name implies, was written for the People of the old covenant. ('Covenant' means compact or agreement, in this case between God and Abraham. God takes the initiative for the covenant, and sets the terms of the agreement, which are for the benefit of the other parties involved.) The Old Testament is the Bible of the Jews, although Christians have tended to regard it as their own personal property. The New Testament was written within the Church for the Church. The Bible as a whole has very great authority because, although it took a long time for its contents to be settled, there was in the end a consensus about them, apart from the Apocrypha (those parts of the Jewish Scriptures which were written in Greek). The authority of the Bible is not intrinsic to its contents, but depends on the Church which authorized it. The central message of the Bible is the record of divine revelation, and so it contains a crucial message for all Christians. But the biblical canon as a whole, in so far as its authors were not miraculously preserved from error, and since they wrote within the limitations of their age and culture, is not supremely authoritative for Christian belief. It needs to be interpreted alongside the other sources of authority which we shall shortly examine. In the Anglican tradition Scripture has an important limiting authority, in as much as anything which 'cannot be proved by most certain warrants of Holy Scripture is not to be regarded as necessary for salvation' (Article VI of the Church of England's Thirty-Nine Articles of Religion agreed in 1562). This is not to say that everything in Scripture is true, but it is to affirm that Scripture contains the essentials of the Christian faith, even if these need reinterpretation in the language and thought forms of each succeeding generation. And it specifically precludes the adulteration of the faith by the inclusion of additional beliefs that are not essential to it.

If it is believed that revelation in the Scriptures is simply confined to the events which they describe together with their inspired interpretation, this would mean that large parts of the Bible could not be regarded as revelatory, since these parts do not refer to events. There is a problem here, because it is not always clear whether the authors of biblical books intended the parts that appear as a record of events to be considered as historical in the modern sense of the word. (For example, in the book of Jonah, a great fish swallows up Jonah, and then after three days regurgitates him alive. This may have been intended as *haggadah*, a moral tale in the Jewish tradition cast into the form of a narrative about God caring for the Gentiles; and Jonah being swallowed by a fish may have been meant symbolically for Israel being swallowed up by world empires, but surviving to preach repentance to the nations.) Furthermore, if revelation is confined to these events, provided that the key of inspired interpretation is to hand, the Scriptures become dispensable if more accurate accounts of the actual events, or more probable reconstructions, can be found elsewhere. This is not to deny that key events may be revelatory, but it suggests that revelation in the Scriptures should not be regarded as confined to events and their inspired interpretation.

Similar difficulties appear if revelation is assumed to be confined solely to the saving activity of Christ. It is easier for us to hold that God discloses himself generally in the world of nature and in normal human intercourse, and that he has also specially revealed himself to those whom he has chosen; in the Old Testament to his chosen people, and in the New Testament supremely through Jesus and his earliest apostles. (Later we shall enquire whether such interaction with God's world is compatible with what we believe about his nature and being; see pp. 124–8.) The mode of this 'special' revelation is varied. God reveals himself through people who have spoken or written in an inspired manner about specially revelatory events or other experiences of God. Their writing may be in poetry or prose, it may be in moral or spiritual terms, it may be by telling stories or by making laws to meet particular situations. Statements are propositional in form, and propositions are necessary if we are to think about moral and spiritual matters. But caution is needed about reliance on particular verses of the Bible. The book of Job, taken as a whole, is an inspired story which illuminates the problem of suffering which is felt by all sensitive believers in God; but that does not mean that we can take isolated propositions from the book, and declare them to be revealed truth. Inspired insight can be gained not only through such stories, but also through symbolic imagery (such as Christ as the vine and ourselves as the branches, in the Fourth Gospel). These images can illuminate the imagination and influence the subconscious mind.[13] This is not to claim that all the Bible is equally inspired, or of equal importance. Some passages are written in such general terms that they hold good as they stand for later generations with very different cultures; but for the most part they need not only to be translated into the language of posterity, but also to be expressed in thought forms and imagery appropriate to each particular culture.

Despite this necessary inculturation, the Bible still provides an authoritative (but by no means infallible) guide for later generations. There is a sense in which the Scriptures provide only secondary revelation: God's primary self-disclosure is in the actual events and through the historical people recorded in the Bible. Yet this does not preclude a degree of inspiration on the part of the biblical authors, nor does it detract from the proper authority of the Bible. But it does save us from the kind of idolatry that worships the Bible rather than God whose activity and inspiration it records.

Tradition

Tradition is a word which may be used in two somewhat different senses. It can describe the process of handing on the Church's way of life and beliefs down the ages from the first Christian century to the twentieth, a process which needs fresh evaluation in each generation. It can also mean the living tradition, derived from the past but contemporary with us now, which an authoritative church (such as the Roman Catholic and the Orthodox churches) teaches through its *magisterium* in the present. We shall deal with the phrase in the latter sense when we come to consider the nature of the Church (see p. 177): here we use it in the former sense.

While we naturally make our statements of Christian belief in today's language, thought forms and imagery, we need great caution before we deviate from the fundamental beliefs of Christian tradition. For example, while today's beliefs about Christian revelation may be more complex (and, as we think, more sophisticated) than those of earlier times, we must not discard the tradition found in the Scriptures which have been central to Christian belief down the centuries. We are not initiating a new religion, but participating in a living stream of faith which began before us and which will continue after us. We have no right to claim that we are wiser than our fathers. We have no reason to believe that the foundation truths of Christianity have been hidden from them and recently disclosed to us. Without our Christian predecessors there would not have been any Christian faith for us to inherit. Our Christian life is lived in continuity with theirs. We may have access to new insights which appear to lead us closer to the truth than those which were enjoyed in the past, but it would be wise to regard these insights as provisional, holding good only for us within the time and culture in which we live.

The claims of tradition upon us are all the greater when they come with the attestation of the whole Church. For this reason the ecumenical Creeds of the Church (the Apostles' Creed and the Creed commonly called Nicene) have particular authority, though we may regret their preoccupation with certain aspects of the faith to the exclusion of others, and in particular their total disregard for what Jesus called 'the weightier matters of the law': mercy, judgement and faith (Matt. 23.23). They were formulated in this way in order to face what were perceived as contemporary threats to the Church's faith. Their authority is such that, far from discarding them, we rightly continue to use them in worship; but we have to interpret them in accordance with our contemporary understanding, which may result in accepting as symbolic clauses which originally were intended as literal (e.g. the return of Jesus on earth to judge the living and the dead). In this way we show our genuine continuity with the past, but at the same time we retain our own integrity today by the way in which we interpret them.[14]

The findings of the Councils of the Church which are commonly known as 'ecumenical' (which originally meant 'worldwide') have also a special claim to acceptance, especially the findings of those Councils which were held before the great schisms between the Eastern and Western Churches, and (later) of the Reformation. When, however, the historical context of these early Councils is examined, it becomes clear that they were not always so 'ecumenical' as claimed. For example, there were several important churches that found themselves unable to accept the 'ecumenical' Definition which was agreed at Chalcedon in AD 451. These early ecumenical Councils were for the most part preoccupied with Christology. Their thought forms, derived mostly from Greek philosophy, are largely alien to people today. It is sometimes claimed that such Councils were miraculously preserved from error. When the political and ecclesiastical backgrounds against which they were held is examined, such a claim involves an extraordinarily high doctrine of providence. According to Article XXI of the Church of England's Thirty-Nine Articles, when General Councils (that is, Councils of the whole Church) take place, 'for as much as they can be an assembly of men whereof all be not governed with the Spirit and the Word of God, they may err and sometimes have erred, even in things pertaining to God'. It would be strange if infallibility were to be given to Councils when it was never claimed either by Jesus himself or by the Apostles in the early Church. Nonetheless, ecumenical Councils, being the considered outcome of church deliberation and accepted as such by our predecessors, have a very considerable weight of authority, in the sense that great caution is needed before we overturn their findings.

We rightly attach this importance to tradition. Yet the very fact that Christian people before us have felt the need to interpret the Christian faith afresh for their generation should encourage us to do the same for ours. Christian doctrine is not to be fossilized for all time in earlier dogmatic statements. All doctrine is necessarily partial and provisional, because people of each age can only grasp those aspects of the truth which are appropriate to the culture in which they live. We should not accept on mere authority, within the internal forum of our own conscience, aspects of Christian doctrine which on other grounds seem to us demonstrably untrue. This leads us to consider the role of experience and reason in our attempt to formulate our Christian beliefs.

Experience

Nobody would be concerned about the formulation of their faith unless they had some personal experience which had given rise to this concern. As we have already noted, an 'I–Thou relationship' is primary and an 'I–It relationship' secondary. There is of course a great variety of human experience, both in our own personal lives, and when we compare this with that of other individuals. In particular our experience is shaped by the culture in which we live, by the temperament we have inherited and by our relationships with other people. There have been those who have regarded 'God-consciousness' as the goal of religion;[15] but formal theology has often fought shy of regarding religious experience as important in the formulation of religious belief, partly because its boundaries are difficult to define, partly because experience is sometimes equated with emotion which is by its nature unstable (and religious feelings are regarded as inferior to religious concepts), and partly because experience is subjective, and may therefore be thought to be the product of the human brain without any foundation in reality.

Yet there is bound to be a subjective element in all religion, because it is about God's relationship to ourselves, and we do not know God as he is in himself, but only in so far as he is in relationship with human beings. Our knowledge of God is personal rather than objective knowledge. (This statement presupposes a particular theory of knowledge which is discussed later in this chapter.) In personal knowledge feelings play an influential part. These are different from concepts, but that does not imply that they are necessarily opposed to them. Feelings often break through from our unconscious selves, and for this reason they are important. If our faith is the response of the whole person to God, then it is bound to include our feelings, because they constitute an essential aspect of what it is to be a human being. Attempts to exclude all feeling suggest a narrowing of faith, and hence a reduced formulation of Christian belief.

It is certainly difficult to determine precisely where religious experience begins and ends, because we live and move and have our being in God, and so all experience is underpinned by him. Nonetheless we may at times be particularly conscious of grace, that is to say, a gracious personal relationship with God in our lives, and this is not to be equated with any other kind of experience. We may feel strongly the presence of providence guiding and protecting us. Silent prayer may reveal to us the presence of God in the depth and centre of our being, an experience found not in excitement but in stillness. Like St Augustine when he wrote that 'our hearts are restless until they find their rest in thee', we may feel conscious of a vacuum in our lives which we identify as the real absence of God rather than his actual presence. By way of contrast charismatic worship may lead to a very different kind of experience of the divine presence, equally authentic: a sense of openness to divine inspiration and feelings of joy and happiness within an overpowering relationship. Mystics further report experiences of the 'dark night of the soul' and a sense of divine union beyond the experience of ordinary people. Sceptics tend to explain mystical experiences of nuptial rapture in terms of sublimated sexuality, but there are important differences, and there are good reasons why this may be refuted.[16]

God is not only experienced as immanent within us, but also as far transcendent to our being. We may experience 'the holy' in a way which makes it irreducible to analysis in terms of anything else. We may be aware of God as a numinous presence, a mystery who both fills us with awe and beckons us on towards him.[17] Alternatively, we may feel so deeply the fragility and contingency of our lives that we become aware of eternity away and beyond us.

Christians also experience Christ in their lives; a few through some visionary experience, most through a sense of his abiding presence and a conviction that their lives are bound up with his; so they speak about 'living in Christ'. He is for them not merely an exemplar, guide and teacher who has brought them into a new experience of life, but also one whom they experience as alive and in vital relationship with them.

These religious experiences are the bedrock on which people's faith rests. They are not the actual cause of faith, which is the gift of God enabling a person to respond to himself; but they often serve to inaugurate faith, and then strengthen and enable it to mature. It is important therefore that religious experience should be given due weight as a source of authority in Christian belief.[18]

Reason

The power to reason is one of the distinguishing features of human beings compared with the rest of the living world. Reason has many functions and differing forms. Reasoning may be inductive or deductive. It may be speculative, and it also may seek to erect a connected structure of belief. It may be critical, content only with the truth, seeking to iron out inconsistencies and to correct errors. All these aspects of reason have a part to play in formulating our beliefs. These need to form a connected whole, and erroneous beliefs need to be purged. At the same time caution must be exercised. How can we be sure that the nature of Christian belief is such that, with the limited capabilities of the human mind, it is possible for us to show the truth and the interconnection of all Christian doctrine? How can we be certain that apparent inconsistencies are not so much real inconsistencies as paradoxes, which are necessary if we are to try to use human language and thought to represent divine realities?

Sometimes reason is contrasted with revelation, usually to the disadvantage of the latter. Revelation, we are told, involves taking things on trust, whereas reason entails thinking them through. A little reflection however shows that this opposition is not so simple as it appears at first sight. The verb 'to rationalize' can be used in a positive sense, meaning simply to explain; but it can also be used in a negative sense, meaning to explain away. Reason can only function on presuppositions and assumptions. Agree an assumption, and the argument logically follows. Agree another assumption, and a quite different argument follows. There is one form of rationality which has as its assumption the acceptance of revelation, and another which does not. Both are valid exercises in reasoning, but because they start from different presuppositions, they reach different conclusions. Thus a person who reasons on the supposition that God acts in the world may accept an event as providential, while another who reasons on an atheist presupposition will reject it. Agnostic or atheistic rationalism is therefore no more rational than the use of reason within religion.

To show the hopelessness of reason as our sole guide in these matters does not mean that it plays an unimportant part in our formulation of our Christian beliefs. On the contrary, it is a vital ingredient. Although we cannot expect human reason to banish all the mysteries with which faith has to deal, we can expect reason to shed more light on them. We must distinguish between mysteries (which become more mysterious the greater the light which may be thrown on them), puzzles (which look like mysteries but which aren't) and problems (which are soluble).[19] But we who live in the post-Enlightenment world cannot genuinely believe what is inherently irrational. Reason may help us to discard what is irrational and to make the necessary distinctions between mysteries, puzzles and problems. Reason can show up flaws in an argument, and thereby lead us to reflect more deeply on the problem under discussion. Reason can lead us to examine whether an argument is intuitive (in which case it is not the result of conscious reasoning) or deductive (in which case it is really only drawing out what is already implicit in its assumptions, and we may then question those assumptions). Or we may come to see that reasoning is inductive, reaching a general conclusion on the basis of particular instances, in which case we have to ask ourselves (in the case of 'miracles') whether we are justified in dealing with special cases which seem to break these general laws.

The fact that faith seeks understanding shows how intrinsic reason is to belief, for there can be no rational understanding without the use of reason. There is an even more profound approach to reason in religion, which is founded on our doctrine of God. Although God is transcendent to us, and his ways are not our ways, yet at the same time he contains within himself all knowledge and understanding. God's reasoning is not like our reasoning, because all possibilities are already present within the mind of God. (God is not omniscient in the sense that he knows things *before* they happen, because God is outside time.) Nonetheless God is not irrational so much as suprarational. Our reasoning about the things of God are a mirror – albeit somewhat misted – of the mind of God himself.

Faith and secular knowledge

1: History

Some religions are totally unworldly in the sense that they have nothing to do with particular people or historical events. By way of contrast, the Christian faith is rooted in history. It is about God who chose a particular person and a particular people thousands of years ago, and who encompassed this people with a special providence, and who through particular events in their history revealed to them something of his nature and of their vocation. It is focused on particular people who belonged to this race, and finds its climax in someone called Joshua (in the Jewish version of his name), who was born and lived during a particular epoch of history, who was the oldest member of a large family, and who, after some thirty years of living a normal village life as a carpenter, attended a holiness crusade led by his cousin, and then suddenly himself engaged in public healing of the sick and in popular preaching of the Good News of God's Kingdom, and gathered round himself followers, becoming such an apparent threat to religious tradition and public order that at a particular place at a particular time by particular people he was put to death. And then, two days later, he was known to be alive, and appeared during a few weeks to certain people in ways that were distinctive and unusual until these appearances ceased, when his followers found themselves given an interior assurance and authority in announcing this Good News. By this time a new movement within Judaism was under way which developed into the Christian Church.

This story is so strange, and the claims made by this person known in his own time as Joshua and to us as Jesus are so singular, that they cannot be blindly accepted, especially as they took place nearly two thousand years ago. They require investigation, and part of that investigation concerns the historicity of these alleged events.

History however is not easy to determine, especially when the events took place so long ago, and when the only documents relating these events were written by people who were obviously prejudiced in their favour, and who wrote not to chronicle history but to strengthen the faith of those who were disciples of this extraordinary man. The historical problems are not made any easier by contemporary concepts of historiography, since the concept of 'scientific history' was quite foreign to those times. (In fact all historiography is bound to contain an element of interpretation, which in turn depends partly on the assumptions held by the historians concerned.[20])

These historical problems inherent in the origins of the Christian faith are also bound up with the study of the documents in which these events are narrated, the linguistic problems they contain, the interconnection of these documents and their transmission down the centuries. This does not mean that the problems cannot be resolved, but it does mean that inevitably we can only reach probable rather than definitive conclusions, and also that there are great differences between the ways in which the alleged historicity of these events is assessed by different historians. To a large extent this depends on the assumptions with which the task has been approached. For example, secular historians of the New Testament period usually bypass the account of the resurrection, either dismissing miracles as impossible or asserting that the supernatural is beyond their terms of reference. Christian historians tend to do likewise if they happen to be contributing to 'ancient history' rather than to 'biblical studies'.

So far as the formulation of Christian belief is concerned, it is not necessary to prove the historicity of these alleged events (which is impossible), but only to show their historical probability and their coherence with other aspects of Christian belief. This is achieved not merely by analysis of the evidence, but by showing the improbability of alternative explanations.

2: The human sciences

In giving a rounded view of Christian belief, we have to come to terms with the findings of the human sciences, and indeed to welcome them in so far as they enlarge our understanding of religion. Anthropology, for example, the study of mankind, its societies and its customs, has amassed a great deal of evidence about the practice of religion in prehistorical times as well as among primitive tribes today. Anthropologists have shown how worship and sacrifice played an important part in the early history of many peoples, whose beliefs, symbols, rituals, sacrifices and other religious practices can illuminate those of Christianity. To primitive man the world was alive and shot through with elemental unseen power. As the human race developed, we find animism (the worship of spirits) giving way to polytheism (the worship of many gods) and henotheism (the worship of one god among many), leading among the mainstream religions to monotheism (the worship of the one and only God). The way in which all these anthropological data are interpreted depends on the assumptions and presuppositions of its interpreters. Anthropology has tended to be positivist in direction, denying any substantial reality to the human soul and regarding religion as a refinement of primitive magic rather than as a developing response to Ultimate Reality.[21] It is interesting to note how different an interpretation of the data can be given by a well-known anthropologist whose presuppositions and assumptions are not agnostic or atheist but Christian.[22]

Psychology has been described as the science of mental life, both of its phenomena and its conditions. It is partly descriptive, 'looking into our minds and reporting what we discover' of 'feelings, desires, cognitions, reasonings, decisions and the like'. It is also partly speculative, building up a logical structure which makes sense of this mass of experience. It has obvious connections with all kinds of religious experience. Within its purview is not only the conscious brain, but also the unconscious and the subconscious and the preconscious; and again there is a connection with religion, noted especially by those who believe that our contact with the divine breaks into our consciousness from the subconscious levels of the mind.

Different psychological theories give expression to very different attitudes towards religion. Freudianism, for example, has a mechanistic view of the mind, seeing religion as a reversion to the infantile, with its old father–son relationship: 'God is the exalted father, and the longing for the father is the root of the need of religion.'[23] The blending of fear and mystery and love, and the fascination of creative energy, which are peculiar to religious experience, are the reappearance in adult life of the emotions of early childhood. Religion is therefore a construct to meet human needs: in reality it is an illusion. Jung, who was once Freud's heir apparent, took from Freud the belief that myths are traces in man of an infantile mode of thought, but he went further back in seeking the origin of belief in divine beings, tracing them not to the infantile situation in the family but to what he called the 'historical collective psyche', or the racial unconscious. 'The collective unconscious is the sediment of all the experience of the universe of all time.'[24] These 'dominants' take shape as gods or demons, and form the basis of all religious sanctions; but they exist within and not outside the psyche. Thus religion, which is the basis of all human achievement, has no objective status outside the human psyche. Jung himself distinguished Christian belief from knowledge. He wrote: 'Nobody can know what the ultimate things are.'[25] Yet in a famous BBC interview, near the end of his life, he claimed not belief but knowledge of God.

These are only two, perhaps the best-known two, of many different explanations of religion in the light of psychology. In one case the writer was an atheist, and the other might be described as a Christian agnostic. The theories of both have been adapted by their Christian followers to fit within a Christian framework.[26] However, a psychological explanation of the mechanisms underlying our experiences does not in itself determine the status or validity of those experiences. For example, the Freudian explanation of how conscience evolves, even if it be correct, does not in itself determine whether its status is purely subjective, or whether conscience helps us to reflect about moral realities.

Despite these fundamental divergencies in various psychological theories, and their apparent hostility to or agnosticism about belief in a transcendent God, there are many aspects of modern psychology which we almost take for granted today and which are of great value in the interpretation of our Christian beliefs. The importance of our early relationship with our parents for our subsequent development, the need for personal self-worth rather than self-hatred, and the necessity of a change of 'sentiment' involving our subconscious feelings if we are to re-align our lives on God; these are just some examples out of many insights which derive from modern psychology.

If psychology is concerned with individual experience, sociology deals with the development and nature of human society and the behaviour and beliefs of human beings within a society. Since the Christian religion is based on a particular community rather than on a book or a set of laws, sociology can shed much light on the function of the Church. It can also investigate what people actually believe and how they act. Sociology cannot however establish the truth or falsity of beliefs, nor the validity or invalidity of religious actions, except perhaps in so far as a belief is unlikely to be true if no one actually holds it. By correlating beliefs with, say, social status or political attitudes, sociology can suggest the influence which one or the other may have on religion, although the sociology of religion cannot by itself determine the truth of such beliefs.[27]

There is another field of enquiry which comes half-way between the human sciences and the natural sciences, namely psychic studies.[28] There are those who would refuse it the dignity of a science, because fraudulent claims have been made on its behalf, and because laboratory experimentation is not always appropriate to validate claims of the paranormal. Nonetheless, paranormal activities and events do take place. It is difficult, for example, to deny the existence of the kind of events for which no natural agent seems to be the cause. Furthermore there have been reputable investigators in this field, the existence of whom is usually ignored by those who work in the natural sciences. There are events described in the Scriptures which are clearly paranormal, and in the New Testament there are passages which, if taken literally, imply materialization, clairvoyance, clairaudience, telepathy, telekinesis, and paranormal healing. There are also paranormal events well testified in the lives of Christian saints. While it is necessary to distinguish the spiritual from the psychic, no rounded statement of Christian belief can with integrity ignore the relationship between the two.

3: The natural sciences

The natural sciences are concerned with understanding the universe and how it functions. Since Christians believe that God creates and sustains the universe, they find that through the natural sciences more and more of God's creation is becoming intelligible to us. Seen in this light, the natural sciences are part of the 'general revelation' of God to mankind whereby he discloses himself in the glory of his creation. This is how many scientists who are Christians look on their work, as contributing to our knowledge of God's world. We now have a far better understanding of God's world, and as a result our wonder deepens as we reflect on his wisdom and power.

It is appropriate in scientific procedures always to look for a material cause for some physical effect, thus ruling out God as the 'primary cause' (although Christians understand him to be the 'secondary cause', upholding and responsible for the 'primary cause'). As secondary agent, God is invisible, so that Isaiah exclaimed: 'Truly thou art a God that hidest thyself' (Isa 45.15). The classic method of procedure for the natural sciences involves the observation of phenomena, the elaboration of a hypothesis which explains the phenomena or some particular action or aspect of the phenomena, and the testing of this hypothesis by repeated observation and experimentation. This methodology, however, is not applicable to all departments of the natural sciences. For example, there is no possibility of testing out cosmological theories about the beginning of the universe, or what happens in Planck time or space (see p. 26), for these situations cannot be reproduced under laboratory conditions. Nonetheless the general method of the natural sciences requires precise observation, the formulation of hypotheses, and the verification or falsification of these hypotheses in so far as this is possible.[29]

There are aspects of the natural sciences which are not dissimilar to those of religion. For example, both inherit a tradition, and in both trust is needed in that tradition. There are other aspects which are very different. Faith in God is different from a mere hypothesis about God. While religions may hope to refine or develop their systems of belief, faith in God is not regarded as provisional in the sense that a better hypothesis may be forthcoming. For the most part the natural sciences are concerned with a different question from that of religion. The latter deals with why things happen, while the sciences are concerned with how things happen.

New ideas in the natural sciences, perhaps surprisingly, often take some time to establish themselves. Nonetheless the atmosphere today is far more congenial to religion than was the case half a century ago. Matter, in its smallest elements, is no longer regarded as a kind of miniature billiard ball, but it is defined by its relationships. An observer, e.g., a scientist in a laboratory, when dealing with particles of the atom, can affect that which he or she observes. Matter is best understood in terms of interdependent and interpenetrating fields of energy, so that there is a sense in which the whole is present in a part. It has been suggested that the universe is gradually unfolding or explicating itself from its original implicate order, in which there existed all its vast potentialities for development and in which everything was enfolded and interconnected.[30] In the past science has considered static systems; but it is now known that in the real world systems are far from static, and can be literally unpredictable, since the minutest variation can have enormous effects. The study of these 'dissipative structures far from thermodynamic equilibrium' has disclosed the extraordinary capacity of matter to organize itself into forms and patterns.[31] The theory of fields of influence, so important in physics, has been extended to biology, and a hypothesis of formative causation has been put forward whereby developing organisms are influenced by morphogenetic fields.[32] Their development is said to be affected by these fields, just as matter may be affected by electromagnetic fields of energy. These hypotheses are not yet generally accepted, but they illustrate a tendency of the sciences to retreat from the reductionism which until recently dominated these areas of research. Although the twentieth century has seen huge advances in the natural sciences, there are still vast areas of ignorance,[33] and it seems likely that when there is more knowledge in these areas, reductionism will become even less credible.

At the same time, there are particular points where religious belief overlaps with scientific hypotheses, and where the two may clash. The Christian religion has a doctrine of creation, which may clash with a scientific hypothesis concerning the origin of the universe. In the natural sciences the principle of evolution is taken for granted even when there is disagreement over its mode, but evolution is opposed by some Christians who take up a position based on the opening chapters of Genesis. The Christian faith holds a doctrine of the human soul, while some scientific hypotheses equate the brain with the mind. Some of these scientific hypotheses presuppose a mechanical explanation of human behaviour, in contrast to most formulations of Christian belief which insist on freedom of the will. So far as Christianity is concerned, according to traditional belief Jesus was born of the Blessed Virgin Mary without the aid of a human father, which seems difficult to harmonize with modern genetic theories of inheritance. The central claim of Christianity that Jesus was raised from the dead is contrary to most scientific assumptions about material bodies. Some of the New Testament accounts of miracles are contrary to the assumptions by which modern science functions. These are some points of contact and potential points of disagreement between religion and the natural sciences, which we shall have to consider later in this book. Those who live at the end of the twentieth century cannot jettison what appear to be the assured results of the sciences, any more than modern Christians can surrender what they regard as fundamental aspects of their Christian belief.

4: Philosophy

A statement of Christian belief must imply some philosophical assumptions, or at least the denial of some philosophical positions which are contrary to belief. For example, logical positivism used to hold that the meaning of a statement is the meaning of its verification, and that any statement which cannot be verified is literally nonsense. Since God cannot in principle be verified, statements about God come within this category. (In fact the foundation statement of logical positivism itself could not be verified, which led to its modification.) To take another example, behaviourism, which denies the possibility of free will, is inconsistent with holding a faith which entails the free response of a person to the grace of God.

The Christian faith is compatible with many types of philosophy. Descartes held a form of philosophy which made a total distinction between the immaterial soul and the body machine. Bishop Berkeley advocated a form of idealism which held that all things, including souls and bodies, exist only in the mind of God. St Thomas Aquinas espoused a form of realism, derived from Aristotle, according to which human beings in the act of perception have a real insight into a thing in itself, while Kant held that things in themselves are forever hidden from mortal knowledge, and that the human mind supplies the categories of interpretation to the raw phenomena of perception. These philosophical positions are very different from one another; but all four philosophers were believing Christians.

Several important philosophical issues are involved in any statement of belief about God. It is possible here to focus only upon one by way of example. It is the question of epistemology (how we know). We cannot hope to validate our knowledge of God unless we have some theory of knowledge about how we can know anything. We live in a period of history in which scientific knowledge is in the ascendant, and the most common view of knowledge is that of which we can be objectively certain, a view itself derived from a popular conception of scientific knowledge. (Despite a high degree of knowledge of the macro-world, the quantum theory forces us to acknowledge that in the micro-world of particles what can be known is influenced even by the observer.) Alternatively there is another kind of contemporary epistemology, popular in some forms of post-modernism, according to which there is no possibility of knowing things as they are in themselves, and the language which we use about reality does not reflect the nature of reality itself, but the way in which we make use of the world around us. Epistemology today tends either towards pure objectivity or pure subjectivity.

Most ordinary people, however, have a common-sense view that we have a real insight into 'what is out there', distorted to some extent by our own subjectivism. This points to another way of considering the way in which we know people and things, and this type of epistemology is primarily neither objectivizing nor subjectivizing. It focuses on the relational aspect between the knower and that which is known.[34] Our relationship to people or things is primary to our knowing them. 'Rational, conceptual knowledge arises out of the knowledge by acquaintance which characterizes our human situation in the world.'[35] This is because we are in a relationship with the universe, and since we are acquainted with it, we can use our intellectual faculties to understand it and to give some account of our knowledge of it. We are not objective and external observers of reality: we are part of it, and our knowledge arises out of this relation. This does not apply merely to our knowledge of things and of people: it applies also to our knowledge of God. In him we live and move and have our being. We are in relation to him whether we acknowledge this relation or not. In this sense we are acquainted with God, and our knowledge of God is by reason of this acquaintance. With such an epistemology we may with confidence attempt to articulate our knowledge of God.

In this introductory chapter we have briefly examined only the prolegomena to our subject. We have considered the relation between faith and belief, and we have looked at the sources of authority which underlie the Christian faith. Because Christianity claims to explain the relationship of God to the universe as a whole and in particular to human beings, we have also considered the particular secular sciences and disciplines with which it inevitably comes into contact. We turn next to consider Christian belief itself.

Notes

1. See Anselm, *Proslogion.*

2. For further reading on faith, see W. R. Inge, *Faith and Its Psychology* (London, 1909); J. Baillie, *Our Knowledge of God* (Oxford, 1939); M. C. Darcy, *The Nature of Belief* (London, 1945); E. Brunner, *Faith, Hope and Belief* (London, 1957); R. Swinburne, *Faith and Reason* (Oxford, 1981).

3. See S. Kierkegaard, *Concluding Scientific Postscript*, tr. D. Swenson (Princeton, 1941).

4. See M. Buber, *I and Thou*, tr. F. Kaufman (Edinburgh, 1970).

5. On Liberation theology, see G. Gutiérrez, *A Theology of Liberation* (London, 1974); L. and C. Boff, *Introducing Liberation Theology* (London, 1989); and also Sacred Congregation for the Doctrine of the Faith, *Libertatis Nuntius* (London, 1984).

6. See Introduction in *The Gospel and Contemporary Culture*, ed. H. Montefiore (London, 1992).

7. On adequacy as a criterion for Christian belief, see essay by H. Montefiore in Doctrine Commission of the Church of England, *Christian Believing* (London, 1946), pp. 146–7.

8. For an exegesis of the traditional view of revelation, see E. L. Mascall, *He Who Is* (London, 1943).

9. L. Newbigin, *The Gospel in a Pluralist Society* (London, 1987), pp. 52–65.

10. See J. Macquarrie, *Principles of Christian Theology* (London, 1966), p. 48.

11. See K. Barth, *'Nein'* in *Natural Theology*, ed. J. Baillie (London, 1946).

12. See W. Temple, *Nature, Man and God* (London, 1934), p. 322.

13. On inspired biblical images, see A. Farrer, *The Glass of Vision* (London, 1948).

14. See H. Montefiore in *Christian Believing, op. cit.*

15. See F. Schleiermacher, *On Religion: Speeches to Cultured Despisers*, tr. J. Oman (New York, 1958).

16. For further discussion, see H. Montefiore, 'Religious experience' in *Reclaiming the High Ground* (London, 1990).

17. R. Otto, *The Idea of the Holy* (Oxford, 1936).

18. For further discussion of religious experience, see W. James, *The Varieties of Religious Experience* (London, 1928); D. Hay, *Exploring Inner Space* (London, 1987) and *Religious Experience Today* (London, 1990).

19. For further discussion, see M. Foster, *Mystery and Philosophy* (London, 1957).

20. For further discussion of historiography, see E. Ives, 'The Gospel and history' in *The Gospel and Contemporary Culture, op. cit.*

21. See for example the closing words of J. G. Frazer, *The Golden Bough*, vol. XI (London, 1936).

22. E.g. Mary Douglas, *Natural Symbols* (London, 1973).

23. L.W.Grensted, *Psychology and God* (London, 1930), p. 50.

24. C.Jung, *Analytical Psychology* (London, 1928), p. 431.

25. C.Jung, *Psychology and Religion* (Yale, 1948), p. 114.

26. E.g. R.S.Lee, *Freud and Christianity* (London, 1948); V.White, *God and the Unconscious* (London, 1952); J.Hannaghan, *Freud and Jesus* (Dublin, 1966); C.Bryant, *Jung and the Christian Way* (London, 1986).

27. See T.T.O'Dea, *The Sociology of Religion* (Englewood Cliffs, New Jersey, 1966).

28. See M.Perry, *Psychic Studies* (Wellingborough, 1984); J.Beloff, *Parapsychology: A Concise History* (London, 1993).

29. According to H.Ellis, *Before the Beginning* (London/New York, 1993) the five primary candidates for appropriate criteria for a scientific theory are: simplicity, beauty, prediction verifiability, explanatory power and unity of explanation.

30. D.Bohm, *Wholeness and the Implicate Order* (London, 1950).

31. I.Pripogine and I.Stengers, *Order Out of Chaos* (London, 1984).

32. R.Sheldrake, *A New Science of Life* (London, 1981).

33. See *The Encyclopaedia of Ignorance*, ed. R.Duncan and M.Weston-Smith (Oxford, 1977).

34. M.Polanyi, *Personal Knowledge* (London, 1962).

35. C.Gunton, 'Knowledge and culture' in *The Gospel and Contemporary Culture*, *op. cit.* p. 85.

chapter 2

Creation

Creation in Judaeo-Christian tradition

'Why is there something rather than nothing?' is a very reasonable question to ask. We live in a contingent world where things come into being and pass out of being. How did it all begin? That also is a very proper question, and some would have us stop there; but the enquiring mind is not satisfied. We desire to know why the universe came to exist. We want to find out whether there is a purpose behind creation, or whether it is ultimately purposeless and meaningless, other than whatever purposes and meanings we read into it in order to make our lives tolerable.

It is part of our Judaeo-Christian inheritance that God is creator and sustainer of all things, and that to him all creation is good. In the second century there arose the Gnostic movement, which has surfaced again from time to time in later centuries, according to which matter is inherently evil, and so God could not have created it: it was the product of an inferior deity, the Demiurge, who fabricated it. The Christian Church fought a sharp battle against Gnosticism, and insisted that God was the Creator; and it won.

Two different stories of creation are incorporated in the first two chapters of the book of Genesis. The first story is a Jewish adaptation of the Babylonian creation myth, edited in such a way that it reflects the strict monotheism which Jewish orthodoxy brought back from the Jews' exile in Babylon. Elsewhere in the Scriptures there is unequivocal testimony to God who created the universe out of nothing ('when I summoned them, they sprang at once into being': Isa 48.13), but according to Genesis 1, it is not so much a story of creation as the formation of the universe out of pre-existent stuff. When God made heaven and earth, we are told, the earth was without form and void, with darkness over the face of the abyss, and a mighty wind that swept over the face of the waters. This was the pre-creation state of affairs, according to the tale. Augustine assumed that there were two stages in creation; first the void, and then the fashioning of the universe, when the Word of God initiated the six days of creation. This began with God saying 'Let there be light' on the first day. The story is an ancient myth: it is not a literal account of creation. The point has been well put by a contemporary Russian theologian martyred as recently as 1990:[1]

Like all myths the story of Creation in Genesis incorporates in the form of a historical story truths which lose their edge when told merely in universals; in this case the truths that God alone called creation into being, and that creation is an ordered sequence with a purpose underlying it. This myth incorporates revelation.

Knowledge about the origins of the Universe naturally took on a form corresponding to the state of thought and to the type of thinking of that distant epoch when Genesis was written. But it is not only a question of epoch. The sacred writer spoke of a mystery which, by its nature, permitted its best expression through symbols.

'In the beginning, God created heaven and earth . . .' These words of Scripture are not the statement of a scientific fact: they proclaim a revelation, they speak of the miracle of creation which related the Absolute to the contingent in a manner which we cannot comprehend. The language of the first chapter of Genesis is the language of myth, in the most elevated and sacred sense of that word. The picture, the image, the symbol, which replace the abstraction, are the way of expressing this which faith requires and which is inherent in the language of all religions.

The intuitive vision which underlies a myth anticipates, so often by several centuries, the development of scientific knowledge. To understand the myth we ought to take account not of their transitory envelope but their essence, their heart.

In its form, the biblical account follows the laws of symmetry which are in accord with the poetry of the Near East. This in itself shows that Scripture does not pretend to give a scientific account of the concrete development of the world. If we then turn to the kernel of the creation story, we will find the thesis of a creation from elementary forces, a creation which contains within itself stages of growth. The word *bara* – he created – is only employed in the Bible when speaking of the creation of the Universe, of Life and of Mankind. To put it otherwise, cosmic creation knew three particular moments determined by the creative Word.

The way in which the ancient Jews made use of an existing myth of creation, and edited it to serve their purposes, should encourage us to do the same with the current theories of creation based upon the contemporary hypotheses of theoretical physics, so long as we keep the same kernel as the biblical myth. Any new paradigm, however, must be considered as provisional, since theories change and no absolute certainty can be achieved.

Modern paradigms of creation

More than one theory about the beginning of the universe is current today. According to one hypothesis,[2] the world did not begin quite at the beginning of time. There was the initial explosion (the Big Bang), but there was no actual 'singularity' when all time and space were imploded into a single point. The smallest unit of time is 10^{-43} seconds, known as Planck time, and we cannot get behind it. At Planck time the universe was only 10^{-33} cm in diameter, and at that size the universe was governed by quantum effects. Under Heisenberg's uncertainty principle, it is not possible in principle to know both the velocity and the position of a particle. So, according to theoretical physicists, when space is contracted to quantum size, time is smeared, and indeed disappears altogether, and becomes another dimension of space. In this situation there is four-dimensional space, but no longer a space–time continuum. The question then arises of the shape of this four-dimensional space. An infinite variety of shapes is possible. On grounds of elegance, Stephen Hawking, with his colleague James Hartle, has chosen a shape which has no hard edge, with the result that there is no origin of the universe at a particular moment when time began. This does not mean that the universe is infinitely old, but simply that time has no boundary as such. After this proto-universe had come into being, its expansion would take place exactly in the same way as if it had come into being at a precise moment at the beginning of time.

There are however problems about such a theory. We do not know whether quantum effects apply to the whole universe when compacted to this quantum size. We do know about quantum effects with particles, but we do not know if those effects held good at a temperature of a million million degrees, when particles and radiation were interchangeable. Again, even though in physics the most elegant solution is thought to be most probably the correct one, we cannot *prove* anything simply on the grounds of mathematical elegance (unless perhaps we were to claim as physicists that God, the source of all beauty, could be assumed to have chosen the most elegant way of creation). Hawking's and Hartle's theory cannot be validated by proof of any kind. It is pure theory; and while it may make sense for theoretical physicists to claim that time can turn into a dimension of space, it is difficult to persuade those who do not share their mathematical expertise that this could happen.

If this is indeed the way in which our universe originated, then this can easily be used as a model of divine creation. God is not temporal. His Spirit is present within the spatio-temporal continuum, but he is transcendent to it. He is eternal. As Augustine wrote, God created the universe not *in tempore* (within the process of time), but *cum tempore* (together with time), which was itself part of his creation.[3] If God is eternal, then there is no essential distinction between creating and sustaining the universe. The vision in the first chapter of Genesis, of God as the author of the universe, still holds. The created universe was not always existent, even if there was not a particular moment when it sprang into being: it is simply that its beginning cannot be determined in temporal terms. The universe is not chaotic: on the contrary, God is responsible for an ordered universe. He has ordained not merely the laws of the universe responsible for its subsequent development but also the laws which produced quantum effects within the initial Planck time. He is the reason why there is something rather than nothing.

This, however, is not the only theory about the origin of our universe. Theoretical scientists explain that there is no such thing as pure nothingness. In a vacuum, random fluctuations occur, and at the micro-level there is indeterminacy, according to the generally accepted hypotheses of quantum theory. Particles and subparticles come into being and disappear almost simultaneously without apparent rhyme or reason. These 'virtual' particles (as they are known) only become permanent when powered by energy. It has been suggested that, in a vacuum, small bubbles of 'virtual' space–time, in the smallest quantum in which it can exist, appear and then vanish in a similar kind of way. (This again is pure theory: there can be no proof that this would happen.) Occasionally a vacuum can become 'excited', that is to say, bursting with energy. This energy would transfer to a 'virtual' bubble of space–time, whereupon it would become a real bubble and expand exponentially. The moment when it became a real bubble would be the moment when time began. Time began when the universe began. Time is a dimension of the spatio-temporal continuum in which we live. It does not exist in its own right.

Theoretical physicists calculate that this proto-universe would have doubled its size every 10^{-34} seconds, so in scarcely more than a trillionth trillionth of a second it would have increased by a factor of 10^{80}, that is to say, to a size of some 30 cm. This period of exponential inflation would only last a very short time, because the vacuum would undergo what is called a 'phase transition', which means that it would revert to its former passive state. But enormous reserves of energy which would have built up inside the bubble would have been released in the form of energy and particles of matter. This was the Big Bang, so big that echoes of it are still found in the universe, in the form of radiation 3° above absolute zero.

These are not the only possible theories, but they are the two which are most favoured.[4]

When the universe exploded, the only restraining force was that of gravity. As a result of the Big Bang the universe is still expanding, although the force of gravity is slowing it up, and (while again there is no certainty) gravity is probably strong enough to prevent an unending expansion, so that the universe will at some point begin to contract, and it will probably all disappear into the nothingness from which it began. When theologians speak of *creatio ex nihilo* (creation out of nothing) this is its meaning in terms of modern theoretical physics, except that physics is only concerned with the process, and not with the author and sustainer of the process. God provides a rational explanation of the fact that there is a creation, that something exists rather than nothing, and that the universe came into being in an ordered way.

According to this theory of the universe's origin, it began with a 'singularity' (when all is infinitely compressed into a point). About this nothing can be said, because the laws of physics only operate in time and space. There was a particular moment which was the beginning of time, rather than the emergence of time from a spatial dimension according to the other theory. Both theories may be used to illustrate in modern terms the work of the Creator.

The expanding creation

As the universe expanded, first particles appeared, then atoms, and then the two simplest elements, hydrogen and helium. Out of these gas clouds there formed over millions of years the stars. Today there are billions of stars, which we find in clusters and even superclusters. There are millions of galaxies. We live on a smallish planet circling round a middle-sized star in a middle-sized galaxy known as the Milky Way, and our home we know as Planet Earth, one among billions of celestial bodies. The whole size of the universe is beyond imagination. Indeed it is even beyond knowledge: for all we know, it may have many domains beyond the one in which we happen to live, and it may extend far beyond its horizon as we know it; and it is still expanding. Instead of the six days of creation, the process of creation has been going on for some fifteen billion years, and the universe is still increasing in size, like a balloon under pressure.

There has been much of what seems like 'fine tuning' which has made this universe possible. In many respects the possibility of its existence was determined by its initial or early conditions. (To give two instances, the distribution of gas in the universe had to be almost uniform, with just sufficient perturbation to enable galaxies to form; and the heat of the Big Bang had to be just right so that there was an orderly expansion.) Again, the constants had to be just right to enable this orderly expansion to take place. (For example, if the strong force which keeps the nucleus of an atom together had been only 2 per cent stronger, the universe would have blown up: if it were slightly weaker, nuclear fusion, which keeps the stars burning, would not have happened.) There are many such coincidences,[5] signal examples to the eyes of faith of the wisdom and providence of the Creator. Planets like the Earth could only form because earlier stars had exploded and scattered their debris in space, and these debris were swept up by a second-generation star like the sun and the planets which are its satellites. This is the source of carbon, which forms the basis of our life systems, and of our heavier metals. Without the probability of exploding stars, there could be no life as we know it on earth today. When the doctrine of creation is seen in the perspective of modern knowledge, far from depreciating it, it gains in grandeur and in our appreciation of the loving care of the Creator.

The creation of life

Life is usually thought to have appeared about four-and-a-half billion years ago on this planet, comparatively shortly after it was formed out of this debris.[6] On this scale of dating, the earliest fossils go back to four billion years ago, if one may trust the conventional methods of dating. These life forms were elementary. The evolution of life on earth has been very rapid in cosmological terms. Until two billion years ago there were no creatures with backbones. 500 million years ago there were no creatures on land. Humanity is a newcomer. Our common ancestor with the apes is probably to be dated five million years ago; and of course *homo sapiens*, a particular species within the hominid genus, appeared very recently indeed.

We do not know how life first appeared on earth, whether it was exported from some other place in space where life had already existed,[7] or whether it came from outer space through a comet,[8] or whether it evolved naturally on earth, or whether it was created directly by a special divine act. Most people think that it evolved naturally on earth; but we do not know whether the emergence of life was inevitable or whether it was exceedingly improbable. We do know that it took place. We see in the evolution of nature a tendency towards greater and greater complexity, and this predisposes us to suppose that the emergence of life somewhere in the universe was likely to happen sooner or later. When the Creator brought the universe into being, he must have intended it to be a place where life could evolve.

There are many puzzles still to be solved about the way in which this evolution took place. We do not as yet have a scenario which describes how proteins and the double helix evolved within an organism so as to enable it to reproduce itself. But evolve they did. Too sharp a line between life and non-life must not be drawn. Viruses to some extent bridge the gap: they can be inert dust or they can reproduce themselves by taking over the cells of other living beings.

Gaia and divine providence

We tend to think in terms of the evolution of species, rather than in terms of the development of the planet as a whole. Until fairly recently the planet was commonly understood to be alive, with Christian tradition following in this respect the views of Aristotle. (St Thomas Aquinas even thought of the heavenly bodies as live intelligences.) As a result of increasing specialization in the natural sciences, such an idea came to appear absurd. How can inanimate bodies be part of a living system? However, the hypothesis has recently been resurrected.[9] Although it has met with strong opposition from scientists who have grown up with the conventional model of the world, the 'Gaia hypothesis' is purely scientific, and it has not been faulted on scientific grounds.

As soon as life appeared, self-assembling cybernetic systems appeared which have kept the earth comfortable for life. So much can hardly be denied. The 'Gaia hypothesis', however, explores the contribution of living creatures to the 'fine tuning' necessary to effect this. (Gaia is, somewhat unfortunately, the Greek name of an earth goddess. The word as used in the 'Gaia hypothesis' is employed in a scientific sense to designate not only the biosphere (that part of the earth where living things normally exist) and the biota (the collection of all individual living organisms), but also the whole planet and its surrounding atmosphere.) Salt has been poured into the sea from rivers and from beneath the oceans, the sun has increased 30 per cent in luminosity and carbon dioxide is pumped into the atmosphere from volcanoes. Despite all this, the salinity of the oceans has been kept constant, the heat of the sun changes little, and the atmosphere is kept just right for the maintenance of life. A little more oxygen and the forests would burn, and a little less and one could not strike a match. The humble marine algae in the oceans contribute to the formation of rain clouds through their emission of dimethyl sulphide which, when oxidized in the air, forms the nuclei around which the rain clouds form. When the Earth is said to be 'alive', this is not meant in the same sense in which plants and animals are alive and propagate themselves, but it does describe the remarkable way in which the biosphere and the biota interact, so that through automatic self-assembling cybernetic systems the environment is maintained comfortable for life (unless human beings interfere unduly with it). The various parts of a living body interact in rather the same way by automatic processes so as to maintain it in life.

It is not impossible that these cybernetic systems may have evolved by chance, but this seems a remote possibility, especially when taken in conjunction with the 'coincidences' that have made possible the evolution of life on the planet. Even if matter is endowed with holistic properties which cause such systems to evolve naturally, the question must be asked: what or who so endowed them? Viewed through the eyes of faith, the 'Gaia hypothesis' (if it be accepted as true) is a yet more striking example of the providence of the Creator. All living things are interdependent, and all depend on the humblest of God's creatures: micro-organisms which break down chemicals in waste substances, and which help in the recycling of essential matter, and one-celled organisms in the oceans which draw off carbon dioxide by forming limestone sediments in the seabed. There is nothing miraculous about any of the ways in which the various cybernetic systems have formed themselves, or in which they function, including those systems in which living organisms participate. But without them life could not have evolved on earth, and without them *homo sapiens* would not have emerged. Gaia is a kind of sacrament through which the power and wisdom of God shines (see p. 185): the outward and visible earth shows us something of the inner working of the Holy Spirit within it. As the Psalmist wrote: 'The heavens declare the glory of God and the firmament showeth his handiwork.'

The probability of the Creator

Scientists used to think of the universe in materialist terms as a great machine. Once in action, it would simply go on and on. Such a view supported a deist conception of God. He had created the universe, as a person might construct a mechanical machine. He had started it up, and he had left it to continue under its own momentum without the need for any maintenance or supervision. We now know that this is a false conception of the universe. 'During this century the new physics has blown apart the central tenets of materialist doctrine in a series of stunning developments.'[10] In fact, from the Big Bang onwards, the universe has developed like an organism rather than a machine. As it has developed, it has manifested greater and greater complexity. It contains within itself a degree of indeterminacy (as chaos and quantum theories illustrate), which endows it with creativity for future development. It appears as though it is structured in such a way that intelligent life which is capable of reflecting on it would appear sooner or later (the 'strong anthropic principle'[11]). It is natural to the eyes of faith to regard all the 'cosmic coincidences', and the self-regulation of Gaia as pointers towards the divine purpose unfolding itself in the universe.

Yet it cannot be said that we have here any kind of teleological *proof*. If there is an infinite ensemble of universes (or an infinite number of domains within our universe), a universe like ours would be bound to evolve by random chance, although of course there is no evidence, nor can there be, of any one other universe than our own. It might be that one universe can develop from a black hole in another, and that our universe is merely one such successful development among others. It is possible also to think of the universe in pantheistic terms, with its progressive self-organization seen as God bestirring himself, as it were, and coming to birth in the development of the cosmos.[12] This changing and developing God can give no explanation for the evil in the world, and it is a strange view of God that he should be subject to contingencies such as those we have already noted. For these reasons a pantheistic view of God is generally regarded as unacceptable. If we think of God as Creator, then as we look at the universe through the eyes of faith, we see both the cybernetic controls of Gaia and the 'cosmic coincidences' of the universe as marks of the signal providence of the Creator. The openness of the universe, and the ability of matter to develop in more and more varied ways and with more and more complex forms show not only that God is the great Architect and Superscientist who planned this universe and brought it into being, but also that his Holy Spirit is immanent within the process, guiding it in a way which does not interfere with natural processes which we think of as the 'laws of nature'.

The cosmic covenant

In the Old Testament the creation story in the opening chapter of Genesis is dominant. But there also are fragments of an earlier and very different creation myth. Recent Old Testament scholarship[13] has uncovered the concept of a 'cosmic covenant' both from the Scriptures (such as the Psalms and the book of Job) and from the book of Enoch, one of the Old Testament apocryphal works which has striking points of correspondence with the older Syro-Canaanite literature found at Ugarit. In the ancient world, rulers made 'covenants' with their people; and the word is used here as an agreement initiated by God which he made with his creatures. Christians use the word most frequently in connection with the old and new covenants (see pp. 70f.).

In this earlier myth the natural forces in the world seem to have been personified, and God imposed his rule upon them, so that all the powers of the universe came under his sovereignty, as part of his kingdom. The covenant consisted in God's prescribing limits for his natural creation. Many examples could be given, in particular the sea which may not transgress its given limits. The point is clearly made in Psalm 74.13–17 with its reference to Leviathan, the great seven headed sea monster which personified the watery chaos before creation:

You divided the sea by your might:
    you shattered the heads of the dragons in the waters.
You crushed the heads of Leviathan:
    and gave him as food to the creatures of the desert waste.
You cleft open spring and fountain:
    you dried up the everflowing waters.
The day is yours and so also is the night:
    you have established the moon and the sun.
You set all the boundaries of the earth:
    you created winter and summer.

Jeremiah in particular speaks of God's 'covenant of the night and of the day' as the bedrock on which God's covenant with David depended. This links God's providential ordering of the natural world with his covenant with his chosen people and thereby with the new covenant in Christ. According to 1 Enoch 69 God binds the elements by the Name of his great oath. In fact the covenant is broken by the wickedness of mankind, and then restored. Of course the early Jews had no idea of evolution: they believed that the natural world had come into being by immediate fiat, and this creation does not describe the actual act of creation, only God's ordering of already existing forces. Nonetheless this ancient creation myth provides a primitive model for God's providential ordering of his world, which is now becoming more and more apparent as modern scientific knowledge begins to uncover the remarkable nature of the 'constants' of evolution and the cosmic 'coincidences' which have made possible the evolution of life on earth; and it is even more important as showing the natural world as an integral part of the Kingdom of God.

The purposes of the Creator

Why did God create? What ends did he have in mind? Here it is only possible to speak about the universe of which we know. There may be other universes, by their nature quite unknown to us, in which God has aims which are necessarily hidden from us. There may be other orders of God's creatures which are immaterial, of which the traditional doctrine of angels is a sign and a pointer. Again there may be other forms of life elsewhere in this universe which are not carbon-based, of which once again we can know nothing. We can only write about those orders of existence which are known or knowable to us.

It is of the nature of love to create. We can find a reflection of this in human love, when two people who deeply love each other want to create another being on whom they can lavish their affection and care. If God's nature is love, then it is congruous with that nature that he should wish to create others to share in his love.[14] It is sometimes alleged that it is impermissible to compare the human love of spouses with divine love, because humans experience love as passionate yearning (*eros*) while divine love is *agape*, a love determined by the will to go to the assistance of those in need. But while the contrast between *eros* and *agape* is accurate,[15] the contrast between human and divine love is not. So far as humans are concerned, it is certainly true that two lovers passionately desire to be united, but it is also true that genuine human love includes the determination of the will to assist the beloved. As for God, there has been a tendency to deny him the feelings of strong emotion. But a passionless God is not the God portrayed in the Scriptures. There God yearns passionately over his creation, and also shows his love in coming to the aid of his people in need through the old and new covenants.

If God created the universe out of love, does this suggest that God is as it were incomplete until he has created it? That does not follow. As we shall see (p. 121), the doctrine of the Holy Trinity symbolizes the divine existence as an exchange of love within the Godhead. God is not a lonely monarch looking for company in order to fulfil himself, but the self-existing self-sufficient Being whose nature is love and who gives expression to that love by creating and sustaining the universe. We are of course tempted to ask what happened before the universe came into being; but the point has already been made that time did not exist before the universe, so the question becomes a nonsense question.

However, love does not create for the sake of creating, without a particular objective in view. When two people procreate a baby, they enjoy the baby for its own sake, but they also have in mind that the baby should grow and develop and enjoy fullness of life. No comparison or 'analogy' between God and humanity can be exact; but nevertheless we are bound to use analogical language in speaking of God. In Christian tradition God has been addressed as Father, going back to the usage of Jesus himself who prayed 'Abba' (Father). If God is our heavenly Father, we may presume that he enjoys and takes delight in his creation, as we find occasionally mentioned in the Scriptures (e.g. Psalm 104.26, NEB). According to Genesis, in creating the universe God saw that it was good, i.e. it has intrinsic value.

In contrast to Hinduism, where creation is regarded as a kind of dance without a purpose, the Judaeo-Christian tradition has understood it differently. God has a particular aim in mind. In the Scriptures this is described by means of a myth in which the primal Man is given dominion over all that lives on the earth, in the sky and in the sea, and acts as God's deputy, and in which he is said to be made, together with the primal Woman, in God's image. There are deep truths implicit in these biblical stories; but somewhat different imagery is required in an age which understands creation as an evolutionary process. The particular purpose of God in creation may best be understood as his bringing into being a process which proceeds under the laws which he has given his universe and which is open and undetermined, and therefore open to the influence of his Holy Spirit. This process is 'fine-tuned' from the very start, so that the development of the cosmos is unlikely to come to an abrupt end before God's main purpose is completed. His particular purpose – or at least the purpose of which we are aware – is the emergence of intelligent beings capable of free and conscious response to his love and purposes, and for their maturation so that they are capable of sharing ever more fully in the life of God himself. It is in this sense of the divine intention that we must interpret such insights in the Scriptures as that in Ephesians that God has 'chosen us before the foundation of the world' and 'predestinated us unto the adoption as children by Christ Jesus to himself' (Eph 1.4–5).

Yet we can only speak of God's purpose generally in terms of intelligent life. It was probable that, given the conditions of his creation, somewhere or other in its vast extent intelligent life would emerge. But we cannot say that it was always God's purpose that *human beings* should emerge, because there were too many contingencies to be certain that this would happen. For example, at the time of the demise of the dinosaurs, the only mammal in existence was a small ratlike creature out of which all other forms of mammalian life have evolved. It is likely that the dinosaurs died out because of catastrophic conditions caused by the collision of a large planetesimal or small asteroid with the earth. If this had not happened, it is unlikely that *homo sapiens* would have evolved. It is improbable that the arrival of a planetesimal at that particular epoch was due to special divine providence. Providence does not work in that kind of way. It usually operates through the normal regularities of nature (see pp. 271ff.), and it opens up the possibility of creative progress out of destructive events. (For example, the Church of England's split from Rome was occasioned by a king's desire for a son and heir, yet out of this destructive event have come the blessings of Anglicanism's distinctive ethos.)

If these intelligent beings who were likely to emerge were to be free to respond or not to God's love, then sufficient freedom had to be built into the whole evolutionary process to enable this to happen. We cannot say that evolution had to follow one particular pathway. There are always different options which may be taken. Nonetheless God is not an absentee spectator, watching (presumably with interest) which paths evolving life is taking. He has made inherent in matter a tendency towards increasing complexity, and he is active within the process, guiding it not through interference with the regularities of nature, but (probably at the macro-level through the unpredictability of dynamic structures, and at the quantum level in ways which are as yet unknown to us) by helping evolving life to take a pathway which leads to intelligent life.

God and Neo-Darwinism

The general picture of evolution (at least in this country) has generally been perceived very differently. The process is said to be purposeless: it has been claimed to be random, in the sense that it is dependent on random genetic mutations which are then 'naturally selected' because they are beneficial to members of a particular species. Darwin's theory of evolution has a beautiful simplicity and an elegance which has commended it to scientists, and which has made it accessible to the public. It combines freedom (through genetic mutation) with determinism (with the genetic make-up determining the 'phenotype' or structure of an individual member of a species). Charles Darwin is now rightly regarded as a great scientist. At first, however, his theory of evolution failed to gain assent, but the discovery of the genetic mechanisms of inheritance together with the laws of genetic inheritance (originally uncovered by Mendel) reinstated it, and have revived Darwin's reputation. Today Neo-Darwinism has become in twentieth-century British culture almost an alternative religion.[16]

Neo-Darwinism is accepted by most Christian thinkers on the grounds that the natural selection of beneficial genetic mutations is God's way of introducing novelty and creativity into the evolutionary process. It is certainly possible that God decided that evolution should take this 'blind' course, in the knowledge that somewhere or other in this universe there might emerge intelligent life. We cannot claim to know the divine will in these matters. But it is not easy to understand how God could have so decided if his nature is infinite love. Instead of guiding the process from within, God would be seen as remote from it. If God did decide in this way to explore all the potentialities of his creation, he would appear to be playing a game of possibilities rather than acting as a purposive Creator.

The general acceptance of Neo-Darwinism is remarkable in view of its lack of credentials. According to the theory minute random changes in the genetic make-up of a creature take place either through faulty replication or through some such effect on the genes as radiation. Most of these mutations are deleterious, and lead either to the death of the creature concerned, or to an inability to reproduce in sufficient numbers to sustain the mutation in future generations. Very occasionally a mutation would be beneficial, and this would favour the individual creature concerned and its offspring, and gradually become built into the species as a whole. Very gradually, over vast epochs of time, the cumulative effects of these occasional beneficial mutations would build up in such a way as not just to benefit the species concerned, but to bring into existence new species which are adapted to their environment, and which therefore flourish.

Darwin himself claimed that natural selection of this kind (of course he did not know about the genetic aspect of mutation) was the *chief* cause of the evolution of species: Neo-Darwinists insist that it is the *only* cause.[17] It is claimed that by this means and by this means alone there have evolved all the millions of species on earth, all the way from primeval one-celled organisms to the huge complexity of *homo sapiens*. The pathway was blind. The mutations were random, but because 'natural selection' ensured that the beneficial mutations were retained, the process gives the appearance of being purposeful.

This theory seems flawed on several counts.[18] Actual evidence of the evolution of even a single species by this means is lacking. The hypothesis depends on the dating of fossils, the interpretation of fossil evidence, and on logical argument. The dating of fossils depends on the dating of the sedimentary rocks in which they are found, and this in turn depends on 'uniformitarianism'. This is the theory that these rocks were gradually formed at a uniform rate over vast tracts of time. But this theory is very hard to sustain against a reconstruction based on catastrophic events on Planet Earth. It comes as something of a shock to realize that the 'geological column', which lists the dates of the various rock strata and which is usually taken for granted, rests largely on supposition and conjecture. Contrary to popular belief, the sedimentary rocks in which the fossils are found cannot be directly dated by radioactive techniques, as they contain no radioactive substances other than those in igneous rocks occasionally intruded into them. Other means of dating suggest a much shorter span. Neo-Darwinism can hardly be sustained if it can be shown that there were not vast tracks of time in which the alleged beneficial mutations could accumulate.

The interpretation of fossil evidence is very ambiguous. For example, a famous sequence of fossils, when closely examined, does not show the progressive evolution of the horse, as usually assumed. Further, there are no fossil remains of any 'missing link' between species. Neo-Darwinism is based on 'natural selection'; but the experience of artificial selection in breeding plants and animals shows that there is a limit beyond which members of a species cannot further be altered. When animals or plants are selected in order to transgress this limit, they cannot reproduce themselves; and the same is likely to happen as a result of natural selection. The Neo-Darwinists' argument that species evolve through cumulative mutation would appear to rest on what has been called the 'statistical fallacy'.[19] Extremely rare beneficial mutations would have to occur *in the right order* in order to accumulate in such a way that evolutionary progress could occur; but the statistical probability of this happening is slight. The odds against these rare mutations taking place at all, when multiplied by the odds against their taking place in the right order, are hugely improbable. Nor is it clear how natural selection could lead e.g. to the long neck of the giraffe, or to thick skin under the sole of the foot. Critics of the theory have challenged Neo-Darwinists to explain a long list of such features in animals and plants, to which they have not yet so far responded.

Neo-Darwinism has relied for much of its strength on the supposition that while genetic information can travel from DNA in the 'double helix' to the proteins of the body, it cannot travel the other way round. But this has now been found not to be always the case. Viruses can act as the means of their transference. Furthermore, far-from-random mutations can occur in bacteria in response to a change in their environment, and computer models suggest that complex systems can tend naturally towards self-organization. Another strength of Neo-Darwinism is that there is not yet a theory of evolution to put in its place. If chance is not the engine of evolution, we do not yet know in scientific terms what is. It may be connected with dynamic structures far from equilibrium, or with quantum processes in the form and structure of biological organisms. It may be something quite different. It seems likely that evolutionary progress has taken place through macro-mutations. However, a theory does not become true because there is no other theory to put in its place. A theory is true because it can be verified, or at least not falsified. The strength of feeling among those who think that Neo-Darwinism has been falsified may be exemplified by the words of a well-known Swedish professor of biology: 'I believe that one day the Darwinian myth will be ranked as the greatest deceit in the history of science.'[20]

It has been necessary to devote so much space to Neo-Darwinism in a book about Christian belief because its influence in the West has been so widespread, particularly in Britain. While we now know that Huxley, its great proponent, was motivated by an anti-ecclesiastical bias,[21] it is important that the theory should only be discarded on scientific (and not on theological) grounds. Our belief in God does not stand or fall by one particular theory. Theologians have manfully tried to incorporate the concept into a view of a purposive God.[22] In particular, there are distinguished contemporary scientist theologians who accept the conclusions of Neo-Darwinism.[23] But the logical effect of applying Neo-Darwinism to religion is either to remove God altogether from the scene, or to make him remote from his creation and totally reliant on chance mutations to achieve any purposes he may have for his creation. This is not to deny that there is a real element of contingency in the creative process; but to make it totally reliant on chance is difficult to combine with the concept of a purposive Creator.

The claims of creation-centred spirituality examined

What doctrine of God does emerge from our consideration of the natural world? We surely want to echo the words of St Paul: 'O the depth both of the riches and knowledge of God! How unsearchable are his judgements and his ways past finding out! For who hath known the mind of the Lord? Or who hath been his counsellor?' (Rom 11.33f.). But we cannot say much more than that. We have seen (by the analogy of human love) that procreation is the natural outcome of human love, but this analogy does not in any way demonstrate that the Creator is loving: indeed there is evidence that could be used to show the contrary (see pp. 133ff.). When we analyse what we can find out about the divine nature from a consideration of the natural world, we can say little more than that we are confronted with Being itself, of infinite power and knowledge and wisdom, existing beyond space and time and yet active and immanent within it. We also can see that in the living world which God has created, self-sacrifice (of a female for her offspring) and death is the rule of life, and that this is the condition under which new life is generated; yet this may not reflect some profound truth about the nature of the Creator, but only illustrate the 'selfish gene' ensuring its survival in the next generation. Without further self-disclosure, we know very little about God. What we do know is inadequate for worship, not does it give us a way of life, except that we ought not thoughtlessly or greedily to destroy the environment of which God is the author and in which we live. But much more than that is needed to determine our life-style and principles of living.

Yet there are those who advocate 'creation-centred spirituality'. There is a great truth to be found here, in that the Christian faith has not in the past taken the material world in which we live very seriously, either regarding it as infected by sin, or despising physical things in favour of spiritual realities. In the material world we do see a real reflection of the glory of God, and we can appreciate more of his wisdom and creativity. Scientific understanding of the universe increases our wonder at the scale and intricacy and interdependence of his creation. It has been a cardinal principle in writing this book that the physical world must be taken very seriously indeed, and we need to express our theology not in terms of pre-scientific myth, but by using scientific models in order to express the eternal truths to be found in those myths.

In fact there has been a long tradition of creation spirituality in the Church,[24] although it has been somewhat obscured by the prevalence of Augustinian spirituality, which has concentrated on the need for redemption from sin almost to the exclusion of the inspiration to be found in the natural world. At the same time, the actual grounds which have been given for a creation-centred spirituality are not very impressive.[25] It is said to be made necessary by our contemporary crises. The ecological crisis, we are told, needs a cosmic spirituality if it is to be surmounted. Certainly a wider vision of God at work throughout his world is required, but even if this were generally accepted, humanity unfortunately seldom takes a right course when this is in conflict with short-term satisfactions. The problem lies in the hearts of men and women rather than in their failure to accept creation spirituality, and the flaws in mankind are too serious to be mended merely by the vision of a 'green view of life'. Nor can what is called 'the scientific awakening' be in itself a sufficient reason for creation-centred spirituality. The natural sciences, as we have seen, are providing us with new models by which to interpret the world, and we need to take some of these into our theological thinking and into our prayers and life-style, shaping these new models so that they conform with scriptural revelation and the Church's tradition. But these sciences cannot show us how to change the human heart so that men and women can carry out a vision which captures their imagination.

Global ecumenism, again, is certainly needed today. We must postpone until later an examination of the relationship of Christianity to other faiths (see pp. 145–50), but clearly we share with most of the mainstream religions a common apprehension of the divine, and a belief in a creator God: what has been called the *philosophia perennis* (the perennial philosophy).[26] But the fact that these faiths share for the most part these common views about the creator of the natural world does not mean that we should concentrate on a creation-centred spirituality. That would be a reductionist faith contracted to its lowest common denominator, something which would be rejected by all the faiths concerned.

It is also said that creation-centred spirituality enables us to reinstate Mother Nature in theologies that have been too long dominated by masculine stereotypes and ways of thinking. We shall be examining gender later in so far as it affects the Christian doctrine of God (see pp. 130f.). Mother Nature is not foreign to the creation story as told in the Scriptures, for God calls on the earth to 'bring forth' or give birth to living creatures. Even when we come to examine the titles bestowed on Jesus in the New Testament, we shall find among them 'the wisdom of God', a female principle in the thought of his day. We may be helped by a creation-centred spirituality, but we do not need this in order to justify the use of feminine analogies when we speak about God. Again, it is said that creation-centred spirituality will encourage 'right-brain thinking'. It is well known that (in right-handed people) the left hemisphere of the cortex is connected with logical processes of thought, while the right hemisphere is connected with form, music, intuition and holistic thinking. We shall argue later the need for imagination and intuition in theology and worship (see pp. 263, 268) but in fact there is already much 'right-brain thinking' to be found in religious practice and worship. For example, the symbol of the crucified Christ has had vastly more impact on millions of people than any particular theory of the Atonement.

Creation-centred spirituality can have the good result of focusing attention on the new scientific models now available to us, which we can use as images by which to express our Christian faith. Its proponents are right to point out that we need to take the work of creation as seriously as the work of salvation. But, perhaps in an attempt to redress the balance, it is sometimes implied that creation-centred spirituality means the exclusion of a fall/redemption model. In fact we need a spirituality that includes both creation and redemption.

Nature as part of the Kingdom of God

There is one important aspect of creation which should be drawn out of the ancient creation myth of the 'cosmic covenant' according to which God set the bounds of the natural forces of the universe, and this should be considered in conjunction with God as the creator and sustainer of the universe. He is responsible for the constants and laws of the universe. Theoretical physicists seek constantly for TOE (the Theory of Everything) which would explain all the constants of nature and all the natural laws (or regularities) on which the whole vast edifice of the natural sciences depend. So far it has eluded them, and they may be on a wild-goose chase. But even if they do succeed in their search, they still need to explain why there is a TOE. Christians believe that God is the Creator and Sustainer of TOE (if it exists) just as he is of the whole creation.

The creation obeys the laws of the Creator. As we have seen, the Creator has given his creation a degree of freedom. It was probably not inevitable that life evolved on this planet. Other bifurcations of the evolutionary process were possible. There was a degree of contingency, since life could not have evolved unless the conditions of climate, etc. were appropriate. It was not inevitable that life evolved in the way in which it has. Evidence from the Burgess Shale in British Columbia suggests that there was an initial multiplication of different forms of multi-cellular animals, followed later by elimination of different types, with the subsequent evolution of species springing from only a few basic anatomical designs, and constrained by the effects of mass extinctions.[27] Within this process there must have been a high element of contingency, so chance played its part in the emergence of humanity. (This freedom, we have already noted, was vital if humanity was to evolve with the capacity for free choice.)

If the natural world enjoys this degree of freedom, and yet obeys the laws of its Creator and Sustainer, it can rightly be called a form of the Kingdom of God. God is its king, and the plants and the animals his subjects; and the forces of nature obey his laws. The interdependence which we have noted as a vital ingredient of nature's ecology shows that there is a sense in which Gaia forms a kingdom or community. Of course plants and animals do not have the freedom of choice in the matter which human beings possess; and furthermore living things require food. Unless they are herbivores which feed on vegetable matter, they are predators which kill other animals for sustenance. This ensures the recycling of nature's resources. It is part of the law of their being, a law of life approved by their Creator, which ensures that nothing in his Kingdom is lost.

What happens to the Kingdom of God after humankind has evolved? To answer that question we need to consider the emergence of mankind and the nature of humanity, to which we next turn.

43

Notes

1. Alexandr Men, *Les Sources de la Religion* (Paris, 1991), p. 141. Fr Men is not generally known in Britain. In Marxist times his books were smuggled out of the USSR and published abroad. After the death of Sakharov he inherited the spiritual leadership of Russia, but he was murdered in 1990 by reactionary forces.

2. See S. Hawking, *A Brief History of Time* (London, 1988). For those who prefer a simplified version, read K. Ferguson, *Stephen Hawking* (London, 1992).

3. Augustine, *City of God*, XI.5.6.

4. H. Ellis, *Before the Beginning* (London/New York, 1993), pp. 94–9, gives five main approaches to explaining the existence of the cosmos: random chance, high probability, necessity, universality and design.

5. For a description of these 'coincidences' see P. C. W. Davies, *The Accidental Universe* (Cambridge, 1982); J. Gribbin and M. Rees, *Cosmic Coincidences* (London, 1990).

6. See W. B. Harland, R. L. Armstrong, A. V. Cox, L. E. Craig, A. G. Smith and D. G. Smith, *A Geologic Time Scale 1989* (Cambridge, 1989). For arguments against the conventional time scale, see R. Milton, *The Facts of Life* (London, 1992), pp. 39–49.

7. Suggested first by F. Crick, *Life Itself* (New York, 1982).

8. Suggested by F. Hoyle and M. C. Wickramasinghe, *Evolution from Space* (London, 1981).

9. See J. Lovelock, *The Ages of Gaia* (Oxford, 1988).

10. P. C. W. Davies and J. Gribbin, *The Matter Myth* (London, 1991).

11. See J. Barrow and F. Tipler, *The Anthropic Cosmological Principle* (Oxford, 1986); and the criticisms of M. Midgley, *Science as Salvation* (London, 1992).

12. See E. Jantsch, *The Self-Organizing Universe* (London, 1980), p. 308: 'The divine becomes manifest neither in personal nor in any other form but in the total evolutionary dynamics of a multi-level reality.'

13. See R. Murray, *The Cosmic Covenant* (London, 1992).

14. For the development of this analogy, see H. Montefiore, 'Love and marriage' in *Reclaiming the High Ground* (London, 1990), p. 19.

15. A. Nygren, *Agape and Eros* (London, 1932). See criticism by C. E. Raven, *Experience and Interpretation* (Cambridge, 1953), p. 42n. For an idiosyncratic exposition of the distinctions between *agape*, *philia* and *eros*, see P. Tillich, *Systematic Theology*, vol. 1 (London, 1953), pp. 310–13.

16. See M. Midgley, *Evolution as a Religion* (London, 1985).

17. C. Darwin wrote in his Introduction to his 4th edition of *Origin of Species:* 'I placed in the most conspicuous position – namely at the close of the Introduction – the following words: "I am convinced that natural selection has been the main but not the exclusive means of modification". This has been of no avail. Great is the power of misrepresentation.'

18. See H. Montefiore, 'The origin of species' in *Reclaiming the High Ground, op. cit.*; R. Milton, *The Facts of Life, op. cit.* Further arguments against Neo-Darwinism (from different viewpoints) may be found in S. A. Kaufman, *The Origins of Order: Self-Organization and Selection in Evolution* (Oxford, 1993) and F. Hoyle and C. Wickramasinghe, *Our Place in the Cosmos* (London, 1993).

19. F. Crick, *Life Itself* (New York, 1981), pp. 89–93; F. Hoyle and C. Wickramasinghe, *Our Place in the Cosmos, op. cit.*

20. S. Løvtrup, *Darwinism* (London, 1987), p. 422.

21. C. Russell, 'The conflict metaphor and its social origins', *Science and Christian Belief* 1.1 (1989), pp. 8ff.; J. R. Lucas, 'Wilberforce and Huxley: a legendary encounter', *The Historical Journal* 22.2 (1979), pp. 313–30.

22. See J. R. Moore, *The Post-Darwinian Controversies* (Cambridge, 1979).

23. E.g. A. R. Peacocke, *Creation and the World of Science* (Oxford, 1979); I. G. Barbour, *Religion in an Age of Science* (London, 1990).

24. E.g. Meister Eckhart, Hildegarde of Bingen, Mechtild of Magdeburg, Francis of Assisi.

25. See M. Fox, *Original Blessing* (Santa Fe, 1983), pp. 12–26.

26. B. Griffiths, *A New Vision of Reality* (London, 1989), p. 10.

27. See S. J. Gould, *Wonderful Life* (London, 1990).

chapter 3

The nature of human beings

The origin of humanity

Human beings like to think of themselves as far removed from animals, but in fact they share 99 per cent of their genetical inheritance with chimpanzees. They also share some of the same characteristics. On the shores of Lake Tanganyika, chimpanzees have been observed to lead a family life not unlike that of human beings, with adolescents playing together and greeting their mothers and friends, and with adults using objects as tools. Our affinities with these and other animals can be demonstrated by tests with blood serum and through a comparison of a particular enzyme protein. This strongly suggests (although it does not of course prove) that human beings evolved from earlier animals. But no 'missing link' between apes and hominids has yet been discovered.

Although the hominids evolved some millions of years ago, *homo sapiens* is reckoned to be very recent in origin. The whole question of dating fossils is very difficult, because of the problems involved in the customary carbon, uranium, argon and other dating methods;[1] and the confidence with which anthropologists see fit to specify the shape and age of a creature when only a few fragments of bone remain strains the credulity of the non-expert. However, there is sufficient evidence to suggest that we do have apes for remote ancestors, who would of course have been tree dwellers. On conventional dating methods, sometime between seven and three million years ago, hominids emerged which stood on two feet. The hypothesis which best accounts for the marked physiological differences between humanity and apes is that our ape ancestors at one stage became aquatic, possibly in the Afar district of Ethiopia near the Red Sea;[2] and when the sea waters were blocked off and eventually evaporated, they emerged on land bipedal, hairless, with subcutaneous fat, salty tears and sweat (and an inefficient cooling mechanism), as well as with certain important sexual differences.

Like other primates, human beings have neocortex (where conscious thinking takes place) comprising 80 per cent of their brains, compared with only up to 30 per cent in other animals. They also evolved larger brains, three times bigger than that of other primates in relation to their size.[3] The most acceptable theory to account for this is that of neoteny, which involves a stretching of the various stages of an animal's development. This would explain the length of human infancy, when the brain (unlike that of other primates) still continues to grow for two years. It so happens that neoteny is a characteristic of aquatic mammals, and near the tropical seashore there would have been the nourishing diet required to supply the needs of the growing brain tissue. When hominids emerged from the waters, they lived on the land, and spread to all continents, before 'Pangaia' became split (through continental drift) into our present continents.[4] They lived first by hunting other animals, then they became pastoralists, and later agriculturalists, until advancing technology completely changed their ways of life.

It may seem to us in retrospect that humanity with its special talents and endowments is the outcome of so many unlikely contingencies that we are simply an extraordinary quirk of nature. However in the sight of God, who is the source of all natural laws, and to whom all potential contingencies are known and from whom no secrets of quantum effects or any other aspects of the universe are hidden, we are one of the providential results of his creative process.[5]

The origin of the human brain

How did human intelligence develop? The evolution of brain power 's related to the ratio of brain size to body weight. (The human brain is at least 100 times the size of the earliest reptilian and amphibian brains.) There is no agreement about how the human brain evolved. Some think that the reptilian brain had superimposed upon it new structures of the limbic system (the seat of the emotions) found in the 'palaio-mammalian' brain, and there was later superimposed (in the case of mammals) the further structure of the cerebral cortex in the 'neo-mammalian' brain where thinking takes place. Others hold that the brain gradually developed in complexity caused by duplications resulting from genetic mutations, or through the differentiation of existing neurones, or (the dominant theory today) through a shift in cell migration in the developing organism.

It has been suggested that the impetus towards development was given some 200 million years ago through the supersession of the need for visual systems required by reptiles by the new need for the co-ordination of smell and sound among the earliest mammals, which were small nocturnal creatures. The cerebral cortex is thought to have evolved further when some 65 million years ago 'modern' mammals evolved, because their daylight hunting required the integration of vision with smell and sound. The further development of the cortex (40 per cent of the brain in modern mammals) enlarged their powers of perception and their ability to make and memorize maps of the environment, enabling the richer diet needed to sustain the enlarged brain, and permitting an increased rate of metabolism. Some connect the development of the brain with endothermy, that is the ability to sustain a constant body temperature, which again required increased supplies of energy derived from the diet.

Such theories are by no means universally accepted. There are those who think that social interaction was as important for the development of human intelligence as energy supplies, and that this explains the fact that monkeys' brains are two or three times the size of those of other modern mammals. It seems that the hominid brain size did not increase greatly in size compared with those of other primates until some two and a half million years ago. However, brain size is not the only determinant. Neural architecture is also important. In the case of humans, the prefrontal zone of the cortex, which is connected with speech centres, is about six times as large as that of apes. With human beings, the cortex accounts for a staggering 70 or 80 per cent of brain volume.

Speech is intimately related to human intelligence, but there is a division of opinion over when speech first evolved, and whether it is continuous with earlier evolution, or whether it depends on neural structures peculiar to *homo sapiens*. Speech was not possible until the hyoid bone evolved which anchors the tongue and other muscles. It is also connected with what is known as 'Broca's area', a bulge in the left side of the brain, which is found among early hominids two million years ago. However the evolution of bodily change which made speech possible does not necessarily mean that speech began at the same time as those changes took place. On the whole, fossil evidence supports the view that language evolved early on, while archaeological evidence points to its later development, with a sudden and dramatic shift in mental abilities a mere 40,000 years ago. Once again, these are deep differences of opinion among the experts.

There is thus much uncertainty about the way in which the human brain evolved from our reptilian forebears. When humanity emerged the brain was sufficiently complex for self-consciousness and introspection to arise. Humanity is made in the image of God, and mental activities focused on the brain play a major part in defining what it means to be made in the divine image (see p. 51). It is therefore important to review the origins of the human brain and its evolution, and to consider the theological implications. Clearly there has been much contingency. At the same time the most primitive form of animal brain contained within itself the potentiality for evolution into the human brain, with its ability to calculate and philosophize and to engage in abstract thought and introspection and meditation on divine realities. Because the evolution of the human brain is dependent on so many contingent factors, its evolution cannot be said to be within God's direct providence. But intelligence and consciousness were almost bound to emerge in the universe sooner or later. 'The details of our mentality will depend on the minor and accidental specifics of evolutionary history, but the emergence of consciousness somewhere and somewhen in the universe is practically guaranteed.'[6] (NASA would hardly be conducting a search for extra-terrestrial intelligence unless such a view were generally shared.) Because of the potentiality of the primitive brain for subsequent evolution so that intelligence and consciousness could arise, this development can rightly be regarded as part of the divine providence (see p. 47).

Biblical accounts of human origin

It has been necessary to spend so much space on the probable origins of the human race because our contemporary understanding is so different from that of the authors of the first two chapters of Genesis, and the accounts in Genesis have dominated Christian thinking ever since the inception of the Church. These Genesis stories are revelatory because they incorporate inspired insights into human nature which are essential for the proper understanding of humanity. But, despite our need of the spiritual truths which the biblical story of Adam and Eve contains, we can no more accept this biblical account as scientific history than we can that of the creation of the universe; and in any case it is unlikely that the biblical story was intended to be a historical account. As human beings living near the end of the twentieth century we are children of contemporary culture. We welcome the extension of human knowledge, including the contemporary accounts of mankind's origin; but we must not accept with them the purely humanistic interpretation which usually accompanies them. We have been careful to interpret them in a way consistent with our faith in God our Creator and Sustainer so that the revelatory aspects of the biblical story still remain intact.

The image of God in humanity

According to the first chapter of Genesis, God made man different from the animals. 'In the image of God created he him: male and female created he them.' What does the image of God mean? Originally some physical likeness may have been intended; but since God is without body or parts, the real meaning must be spiritual. In some important ways humanity resembles God. Our most striking characteristic, contrasted with the animals, is our intelligence. Physiologically speaking, this derives from our enlarged brain, and the anatomical developments which made speech possible;[7] but theologically speaking we rightly call these changes providential (see p. 36). (In the same way ventro-ventral sex — that is, intercourse that takes place face to face and not from the rear – which probably derives from our aquatic ancestry, has made possible personalized sex: this again is providential.) In God are hidden all the treasures of wisdom and understanding, and human beings are in God's image in so far as they mirror this. Animals of course show incipient marks of intelligence. They can communicate by sign language or by sound and ultrasonics. Chimpanzees can count and baboons can practise deliberate deceit. But only human beings are capable of conscious thought. They alone can develop concepts and ideas, and they alone are able to unravel the secrets of God's world. It is extraordinary that they have achieved so much by using only a fraction of the neocortex which they have evolved. Intelligence is part of what is entailed in being made in God's image, reflecting, however faintly, the fullness of wisdom and knowledge in God.

Another characteristic which is unique to human beings is the moral faculty. Human beings may differ in their views of what is right and wrong, but only human beings are capable of free moral choices. Animals may be conditioned to certain types of behaviour, and even to show signs of discomfort if they transgress them. They inherit social instincts which help to regulate their actions. But they are incapable of free moral choice. Human beings may not always decide to act in a moral way. They may determine to act immorally. But a human being who is entirely amoral is rightly regarded as in this particular respect subhuman. One of the most important truths of revelation given by God, as we shall see later, is the disclosure of his nature as righteous (see pp. 106f.); and this is mirrored in the human moral faculty which can distinguish right from wrong.

A further unique characteristic of human beings is their capacity for personal relationships. In many animals there is pair-bonding, occasionally for life. There is often a special relationship, at least during infancy and adolescence, between a young animal and its mother, on whom it may depend for food and protection. The origins of personal relationships which humans enjoy can certainly be seen in the animal world. But the development of speech and intelligence, the ability to make moral choices, the refinement of their emotions and feelings has enabled human beings to engage in depth in personal relationships, which find their apogee in the experience of human love between two persons. Most importantly this faculty enables human beings to have a personal relationship with God, and mirrors to some extent the nature of divine love itself.

Intelligence, the power of free moral choice and the ability to make personal relationships are all part of what it means to be human. These abilities may be gravely impaired, but they cannot be removed without extinguishing essential aspects of humanity. It follows therefore that sin (that is, disobedience to God's will) cannot obliterate them. The early Fathers distinguished between likeness and image; and this distinction is helpful. We behave in a way which is very *unlike* God; but we cannot extinguish his *image* in us and still remain human. It is this image which raises human beings to a different category from the animals. Intelligent life is rightly regarded as part of the divine purpose behind the evolutionary process. This is not to say that God does not have other purposes. Nor is it to assert that humanity cannot commit collective suicide by its follies and futilities. It is however to claim a very special dignity for each individual of the human race. It is this dignity that forms the basis of what is often called 'human rights', and which means that a human being should always be treated as an end and never merely as a means (see p. 245).

The dominion of man

According to the second chapter of Genesis (unlike the first chapter), man was not created at the same time as the animals. Adam was lonely. The animals were created for his companionship, but they did not suffice. And so Eve was formed out of his rib. This myth declares that man was prior to woman, whereas recent scientific research suggests that the female developed prior to the male. The biblical story has abiding value because it shows the close companionship and kinship between humanity and the animal world, and it also demonstrates the close bodily affinity between man and woman, and their deep need for each other.

The myth predates by many thousands of years the recent sexual revolution, according to which woman has the same status as man. It is man in Genesis 2 who has power over the animal kingdom, which is shown by his naming of them. In the first chapter this dominion is more explicit, but the dominion there is shared between man and woman, deriving from their status as together created in God's image. It is because of this resemblance to God that they are to act as God's deputies, and to have power over all living things. They are to be fruitful and multiply and fill the earth. This has often been understood as a licence to exploit the earth and its contents as much as they wish; but in fact this dominion over nature is given to human beings created in God's image, and God therefore requires them to use it with God-like responsibility. The command to multiply belongs to an age where life was brutish and short, and where man's hold on life was fragile. It was not a command to go on multiplying in such a way as to endanger the earth over which they hold dominion. This dominion is a *de facto* reality, but unless it is exercised in such a way that the interdependence of all living things is recognized and honoured, mankind will bring retribution upon itself. The spiritual insight about man's dominion in Genesis is of abiding value and truth. But the Bible itself ought to prevent a too exclusively anthropocentric view of the world. There are passages where other animals have an importance in God's eyes equal to that of mankind (e.g. Psalms 104 and 108). Above all, when Job's God takes him on a tour of all creation (Job 38–41), he constantly humbles Job by rubbing in that he does not understand *anything* about God's creatures. 'Job would not have stood a chance if he had tried to reply "You have subjected all these to me". The same Bible contains the subjection of all creatures to humankind *and* their autonomy as God's creatures, which is for us to respect.'[8] Our modern knowledge of ecology shows the interdependence of all life, and it confirms the need to supplement the biblical doctrine of man's dominion over the natural world with the other biblical doctrine about the intrinsic goodness of all God's creatures.[9]

Human nature

According to the story as told in the second chapter of Genesis, 'the Lord God formed man of the dust of the ground, and breathed into his nostrils the breath of life; and man became a living soul (*nephesh*)'. The Israelite conception of man is made clear through this myth of creation; and even though the myth is adopted from other nations, it still preserves the essential stamp of the Israelite manner of thinking. 'The text does not set out to analyse the elements of man, but to represent his basic character. The basis of its essence was the fragile corporeal substance, but by the breath of God it was transformed and became a *nephesh*, a soul. It is not said that man was supplied with a *nephesh* and so the relation between body and soul is different from what it is to us. Such as he is, man, in his total essence, is a soul.'[10] Humanity is a unity. Mankind is psychosomatic. The soul is not something added to the body, or separable from the body. Man became a living person (which is perhaps the best rendering of *nephesh* in this connection). So humanity is on the one hand purely material ('dust thou art, and to dust thou shalt return'), and on the other hand entirely spiritual (he became a *nephesh*). One cannot do something to someone's body that does not affect the *nephesh*, and one cannot do something to the *nephesh* that does not affect the body. This is an inspired insight into the nature of human personality. Furthermore, life, human life, is seen as the gift of God. According to contemporary thinking, life is something that arose naturally from a particular complexity of matter, although as we have seen there is still mystery about how it actually originated. But, however it arose, it is still the gift of God. The imagery of God breathing into the nostrils of primal man symbolizes the assumption that human life is participation according to its mode in the eternal life of God himself.

These are revealed insights into human nature. But the passage does not in itself solve psychological questions about the functioning of human consciousness and the operation of human personality. It was not intended to do that. It is sometimes wrongly assumed that the Scriptures not only reveal to us crucial insights about humanity's basic nature, but also that we should adopt today the primitive psychology of ancient Israel. We must not assume, as did the ancient Israelites, that, because a human being is a totality, the soul or *nephesh* collapses when the body disintegrates at death (unless the body is resurrected with its accompanying *nephesh*). Nor does the passage license us to assume that mind and brain are simply different aspects of the same totality.

The soul

We have today a fairly complete picture about the way in which a human body develops within a woman's womb:

A newly fertilized egg, a corpuscle one two-hundredth of an inch in diameter, is not a human being. It is a set of instructions sent floating into the cavity of the human womb. Enfolded within the spherical nucleus are an estimated two hundred and fifty thousand or more pairs of genes, of which fifty thousand will direct the assembly of the proteins and the remainder will regulate their rates of development. After an egg penetrates the blood-engorged wall of the uterus, it divides again and again. The expanding masses of daughter cells fold and crease into ridges, loops and layers. Then, shifting like some magical kaleidoscope, they reassemble into the foetus, a precise configuration of blood vessels, nerves and other complex tissues. Each division and migration of the cells is orchestrated by a flow of chemical information that proceeds from the genes to the outer array of proteins, fats and carbohydrates that make up the substance of the constituent cells.

In nine months a human being has been created.[11]

This describes the physical development of a human being. But it leaves no room for the development of a human soul. When the foetus reaches a sufficient degree of complexity, quickening takes place, and after further development, birth supervenes. The resultant human being has a purely physical nature. This view of humanity is part of the materialist outlook.

Materialism is a common assumption that lies behind much recent scientific writing. Reductionist theories have reduced a human being to a bundle of behaviour patterns, after the model of a rat in a box which learns to manipulate a lever in order to satisfy its desires. A sociobiologist has written: 'The brain exists because it promotes the survival and multiplication of genes that direct its assembly. The human mind is just a device for survival and reproduction, and reason is just one of its learning techniques.'[12] Materialism lies at the root of such viewpoints. Derived from positivism, it results in a reductionist view of the human brain. There has recently been a quickening in the pace of scientific investigation of the brain, usually (but not always[13]) by those who hold reductionist views. But it is hard to account on reductionist grounds for the freedom of the will, and as a result those who identify the brain wholly with the mind tend to be determinists.[14] As a well-known Professor of Physiology has written: 'I should be uncomfortable to feel that I was not in control of my life or to feel that I was not responsible for my actions. But I believe that the "I" in me is the operation of a mind, which is itself the operation of a brain, constructed solely by genes and environment. I find that notion just as wonderful as, and in many ways more satisfying than, the empty illusion of a spiritual self."[15]

Descartes sharply divided the soul from the body, but Cartesian dualism has long been generally abandoned. Yet there still remains for many people the concept of the self, a seat of consciousness not to be identified *simpliciter* with the human brain. Recently, however, theories have been produced to account for the experience of consciousness on materialist lines.[16] The stream of consciousness is said to be an illusion: rather there are many streams of consciousness created by circuits within the human brain functioning rather like parallel computers combining to mimic a single serial machine. Attempts are even made on Darwinist lines to explain how such a brain came into existence. These theories in no sense constitute proofs or even demonstrations: in large measure they are the working out, in scientific terms, of the materialist assumptions of their authors.

Some theologians also believe that the soul has no existence apart from the body, holding that consciousness could only be regained after death in some kind of reconstituted body. Most, however, continue to believe in the existence of the soul. If it is to be in some way distinguished from the body, when are the two conjoined? This is a matter over which Christians are divided. There are those who think that the soul is added to the body when a human sperm first fuses with a human embryo. Others think that it is added when the fertilized ovum first embeds itself in the lining of its mother's womb. St Thomas Aquinas, following Aristotle in this matter as he did in many other ways, believed that a human being is not created until the human soul is infused into the body, after forty days in the case of a male, and ninety days in the case of a female, whom he regarded as a failed male. (Contrary to popular understanding of the matter, the Roman Catholic Congregation of the Faith, in a Declaration on Abortion in 1974, made it clear that 'the question is a philosophical one'.)

If we do not know how the 'animal soul' evolved, which gives to animals their primitive levels of consciousness, we are unlikely to explain the exact relationship of the human soul to the body or the way in which it evolved.[17] According to our contemporary understanding of the growth of personality, it is easier to think in terms of process. As the growing foetus achieves an increasing complexity of development, it attains new qualitative levels of existence with 'new stages and expressions of being welling up from within'.[18] The soul of a human being could develop out of the growing complexity of the body, and could eventually be separable from it. Aquinas, following Aristotle, thought of the soul as the form of the body. As the body developed, so also did its form. Consciousness and self-consciousness developed, and also the 'unconscious' and the psychic faculties of personality. We shall consider later whether after death the soul could exist for a time on its own, waiting to be 'clothed upon' with its new resurrection body (see pp. 226–8).

The idea of the soul is found in most mainstream religions. Judaism and Islam both believe in its existence. Although Buddhism does not have a metaphysical concept of the soul, *vinnana* persists, a kind of 'karmic deposit' from previous lives, an unconscious dispositional state. According to the Hindu Vedanta, the soul is a substance, a spark of *Brahman* immersed in *maya*. Differences of detail must be expected within the different religious traditions, each of which enjoys its particular cultural milieu. But the existence of a soul which can exist in some form apart from the body, and is not to be wholly identified with it, forms part of what might be called the *philosophia perennis* (see p. 148), and is not lightly to be disregarded. On such a view, the soul is to be regarded as co-extensive with the body, so that the two interact in everything that a person does.

The interaction of the soul and the body remains mysterious. In some respects the soul can even extend beyond the physical body. Beyond the personal unconscious, Jung developed the concept of the collective unconscious, so that all share in the archetypes which are part of mankind's inheritance. At the personal level, the interaction of mind with mind is evidenced by paranormal phenomena.[19] Hypnotism and extra-sensory perception strongly suggest this. Poltergeistic activity is often connected with young people in emotional turmoil, as though their psychic energy is disturbed and escapes beyond the confines of their bodies. Telepathy, clairvoyance, clairaudience and other phenomena, although denied almost in principle by the reductionists, have massive testimony. Again, the evidence of special powers granted to saintly people to influence not merely people with whom they are not in touch, but also material objects, is very strong, if viewed without bias. It is as though at the unconscious level we are not totally separated from each other. 'Like islands of an archipelago, joined together underneath the sea that separates them, we are knit together by invisible and unconscious ties.'[20] The soul is moored to the body, and coextensive with it, and yet it is capable of extension far beyond it. The idea is not very far removed from Bohm's idea of the implicate order with everything intimately inter-connected. (The hologram is sometimes given as an example of the way in which the whole may be present in a part: it gives the appearance of a three-dimensional image which persists even when part of the hologram is removed.)

At this unconscious level we are not only linked with other people but also with God. There is much testimony from mystics that they have found God within themselves, in the very centre and ground of their being. Those who are alienated from their selves at this deep unconscious level are likely also to be alienated from God. Experience suggests different levels of consciousness, rather like those experienced by infants as they develop into children. Beginning with the oceanic, in which a person is engulfed in nature and feels one with the universe, the primitive levels of consciousness have much in common with later mystical states of consciousness. The unconscious plays a great part in our conscious states, affecting our moods and our feelings. Repression of conscious feelings may build up pressure in the unconscious, resulting in what seems to be demonic behaviour. But an integrated unconscious is the source of creative imagination, the fountainhead of scientific discovery and of art, and also of religious inspiration. It is at this level that psychic activity probably takes place. However, the mystics have always warned against regarding this level as divine. Here both good and evil forces operate. The divine, which upholds the whole personality, is at the centre of personality. The material or 'gross body' is distinguished from the psychic level (or the 'subtle body' of Buddhism and the Great World of Hinduism), and this may perhaps be identified with the etheric body of which psychics sometimes speak. But this level is not to be confused with the very deepest level of the soul, where we can be confronted by divine Reality itself.

It is sad that Christian theologians, as well as sceptical reductionists, tend to ignore or dismiss this massive testimony to the extension of human personality outside the limits of the body, and to the depths of the personality below the level of conscious thought. Relying on logic for their arguments, and distrustful of intuition, feelings and higher states of consciousness, they prefer a 'left brain' approach to their work, which substitutes argument for symbol and which enables them to have dialogue with sceptical positivists. As a result they tend to have an attenuated and even desiccated doctrine of the human person.

Yet the soul is intimately linked to the body. The brain does play a crucial part in processing information, in storing it, and in collating it. Injury to the brain often means injury to the mind. Degenerative diseases of the brain, like Alzheimer's, result in the deteriorating functioning of the mind. Perhaps we might think of the brain as a complex receiver and transmitter of radio waves, or better, like the hardware of a computer, whose software when it is removed awaits re-embodiment in another compatible computer. The analogy is by no means precise, but it gives some indication of the possible relationship of soul to body. The software certainly has a kind of reality of its own, but it needs to be embodied in hardware to be usable. The soul has a reality of its own, but it needs to be embodied in a body in order to be more than passive, and to function creatively.[21]

Man and woman

Men and women share the same human nature. Their differences are small compared to their similarities, and lie in their differing evolutionary histories. A woman's body is adapted to child-bearing and child-rearing and a man's body is adapted to hunting for sustenance, and also (in the primitive days of the hominids) to hunting for mates, which favoured the survival of the human species. It seems likely that the brains of the two sexes evolved in somewhat different ways, related to these different functions. Because of their differing functions, men tend to be more aggressive than women, for aggression was needed for both types of hunting mentioned above, while women needed the qualities necessary for nursing infants and giving to children the love that they need for their proper maturation. Although there are many different types of temperament and character within either gender, it is fair to say that in general their stereotypes differ, although these differences are very greatly influenced by the culture in which people happen to be living.

According to the creation myth in Genesis 1, men and women are created together in the image of God. There is no hint here of subservience of one sex to the other. In Genesis 2, however, only man is said to be made in the image of God (although 'man' may be regarded as a generic term for a human being, including women as well as men). After Adam's and Eve's transgression, God is said to have pronounced punishment on them both. Eve is told that her labour and groaning will be increased (which suggests that even in the Garden of Eden her life was not without its problems), and that in future childbirth will be painful (up to this point she had borne no children, and she would not have observed pain in travail in the animal kingdom). She was also told: 'You shall be eager for your husband and he shall be your master.' This presumably has a sexual connotation, which may somewhat surprise those who assume men achieve orgasm more easily than women. The mastery of a husband over his wife is here pronounced to be a punishment for transgression.

In fact, the mastery of men over women in primitive societies was an inevitable consequence of the function of women. Men were generally taller than women, and almost always stronger. A man could therefore generally impose his will on a woman as the 'weaker vessel'; and he did. Furthermore a woman was at a disadvantage because she could not control her fertility. In primitive societies it was (and still is) true that a husband is the master of his wife. However, women can now control their fertility, and brain is needed in modern society more than brawn; and so women are not at such a disadvantage. During this century the largest revolution that the world has ever seen has begun to take place, which involves just over half the human race. Humanity is beginning to return to the truth revealed in Genesis 1, that men and women, although different, are equal in the eyes of God. Therefore they should have equal status in the eyes of mankind, for they are created together in the image of God.

The individual and the community

The fact that human personalities seem to overlap at the unconscious level is an indication that we are not merely individual persons, but that we belong together. Human beings, apart from the exceptional hermit, need personal relationships with other people in order to fulfil their personality. (Even hermits met together on the Lord's Day for the eucharist.) Human beings need some form of community, which is different from a mere crowd where the individual merges his personality with others, to which crowd behaviour can bear witness. A community is a body of people to which the individual freely contributes, and from which the individual can draw strength and values and a way of life.

There are as it were concentric circles radiating from the individual. There is the family to whom the individual is linked by common genes as well as by close association (although not so close in most 'developed' Western countries as it was in the days of the extended family). There is usually a circle of friends to which the individual is linked by common interests as well as association. There is for most people the community of the workplace or school. There may be communities of special interest or peer groups with their distinctive subcultures. There is the local community in the area where the individual resides. There is the larger community of the region or area where the individual shares in a common culture, and there is the community of the country to which the individual belongs. For Christians there is the community of the Church where individuals are joined together in their common unity with Christ. Above all, there is the whole human race in which the individual is bound in solidarity with all mankind in the bundle of life. These communities are not merely associations: they have a reality of their own. We may expect therefore that God deals with persons not merely as individuals but as members of various communities, and that if he has relationships with individuals, he will also have them with the countries and other communities to which they may belong.

Original sin and grace

Human beings are capable of great heroism, goodness and unselfishness; but they are also capable of great injustice, evil and selfishness. This applies not simply to individual human beings, but to whole communities. Traditional Christian doctrine has looked to the primal man and woman for the origin of what seems to be a curse inflicted on all mankind, under which they all suffer through their inability to respond positively to God's will. The story of Adam and Eve in the second chapter of Genesis, even if originally it was concerned with the loss of the chance of immortality,[22] has been understood in the tradition of the Church to provide the cause of this universal curse.

It must be said, however, that there are hints in the Bible of an origin of evil earlier than the sins of Adam and Eve and their descendants down to the time of Noah when God decided to reconstitute the earth. According to Genesis 6, the sons of God came down to earth and took to themselves the daughters of mankind, and it was after this took place that the events of Noah's lifetime are recounted. The story as we have it is clearly truncated, and there are hints elsewhere in the Bible (as well as in Old Testament pseudepigrapha, that is to say, in those writings which failed to gain acceptance in the Old Testament canon) of an earlier myth, partly but not wholly obliterated in the biblical texts, whereby the lesser gods revolted against the Most High God, and brought down to earth their rebellion, thus inaugurating the sins of humanity. This gave rise to the story of the Lucifer and the fallen angels. Certainly it is the experience of those with psychic gifts that there are non-human forces of evil, in addition to evil in humanity. It is understandable that this ancient myth was suppressed, because the Bible is concerned to emphasize human responsibility; yet the myth does provide a larger framework in which to understand the perplexing problem of the origin of evil. The idea of a 'precosmic fall'[23] has even been suggested.

The actual story of Adam and Eve may be intended to represent humanity in general. It has no reference whatever to the entail of this curse upon others, but the later stories of Cain and others show that they too suffered from the same weaknesss as that of Adam and Eve. The actual transgression of Adam and Eve was disobedience to the law of God not to eat of a particular tree in the garden of which they were stewards. The punishment was death (but not immediate death). The tree of knowledge was such that anyone who ate of its fruit would know the difference between good and evil. They would lose their innocence and become aware of their sexuality. For this transgression Adam and Eve were banished from the garden. In particular Eve was punished by pain in childbearing, and by subservience to her husband, while Adam was punished by hard and unremitting toil at a refractory earth. And of course they both died, not immediately but in due time. The gift of immortality was denied to them, because their banishment from the Garden deprived them of the opportunity to eat from the tree of life (Gen 3.24).

This ancient folk tale reveals important spiritual truths. It shows the nature of temptation. In this case the woman listened to the blandishments of the serpent (which suggests that the origin of evil is non-human), and the man was persuaded to follow the example of another person. This shows the tendency of human beings to be led into evil and then to blame others for their actions. In this case Eve blamed the serpent and Adam blamed Eve, whereas we are all individually responsible for our actions. It shows too that transgression brings its own inevitable nemesis, and a feeling of guilt, induced by the conviction of God's anger.

However, the central thesis, that to obtain knowledge of good and evil was a sinful error, is surely false. The passage of mankind from primal innocence to moral consciousness was a great step forward. It was not exactly 'to be as gods', but as we have seen it was part of what it means to be created in the image of God. Blind obedience to a command does not have the same moral value as informed and responsible choice. Innocence, regarded as a state in which moral consciousness has not yet evolved, is a lower state of being than full human adulthood, in which a person makes responsible choices on moral grounds. So if this was a fall, there was a 'fall upwards'. Mankind gained the potentiality of greater good.

The early Fathers did not think that Adam's sin was entailed on subsequent humanity. Individual sin was regarded as the free act of the human will, a repetition rather than the consequence of the primal sin. The very phrase 'original sin' did not enter their vocabulary until Tertullian at the end of the second century. This view was strenuously maintained against the Gnostics with their distinction between the élite and the rest of mankind. The moral powers of human beings may have been thought to be enfeebled by the Fall, but with one voice the early Fathers held, up to the time of Augustine, that they were not lost.[24] It was Augustine who believed that the effects of the Fall were so great that the power of spiritual good was totally lost. He interpreted Romans 5.12 in its Latin translation to mean that in Adam all have sinned and all have been condemned, although that is not the meaning necessitated by the original Greek. As a result of this taint, the whole human race in its natural state is powerless to choose what is good without a radical new start from outside. No doubt Augustine was generalizing from his own personal experience, but the effect of his thinking has cast a shadow on Christian thinking ever since. Augustine looked forward to the restoration of the freedom of the will in such a way that while a person will be free to choose evil, that person will be unable to consent to such a choice. Such a person will be unable to sin. That may be our future destiny, but it is certainly not our present experience, whether we are Christians or not.

Pelagius, a British lay monk, who opposed Augustine, evidently spoke also out of his Christian experience. He was revolted by Augustine's insistence that in a situation where no one could opt for the good, God predestined some to a fresh start (with the unspoken corollary that others were predestined to hell). He insisted that people are unaffected by Adam's fall: that they do therefore have complete freedom whether or not to choose evil. He believed that human perfectibility is possible given the will, and that the grace of God is always given to those who make the effort.

Both Augustine and Pelagius were wrong. We are partly constricted in our choices. Sociological surveys show the probability of similar choices by others in similar situations. But they do not show the inevitability of every choice being identical. We are not wholly restricted. Individuals do have freedom to choose. The idea that God predestines us on a certain course is contrary to a doctrine of God according to which God is beyond time, and wills all men to be saved. (It is difficult for us to imagine God as beyond time, but time belongs to the space–time continuum, and only came into existence with the creation of the universe.)

On the other hand the idea that all people are unaffected by what was thought to be original sin is equally false. While we cannot accept the transmission of guilt and sin from Adam and Eve, nonetheless the human personality is wounded and lacks the fulfilment of its potential. Because God loves all without respect of persons, the grace of God is not limited to those who profess Christ. The word 'grace' is derived from the Latin *gratia*, one of whose meanings is free gift. Grace is the free gift of God, which does not add to our being, but which enables it to reach a fuller potential. The best secular illustration is to be found in the mutual love of husband and wife, where the love and support of the one enables the other to reach her or his potential and to achieve what would otherwise be impossible. Grace works in co-operation with the will. But we must not confine our concept of the will to the conscious self. There can come a time when the unconscious self can stage an internal revolt against the aims and motives of the conscious will, and the grace of God co-operates with such an unconscious attempt at greater integration of the self. Wholeness of personality, which is our goal, involves the integration of unconscious and conscious desires.

The concept of prevenient grace (that is, grace which precedes the movement of our will) is often wrongly understood, for God's help is omnipresent to all humanity at all times. Certainly God can put in our hearts good desires, and in that sense his grace is prevenient: it goes before us. But in human decision-making, God's grace is not irresistible: it co-operates with the human will to do good, and the grace to carry out a good action is given in the act of carrying it out. Grace is often experienced in terms of strength and power, but this experience is the outcome of a gracious personal relationship between a person and God.[25] That relationship may be one-sided (when a person is not actively aware of it) or two-sided (when a person uses the will consciously to co-operate with God).

If sin and guilt are not transmitted from Adam, why are they so rampant? Any survey of today's world would be bound to record much sin and evil, on the part of both individuals and nations. How does this occur? The Jewish view is that human beings are created by God with both a *yetser hara'* and a *yetser hatob* (the evil and the good inclination). Christian theologians, by contrast, have traced the origin of evil from the sin of Adam and Eve, although Origen held that souls were pre-existent in heaven, and after their rebellion against God are banished to earth and joined to an earthly body. In the West the common view was traducianism, that is to say, a person's soul, like the body, was regarded as derived from parents and originally from Adam, as it were a chip of the old block. More popular in the East was a form of creationism, according to which each soul was created *ex nihilo* and joined to a body derived from Adam, from whom original sin was derived. According to this view, evil resided in the flesh, which contaminated the soul.

The traducian view that original sin derives from Adam's sin is contrary to the received view of the non-inheritability of acquired characteristics. (We may inherit features of a parent's endowment, such as the colour of our hair or intellectual ability, but not characteristics that have been acquired, like a limp or broken nose.) But if the traducian view is combined with the belief that humanity has evolved from the animals, it accords with modern genetical theory; for if we do not inherit a tendency to do evil from our genes, it is difficult to see how such a tendency could be passed on. Many species of animals belong to groups or packs, and within the group altruistic conduct can benefit the group as a whole, and may have been bred into the genes. The 'selfish gene' often has most to gain through this altruistic behaviour. At the same time animals are essentially self-regarding, concerned with getting sufficient food to eat and with propagating themselves in their offspring. These self-regarding instincts are still strong in human beings who inherit an animal nature. In this sense the tendency towards selfish conduct (which is part of what is meant by original sin) is a traducian inheritance from our animal past.

There are those who have regarded original sin as merely an evolutionary hangover.[26] But the matter is more complex than that. In the first place, infants have to be self-regarding, or they die. Those who were not self-regarding did die, and so those who survived and grew up to reproduce themselves inherited in their genes a tendency to be self-regarding. This self-regarding nature continues to manifest itself late in life, especially in a species whose infancy has been prolonged through neoteny (that is, when what was originally a short phase of life becomes prolonged). In particular the sexual instinct in humanity is very disruptive of morality. It is an instinct only with difficulty brought under control, and seldom completely so. This is hardly surprising. Our evolutionary development has been such that *homo sapiens* has been described by a zoologist as 'the sexiest primate alive'.[27] It has also been shown that the species is in transition from polygyny (marrying many women) to monogamy.[28] This partially explains human failures to live up to sexual ideals. Furthermore, if any truth be granted to Freudian theories, the Oedipus complex (when children try to supplant their father for their mother's love) may be an inheritance from a distant prehistoric past; and sexual fantasies, which are very common, may well be the outcome of sexual instincts repressed below the level of consciousness.

This however by no means wholly explains original sin, which is concerned not merely with concupiscence, or with an inability to control instinctual desires, but also includes a tendency towards the other five of the seven deadly sins, i.e. pride, envy, covetousness, anger and sloth. Here we can be helped by modern psychological insights. Many of these tendencies are the result of our lack of feelings of self-worth, and our attempt to give ourselves value by other means, that is, puffing ourselves up with pride so that we manufacture value for ourselves, desiring to be someone else whom we judge to have the value which we lack, or desiring to give ourselves value by possessing something that belongs to another. Anger is known to be a form of depression, when our rage externalizes our emotions to cover up our inner feelings of valuelessness. Sloth or accidie is deadly because our valuelessness has made us give in and collapse into passive helplessness. The inner feeling of worthlessness, which lies at the heart of the seven deadly sins, is the result of a failure to be loved, or failure to perceive that we are loved. These feelings often have their origins in infancy, and may be exacerbated by the wounds of adolescence when we break away from family bonds in order to try to find our own identity. We feel alienated from our true selves, and since we find God in the ground of our being, we feel alienated from God. We find ourselves trapped within that state of being so well described by St Paul when he wrote: 'The good that I would I do not: but the evil which I would not, that I do' (Rom 7.19).[79]

Even this does not fully explain original sin in our human make-up. Animals can only feel: but human beings can reason, and the reason can serve these negative feelings and emotions. It can be deeply corrupted. We can inherit from our culture not merely negative emotions but also wrong-headed prejudices *Homo sapiens*, as a result of such influences, is one of the few species which engage in internecine fighting and actual murder. For example, many species use a show of force against an opponent of the same species, say in rivalries during courtship, but usually the weaker gives way, whereas among human beings such rivalry can result in injury and murder. Tribalism and nationalism can result in massive bloodshed and slaughter. Racialism has resulted in a Holocaust. Our past bears upon the present, and our intellectual sophistication, far from curbing our negative emotions, can feed them and give them horrible expression. In this sense, and in this sense only, mankind is totally corrupt, in that there is no part of the human personality which is exempt.

But human beings are not totally corrupt in the sense that no good remains in them. We have already noted that the natural man or woman is capable of great goodness, kindness, generosity and beauty of soul. The annals of history and the records of biography testify often to the innate goodness, and sometimes even to the heroism and self-sacrifice of human beings. While there are some who are born with a character which seems to predispose them to evil, there are others who seem to have an innate tendency to be kind and good. We are all a curious mixture of very good and very bad. The doctrine of mankind's total corruption is itself a corrupt doctrine, for there is a certain pride in claiming that we are worse than we really are.

Nonetheless the human predicament is one in which help is urgently needed, even if our sickness is such that we are not always aware of our need. We do need to be healed of our wounds and made more whole. There is no golden age to which we can return. We cannot retreat into pre-human innocence. We cannot escape from our humanity by release from the burden of the flesh. Evil affects the whole human personality. It is as persons, and only as persons, that we can hope to gain wholeness. It is as human persons, with all our animal instincts, that we need to gain control of ourselves without repressing those instincts so that they break out irrepressibly. It is as human persons that we have to regain a true sense of our worth as created in God's image. It is as human persons that we have to accept our childhood and adolescence without repressing them or being at their mercy. It is as human persons that we have to overcome our sense of alienation. It is as human persons that we have to live with the past history of our species, our race and our culture in such a way that these do not dominate us. It is as human beings that we have to cleanse our minds and imaginations from the false prejudices and hatreds which have infected us.

We say we have to do these things, but we cannot do them. Mankind's history is the history of our abject failure. If we cannot do this ourselves, we can only look to God for help.

Notes

1. See R. Milton, *The Facts of Life* (London, 1992), pp. 30–49.

2. See E. Morgan, *The Scars of Evolution* (London, 1990), pp. 51–2.

3. R. Passingham, *The New Scientist* (4 November 1982), p. 288.

4. On the uniformitarian model, Pangaia (the name given for the original single land mass on earth) split aeons and aeons ago, before the evolution of species had developed very far. See R. Milton (*op. cit.*, pp. 65–6) for the argument that species had already developed when the continents formed as the result of a catastrophic event such as the splitting of the Wisconsin ice cap 10,000 years ago.

5. K. Ward, *A Vision to Pursue* (London, 1992), p. 146.

6. P. C. W. Davies, 'The mystery of consciousness' in *The Proceedings of the 5th International Conference on Thinking* (Melbourne, 1993), p. 9.

7. For a summary of the evolution of the brain, see *The New Scientist* (5 December 1992).

8. R. Murray, *The Cosmic Covenant* (London, 1922), p. 163.

9. See H. Montefiore, *Preaching for Our Planet* (London, 1992).

10. J. Pederson, *Israel* (Copenhagen, 1926), vol. i, p. 99.

11. E. O. Wilson, *On Human Nature* (Cambridge, Massachusetts, 1978), p. 53.

12. E. O. Wilson, *op. cit.*, pp. 2–3.

13. E.g. J. Eccles and K. Popper, *The Self and Its Brain* (London, 1954).

14. E.g. R. Cotterill, *No Ghost in the Machine* (London, 1989).

15. C. Blakemore, *The Mind Machine* (London, 1988).

16. See D. C. Dennett, *Consciousness Explained* (London, 1991); J. Searle, *The Rediscovery of Mind* (Boston, 1992).

17. R. C. Swinburne, *The Evolution of the Soul* (Oxford, 1986), p. 183.

18. J. Mahoney, *Bioethics and Belief* (London, 1984), p. 78.

19. See M. C. Perry, *The Resurrection of Man* (Oxford, 1975), pp. 18–39.

20. C. Bryant, *The River Within* (London, 1978), p. 95.

21. For further discussion, see H. Montefiore, 'The premature demise of the soul' in *Reclaiming the High Ground* (London, 1990), pp. 113ff.

22. J. Barr, *The Garden of Eden and the Hope of Immortality* (London, 1992).

23. N. P. Williams, *The Ideas of the Fall and Original Sin* (London, 1939), p. 194.

24. J. Bethune Baker, *The History of Early Christian Doctrine* (London, 1938), p. 307.

25. On grace see *The Doctrine of Grace*, ed. W. T. Whitley (London, 1932).

26. See F. R. Tennant, *The Origin and Propagation of Sin* (Cambridge, 1902), pp. 139–50. For further discussion of this, see N. P. Williams, *op. cit.*, pp. 530–7. I have not discussed Dr Williams's own theory of a pre-cosmic fall, since it accords ill with modern cosmology.

27. C. Morris, *The Naked Ape* (London, 1967), p. 63.

28. E. Morgan, *op. cit.*, p. 147. The reasons adduced for this are: (1) In a harem-type group, when one dominant male is accompanied by several females, he has to fight to maintain his position. Males therefore need to be stronger than females and taller. The male gorilla (which is promiscuous) is twice as heavy as the female and has strong canines. The difference in size and weight between men and women is only 20 per cent, and they have similar canines. With gibbons (which are monogamous) there is no difference between male and female in size or in canines. (2) For hasty copulation in promiscuous activity abundance of sperm is needed. A man's testes are larger than that of a chimpanzee (a few of which are monogamous for a period) but nothing like so large as that of the promiscuous gorilla.

29. For a longer discussion, see H. Montefiore, *Awkward Questions on Christian Love* (London, 1964), pp. 69–96.

chapter 4

The person of Jesus

The need for revelation

What we can know about God in the natural world is quite insufficient to enable us to worship him with mind and heart, for it only leads us to believe that he exists. It does not give us sufficient grounds for beliefs about God's nature. Any assumptions about this in earlier chapters of this book have derived not from the world of nature, but from God's self-disclosure in other ways. Without any divine self-disclosure we would have no real basis for conduct, except a utilitarian ethic which in essence is self-regarding. We would have no real grounds for holding that there is any purpose in life, other than the purposes for which we ourselves order our existence. It could even be that God's nature is such that he has no goodwill towards us, that he has created a universe in which he deliberately wills us to suffer, and that far from being indifferent to our welfare, he is actually malevolent towards us. In such a case we would not expect him to help us in any way: on the contrary, he might torment us. But if God's nature is pure love (a conviction that accords with human experience of love as the highest human experience, a 'given' which is not to be depreciated by reducing it to mere emotion), it is congruous that God, in his love for us, should reveal himself to us in a way by which we can truly know him. We would expect him to disclose to us something of his nature, his purpose for our lives and a way of life that meets the demands both of our human nature and of his will for us. Since God wills all to be saved (1 Tim 2.4) we would expect him to disclose himself to all in accordance with their own particular situation, even though this means through non-Christian religions which are 'incomplete, rudimentary and partially debased'.[1] But this is in itself insufficient. If his self-disclosure is to be adequate to reveal him to human beings, it seems congruous that he should make it through the medium of human personality, for this is the mode of existence which human beings understand best, and which (since humanity is made in his image) is able to reflect his nature. This is what he has done.

Revelation under the old covenant

God's special self-disclosure began thousands of years ago with a call to the patriarch Abraham to leave Ur of the Chaldees and to sally forth without knowing his destination; and he was led to the Holy Land which we now know as Israel. Basic to Jewish and Christian belief is the covenant which God is believed to have made with Abraham, which included the promise that in him all the nations of the world would be blessed. No doubt the historical narratives about the patriarchs recounted in Genesis are part of the folklore of ancient Israel, representing tribal migrations. The stories have been embellished and altered: they are narrated graphically, and with telling details. They seem likely also to incorporate tales about individuals which were carefully preserved in those far off days by word of mouth.

Out of these early beginnings there developed the tribal groups of Israel, who were taught by God to regard themselves as his Chosen People. Out of an original henotheistic faith there developed a conviction that God is one, still repeated daily in the Jewish *Shema'*. But there was no steady progression in God's self-revelation to his people. His people learnt through success and failure; and there were many regressions both to idolatry and to immorality. Certain individuals stand out in the long history of the Jews. Foremost is Moses, who led God's people out of slavery in Egypt into the freedom of the promised land, and gave them the laws of God. Even though the biblical accounts of their escape and of their wilderness wanderings and subsequent conquest of the Holy Land have been idealized, we cannot doubt that historical events, including a historical person of great stature, underlie them. Later the character and long rule of King David, who unified the tribes of Israel, gave rise to a widespread belief in a coming Messiah, an Anointed One who would fulfil all that David himself, for all his greatness, could not achieve.

A succession of prophets (who forthtold about God as much they foretold about him) deepened the Jews' insight into God and his ways. All looked forward to a future reign of peace. The greatest was Elijah who was believed not to have died but to have been taken into heaven. Among others were Amos who spoke of God's righteousness, Hosea of his covenant love for his people, Isaiah of trust in the faithfulness of God, Jeremiah of the inevitability of national disaster. There ensued a period of exile in Babylon in which the Israelite faith was deepened and (through 'Second Isaiah') monotheism trenchantly affirmed. After the return from exile under Persian rule, there began two movements, one of which resulted in the Jews becoming the 'people of the book', and the other leading to lurid prophecies of the imminence of the End, with its vindication of the People of God at the hands of God. During the Jews' successful struggle against the Seleucid dynasty of Antiochus, they came to believe in the atoning sacrifice of martyrdom. After a very brief period of independence, the first for nearly six hundred years, the Roman Pompey entered the Jewish Temple, and Roman vassaldom began. Such was the situation in which Jesus of Nazareth was born: a situation characterized on the one hand by vivid apocalyptic expectations of imminent vindication, and on the other by a meticulous observance of Torah, the Law as interpreted by tradition.

Revelation under the new covenant

In Jesus God disclosed himself in a fully personal way; not through the writing of a book and not merely through the words of a prophet or the wisdom of a sage, but above all through the life and death of an extraordinary human being. It has been necessary to recall the earlier history of the Jews, because Jesus marked its culmination, and because it provides the framework by which Jesus understood his own vocation and by which his work was interpreted by the earliest Jewish Christians, together with the symbols through which it was imaginatively approp riated. Jesus was the Second Moses who brought his people out of darkness into the glorious freedom of the children of God. He was the prophet 'like unto Moses' who it was prophesied would come, and, without demolishing the Torah, he gave the new law of love. Like Elijah the prophet who was believed to return before the Last Day, his coming triggered belief that the Last Days had already begun, and that after his death like Elijah Jesus ascended into heaven. (The story of the Transfiguration however shows his superiority both to Moses and to Elijah.) Jesus was the Son of David (literally a descendant of David, according to St Matthew), the long-awaited Messiah who would redeem his people. It was prophesied by Samuel to David about one of his successors: 'I will be his father and he shall be my son' (2 Sam 7.14). Jesus was that Son of God. Like the later prophets Jesus taught about the righteousness and the love of God, about the need for trust in the faithfulness of God and the inevitability of national disaster. And his death was interpreted as a martyr's death, an atoning sacrifice for sin. Thus he fulfilled the expectations aroused by the writings of the Old Testament.

The virginal conception of Jesus

About Jesus there are inevitably many unanswered questions. In particular the learned are divided about how much can be known with reasonable certainty about Jesus' life and ministry. It is currently fashionable for New Testament scholars to hold a minimizing view, tending to ignore the judgement of those secular historians who regard the Gospels as containing better history than the writings of contemporary pagan biographers in the ancient world. Nonetheless there are solid grounds for witholding assent to the historicity of some Gospel accounts, in particular to the conception of Jesus. It is by no means certain that Jesus was really born in Bethlehem by what is commonly known as the 'virgin birth' but which in fact refers to his virginal conception.

The case for and against this cannot be argued in great detail here.[2] Yet the main points can be summarized, so that the complexities of New Testament scholarship may become apparent. Jesus' virginal conception is only mentioned in St Luke's and St Matthew's Gospels; and St Paul certainly did not know of it (Rom 1.3f.). But the argument from silence in most books of the New Testament proves nothing, neither does the fact that it is not mentioned in St Mark, the earliest Gospel. It is very difficult to reconcile the infancy narratives in St Matthew's and St Luke's Gospels, which only agree on the fact of Jesus' birth in Bethlehem; but that again neither proves nor disproves that he was virginally conceived.

Detailed examination of St Matthew's Gospel shows that Jesus' virginal conception is almost taken for granted in that Gospel, which suggests that it had long been known in the circles from which the Gospel emanated. The tradition certainly could not have arisen from the verse of the Greek translation of Isaiah which the evangelist cites as his 'proof text' (Isa 7.14). Yet it seems to have been unknown to the source from which the Matthaean genealogy of Jesus was taken. This is apparent from certain awkwardnesses of expression, and from the strange insertion of four women (in addition to Mary) in the genealogy, three of whom were well known for sexual irregularity. It is hard to account for their insertion unless it was to show how divine providence overrides any sexual irregularity surrounding the conception of Jesus.

The emphasis in Matthew's narrative is on the legality of Jesus' descent from David rather than on his virginal conception. The evangelist is fond of describing supernatural communication through dreams, and his account of the virginal conception is entirely dependent on a dream in which Joseph is told not to terminate the betrothal between himself and Mary when she was found to be pregnant. But Joseph would not have been able to arrange the quiet ending of his betrothal which he is said to have intended, for betrothals could not be terminated informally, and the scandal of Mary's pregnancy by someone other than her betrothed – regarded as on a par with adultery would inevitably have been rife in a small village. Doubts have also been cast on the historicity of the other Matthaean infancy narratives (the visit of the magi, and the flight into Egypt). But the possibility remains that the virginal conception was a historical fact even if the infancy narratives in Matthew are *haggadah* (a pious tale with a moral purpose rather than history).

In St Luke's Gospel there are also difficulties. All his infancy stories, which are cast in a distinctive 'Old Testament' style, incorporate images and phrases drawn from the Old Testament which show that Jesus is the Messiah and Son of God, and that Mary carried Jesus in her womb just as the Ark according to the Old Testament contained the presence of God. The question arises whether these narratives are also *haggadah*, written with imaginative insight by a gifted author. In particular, doubt is cast upon the story of Jesus' birth in Bethlehem, since the Roman census which brought him there took place many years later, and in any case registration always took place at the place of residence, not the place of birth. The story of the Annunciation does not explicitly mention a virginal conception: the imagery is that of God immanent in Mary. It has been suggested that the actual words of annunciation are a later interpolation into the narrative, but there is no textual evidence for this, and after the prophecy of the miraculous birth of the Baptist the announcement of an ordinary birth for the Messiah would have been an improbable anticlimax. St Luke intended to allude to a virginal conception. In contrast to St Matthew, who describes the virginal conception from a man's point of view, St Luke writes in his infancy narratives from a woman's angle, and it has been suggested that he heard the stories when he visited Jerusalem with St Paul, or earlier when he lodged for some time in Caesarea in the house of Simon the tanner, who had four daughters all of whom 'prophesied'; and that he later added these stories to the original text of his Gospel.

Those who deny the historicity of the virginal conception have to explain how all these stories originated if they are not historical, and in particular how the story about the birth at Bethlehem could have grown up from one obscure verse (Mic 5.2). On the other hand, upholders of the virginal conception have to show how the story reached St Matthew and St Luke if it was apparently unknown to Jesus himself and his Apostles. Opinion is divided on whether there was sufficient time between the alleged events and the writing of the Gospels for these stories to arise and gain currency.

The two strongest arguments against the virginal conception are that in the Gospels Jesus himself never referred to it and that Mary at one time thought that Jesus was out of his mind, when he first began his public ministry with healings at Capernaum (Mark 3.21). It is hard to understand how she could have agreed with the rest of his family to fetch him away on this account if she knew that she had born him by supernatural agency.

The virginal conception of Jesus raises questions concerning his humanity and his divinity. There are those who think it inappropriate for one who was to be recognized as the expression of God in human personality to be born by normal human intercourse. 'Without endorsing any of the older theories which linked human sinfulness with sexual generation, would not the child of human parents inevitably share our imperfect human nature?'[3] Others, however, think that it is not only appropriate but prerequisite that Jesus should have been conceived in the normal way, as otherwise he would not have been a fully human person. What of our modern knowledge of genetics? To be a human person, Jesus would have had to have twenty-three father-derived chromosomes (including the specifically male chromosome) as well as twenty-three mother-derived chromosomes. Even if the former were provided by supernatural agency, they would have had to be *human* chromosomes or Jesus would not have been a human being. It follows therefore that, if Jesus was virginally conceived, this does not in any way prove his pre-existence. If half his human chromosomes were not derived from Joseph, but were provided by supernatural agency, what male inheritance would they have signified? We have no means of knowing. Whereas God doubt-less could have initiated a virginal conception (as takes place naturally in certain species), it is clearly doubtful whether he actually did.

Whether he did or not leaves entirely unaffected the great spiritual truths which underlie the accounts, namely that with Jesus a new start was made for all mankind, and that Jesus is rightly called the Son of God, for he was in the closest filial relationship with his heavenly Father.

The historical Jesus

Not all the facts about Jesus' life and ministry are so doubtful. It is sufficiently certain[4] that he was brought up as the eldest of a large family in the village of Nazareth in Galilee, and worked there as a carpenter until his thirties, when he joined the holiness movement of his cousin John. He later left this movement to start his own, proclaiming a more positive and joyful message that with his coming God's Kingdom had drawn near. He used parables to drive home this message and was widely welcomed as a teacher and prophet, performing many healings regarded as miraculous. He became the friend of those despised by others, teaching that God loves everybody. He disclaimed knowledge of the exact date of the End, but foretold great suffering for himself, his followers and his people. At one time there was an attempt to make him king, which Jesus himself refused, escaping from the crowds into the hills. It seems that from that time onwards he no longer continued a public ministry, but remained within the circle of the Twelve he had chosen to be with him and to work on his behalf. Within a short period (it is uncertain whether his ministry lasted three years, or only one year) he was put to death as a suspected rebel under Pontius Pilate, who was governor of Judaea from AD 26 to 36. Jesus believed that his own death lay within the good purposes of God, and despite his previous active ministry, he was remarkably passive after his arrest in the face of the authorities' accusations.

The resurrection of Jesus

The Apostles were amazed to find that Jesus was alive from the dead. It is important to consider in some detail the resurrection of Jesus, which is an *articulus stantis et cadentis ecclesiae* (an article of faith by which the Church stands or falls). Without the conviction of his resurrection the Church would never have come into being. The disciples would have fallen away and Jesus would be just one of a number of charismatic religious leaders of the period, probably less well known than his cousin John the Baptist. It was the resurrection that marked him out as One approved by God who thereby vindicated his death.

That he did really die after so short a period on the Cross has been denied; but this may be confidently refuted, the Fourth Evangelist personally vouching for the certification of his death by the Roman authorities. After his death, his followers were downcast and depressed by the apparent failure of his mission, but he amazed and transformed them by a series of appearances. These appearances are found in all the Gospels except for St Mark (unless the 'longer ending', which certainly was not part of the original Gospel, is judged to contain authentic and independent material). He seems to have been able to appear and disappear at will, and to pass through closed doors; and he was not always immediately recognized, as though his material body had been subtly changed into another kind of body. It is difficult to reconcile the various appearances in the various Gospels. In St Luke these take place in Jerusalem and its environs, in St Matthew in Galilee and in St John in both. These differences are probably theologically motivated. The stories are markedly different from accounts of theophanies in the ancient world. Despite differences of content, they contain for the most part a common pattern, a brief and unadorned account in which the emphasis is not so much on the miracle of his resurrection but (after Jesus has been recognized) on his giving his disciples orders for the future. In addition to the stories of Jesus' post-resurrection appearances, there is also a list of such appearances given by St Paul (1 Cor 15.5–8), which includes some not reported in the Gospels. Testimony to Jesus' resurrection is also found in most of the speeches in the Acts of the Apostles, some of which seem based on early sources in Aramaic (the spoken language of the Jews at that time). These appearances are said to have been spread over a period of some forty days (a traditional biblical period of time) until at a final appearance he seemed to be carried upwards into the clouds. It is likely that this account was influenced by the Old Testament story of Elijah's ascension into heaven (2 Kings 2.11) and by the account of the angel Raphael in Tobit 12.16–21.

In addition to appearances of the risen Jesus, there are also accounts of the tomb in which he was buried being found empty. (It has been alleged that as a common criminal Jesus could not have been buried in a private tomb, but in a plot kept by the Jewish authorities for criminals; but Jesus was put to death by the Roman authorities, and it was not unknown for the Roman governor to grant a body for private burial.) There is some disagreement in the Gospels about the reasons which brought women to Jesus' tomb very early on Sunday morning, where they found the stone rolled away and the tomb empty. It is unlikely that they came to complete the burial rites, since they would not have been able to roll away the heavy stone unaided. It is more likely that they came to grieve at the tomb early in the morning, before people were about. In Jewish law a woman's testimony was not valid evidence, which suggests that the stories about Mary Magdalene and the other women finding the tomb empty are historical, as also the account of Mary Magdalene as the first person to meet the risen Jesus. It may be noted that, if the story of the Empty Tomb is accepted, two miracles are involved; the rolling away of the stone (without which the tomb could not have been known to be empty) and the resurrection of Jesus. Although both of these would have been extraordinary events, we shall consider later the possibility that a higher spiritual law can override normal physical regularities (see p. 273).

Various alternative explanations have been attempted: that Jesus recovered consciousness in the tomb and escaped (but the stone could not be rolled away from inside); that the women in the early dawn of Sunday morning went in error to the wrong tomb (but they had only left it at dusk on Friday evening); that the Jews had stolen the body (but why did they not produce it?) or that the disciples stole it (but there is no hint of Christian veneration at a martyr's grave). These alternative explanations seem more difficult than acceptance of the tradition. The testimony to Jesus' resurrection can be traced back to within three or four years of the event itself, assuming that St Paul's conversion took place not long after Jesus' death. Paul also gives sworn testimony that he conferred with Peter in Jerusalem some two or three years later, and their conversation is bound to have included the resurrection (Gal 1.18–20).

Might all these testimonies to Jesus' resurrection have evolved to show that good conquers evil or that the memory of Jesus inspires people to noble thoughts and deeds, or as a parable of the supreme value of self-sacrificing love? Such a myth could surely not have developed so quickly. Was it the result of subjective hallucinations? Mass hallucination of this kind is very rare indeed, and only likely to happen when people are in a highly emotional or expectant state, which (apart from Paul) cannot be predicated of the other earliest witnesses. A possible alternative to physical appearances of Jesus (objective enough be photographed) is the analogy of 'veridical hallucination', a rare but not unknown phenomenon when at the moment of death or shortly after death a person appears to a loved one. This would account for the fact that Jesus appeared fully clothed, and it could be a pointer towards the mystery of Jesus' resurrection.

Some Christians who attest the resurrection of Jesus do not believe that the tomb was empty. The objection is raised that it would have been immoral of God to initiate this type of 'laser beam' miracle when he did nothing to prevent Auschwitz, or to stop death and suffering from war, earthquake, pestilence, drought or hurricane. Such an objection suggests that earthly health and safety are more important than spiritual salvation. It also precludes the concept of 'miracle' as the effect of spiritual laws overriding physical norms. A spiritual objection to Jesus' 'bodily' resurrection is that his resurrection would have been different in kind from that of other human beings, a difference which would be partly overcome if the analogy of 'veridical hallucination' were adopted.

It is also suggested that there is evidence in the New Testament which counts against a 'bodily' resurrection. Paul includes the appearance of Jesus at his conversion as the last item in his list of resurrection appearances, and although the various accounts of this differ in details, none of them suggest that Paul actually saw the body of the risen Lord. This leads some to believe that all the appearances of Jesus were of this kind. However Paul insisted that Jesus was dead and *buried* (Rom 6.4). Why this emphasis on burial unless Paul believed that Jesus had risen from the tomb in which he had been buried? Christians who believe that Jesus' resurrection was purely spiritual hold that the tradition of the Empty Tomb derived from Psalm 16:10 'Thou wilt not leave my soul in hell, neither wilt thou suffer thine Holy One to see corruption' (cited twice in speeches in the Acts). It is difficult to see how a 'myth' about the Empty Tomb and the Gospel stories associated with it could have developed from this single text in such a short period of time, possibly within the lifetime of witnesses.

The mode of Jesus' resurrection is of very secondary importance compared with the fact of his resurrection. Even when account is taken of the fact that the Gospels were not written as biographies, but to strengthen faith, there is excellent evidence for the resurrection of Jesus both in them and in the rest of the New Testament. Equally important is the fact that without his resurrection it is not possible on psychological grounds to account for the sudden transformation of mood of the earliest disciples from despair and doubt to joy and confidence, with the consequent coming into being of the Church, to say nothing of the spiritual experience of the risen Christ since then of countless Christians down the centuries.

It has been necessary to deal at some length with the evidence for the resurrection of Jesus because it is so central to the Christian faith.[5] At first the early Christians were more concerned with the fact than with its meaning; but they came soon to understand it as the sign that the Last Things were already beginning, that it was a vindication by God of Jesus' saving death, that it declared him to be Son of God, and attested him as Lord and Messiah. We shall investigate the Christian doctrines of the Last Things later (see pp. 219–37). Later in this chapter we shall consider his filial relationship to God. He was indeed Messiah, although he refused to use the title, preferring the enigmatic title Son of Man, because in his day the concept of Messiah held political connotations of earthly glory. Christians rightly call Jesus Lord because he is the authentic expression of God in terms of human personality.

Christology in the primitive Church

It was the certitude of his early disciples that Jesus' death had been vindicated by his unlooked-for resurrection that enabled the Jesus movement to 'take off' after his death. He was to be worshipped as Lord, and whatever else the title may have meant, it was associated in the New Testament with Psalm 110.1: 'The Lord said unto my lord, you shall sit on my right hand.' The risen Lord was in the closest association with God. Also, as Paul wrote in the opening sentences of his letter to the Romans, 'He was declared Son of God by a mighty act in that he was raised from the dead'. Although Jesus had left behind him no instructions to found a Church after his death, his followers were convinced that they were strengthened by God to celebrate and proclaim the good news about Jesus with confidence and assurance. We find within the New Testament an account of the early history of the Church and a collection of letters from the Apostles to various Churches. Interestingly enough, the word most used by Jesus to describe himself (the Son of Man, which, whatever else it signified, must have emphasized his humanity), is never once used by them. They preferred the terms Lord and Son of God, whatever these may have meant. Jesus himself seems to have denied that he was simply God: 'Why do you call me good? No one is good except God alone' (Mark 10.18). But he knew himself to be called and inspired by God, a prophet and more than a prophet; and he was conscious of being God's son, an intimate sonship which put him in a special relationship with God. He knew that he had been chosen for a special purpose in which God was acting through him.

Very seldom in the New Testament (and then always ambiguously) is Jesus described simply as God. He is the Christ of God, the Word of God, the Son of God, the Wisdom of God; but not just God. According to the prologue of St John's Gospel, the Word in the beginning was with God (in Greek *ton theon*, God with the definite article), and the Word was God (*theos*, without the definite article). The distinction is clear: Jesus was divine but he was not God. Again, writing to the Philippians, Paul writes that Jesus was 'in the form of God' (i.e. his nature was divine), but 'he did not think to snatch at equality with God' (Phil 2.6). Again, he is regarded as divine, but not God himself.

In the time of Jesus the one God was believed to use more than one means of showing himself. 'The fundamental point is that Jewish monotheism did not at that period involve the utter solitariness often assumed by modern theists.'[6] Despite Exodus 6.2 there is some evidence to show a long-standing Jewish tradition that El, the unknowable God most high, was not identical with Jahweh who was originally believed to be the eldest of his sons. The 'second God' was known by a multiplicity of titles and had appeared in human form (Ezek 1.26; Dan 7.13). It must seem strange that Christology developed so early on in New Testament times until it is realized that this theological structure lay ready to hand by which to interpret the life and ministry of Jesus.[7]

This distinction between God and a 'second God' who makes known the otherwise unknowable God most high, is no longer acceptable to us today. But it is found in the Fourth Gospel: 'No one has ever seen God; but God's only Son, he who is nearest to the Father's heart, he has made him known.' At the outset, before theological reflection had properly begun (if we may take the opening chapters of Acts as containing some authentic material about the very primitive Church), the risen Jesus is described in terms which are clearly functional (e.g. servant, leader, saviour, Messiah [Christ]). The title *kurios* (lord) although it can mean simply 'Sir', was believed in these early days of the Church to have been bestowed on Jesus when he was raised to the heavens (Acts 2.34f.). Paul later gave expression to the same belief, when he wrote that God had bestowed on the risen and ascended Jesus 'the name that is above every name, that at the name of Jesus every knee should bow – in heaven, on earth and in the depths – and every tongue confess, "Jesus Christ is Lord", to the glory of God the Father' (Phil 2.9–11). Even here, the Lord is subordinate to God most high.

There is no single New Testament Christology. Although there is a general convergence, and similar titles for Jesus are used by different writers, there is also a certain pluralism. The Epistle to the Hebrews, probably an early Epistle, uses high priesthood as its main category by which to describe Jesus. In this Epistle there is, however, as well as an unequivocal assertion of his humanity, a striking emphasis on his divinity as well. Here too the Son is subordinate to God. The unknown author used a verse from a psalm to show both that Jesus is divine, and that he owes his divinity to his Father, addressing Christ as God in the words: '. . . therefore, O God, thy God has set thee above thy fellows' (Heb 1.9). The Jewish tradition of a 'second God' probably helped the formation of this Christology.

Paul does not give any indication that he is innovating when writing about the risen Jesus. By the time he wrote his extant letters, Christ (the Greek word for Messiah) had almost become Jesus' proper name. 'Saviour' was a title much used in the pagan Hellenistic world, and its attribution to Jesus probably refers to the conviction that through him sins were forgiven. Paul's evident belief in a pre-existent Being who was incarnate in Jesus suggests also the influence of the 'second God' tradition. Jesus' filial consciousness and his knowledge of his intimate and close relationship with his Father, together with the 'second God' tradition, probably helped to form the early conviction that Jesus was the 'Son of God'. Here again the Son ultimately hands over his kingdom to the Father (1 Cor 15.28).

The Fourth Gospel contains some early material, but the Gospel as a whole is clearly the fruit of profound reflection on the role and status of Jesus. The Fourth Evangelist by his emphasis on the flesh of Jesus underlines his humanity. His favourite term to describe Jesus is 'the Son'. The relations of the Son and the Father are very close: indeed they are 'one thing' (John 10.30). Nevertheless the Father is greater than the Son: 'My Father is greater than I' (John 14.28). Jesus is the mediator between God and humanity. He always does his Father's will, and he continually points people to the Father both by his words and by his life. He is, as we have already noted, divine; and acknowledged as such by Thomas after the resurrection: 'My Lord and my God' (John 20.28). In the Book of Revelation there are many images used to describe the exalted Jesus. He is the Lamb, the Scion of David, the Lion of the tribe of Judah. Jesus is clearly divine (the four and twenty elders fall down before him), but he is subordinate to the One who sits on the throne, the sovereign Lord of all (Rev 5.13). We may conclude from this brief sketch of Christology in the New Testament Church that while Jesus on earth was believed to have been a real human being, the risen and ascended Jesus was believed to be a pre-existent divine being who at the resurrection was given the highest honours in heaven. It is likely that the Jewish tradition of the 'second God' influenced this Christology, based though it was on the actual facts of his life. The high Christology of the New Testament must be seen within its historical perspective. 'Because the first Christians see God's redemptive revelation in Jesus Christ, for them it is his very nature that he can be known only in his work – fundamentally in the central work accomplished in the flesh. Therefore in the light of the New Testament witness, all mere speculation about his nature is an absurdity. Functional Christology is the only kind that exists.'[8]

The Hellenization of Christian belief

Jewish Christology was a Christology of function in terms of history rather than a Christology of status in metaphysical terms. The earliest Christians identified the work of Jesus in history as the work of God. When the leadership of the Church passed from Jewish circles into the Hellenistic world, there was a change of emphasis. Instead of asking 'What is Christ's function?' the question became 'What is his nature?'.[9] There was a category change, as a result of which metaphysical questions began to be asked about his status. The Johannine concept of the Logos (the Word), when later separated from its Jewish origins and transposed into Hellenistic categories of thought, was widely used; but it could not bear the weight that was put upon it as a metaphysical explanation of Christ's divinity. Equally deficient was the view that Jesus had started out simply as a man, and then at his baptism had been raised to divine sonship (Adoptionism). There developed the conviction that Jesus was God and man conjoined in one being, that is to say, the belief that Jesus was not just divine, but the God-man, God himself incarnate in human personality. This had already been prefigured by Paul's assertion that 'it is in Christ that the complete being of the godhead dwells embodied' (Col 2.9). Christian metaphysical thinking in the Hellenistic world followed up this lead of St Paul, while Jewish Christianity was dismissed as Ebionism, a word which signifies a 'cheap' view of Christ. We only know about it from orthodox sources which alleged that he was regarded by the Ebionites merely as a human messiah who came to purify the Law.

How could Jesus be both God and man? We have to start at the one point on which there can be no reasonable doubt, the full humanity of Jesus. Jesus had been undeniably a human being, with human limitations such as thirst and the need for sleep, and even limitations of knowledge about the time of the End. But in the Hellenistic world the starting point was divinity: how could God who was 'impassible' (incapable of suffering) be joined to suffering human nature? How could God become incarnate unless he relinquished his godhead? The subtlety of Greek metaphysics was brought to bear upon these intractable questions. For some the solution was to assert that Jesus only *seemed* to be human: he was really a divine being in a disguise (Docetism). Gradually other false solutions were also discarded. One of these was that God the Father was incarnate in Jesus (Patripassianism): the pre-incarnate Son was one with him, and yet distinct. Another was that Jesus was not really God: he was an emanation from the godhead (Gnosticism). The most dangerous and long-lived was that Jesus must have been of similar substance as the Father (and not of the same substance): he was on the manward side of the godhead, so that there was a time when he was not (Arianism). Orthodoxy maintained that Jesus was truly a man; that he was the incarnation not of the Father but of the Son; that the Son was of the same substance of the Father: he was no emanation from the godhead, but the Father eternally generates the Son (whatever that phrase could mean).

Christology in its orthodox formulation

If Jesus was both fully God and fully man, he could not have had simply a divine soul (Apollinarianism), but a human soul as well. However different godhead is from humanity, the two natures of Jesus cannot in Jesus be separated (Nestorianism): they were conjoined in one integrated being. At the same time the two natures, divine and human, were not assimilated to one another so that Jesus' human nature was deified by its union with the divine nature (Eutychianism). Even though there was one unified being, with the godhead at the centre of this being, assuming to itself the manhood, the two natures were still distinct. So the way was prepared during the early centuries of the Church for the definition which was agreed at the ecumenical Council of Chalcedon in AD 451. This has been the touchstone of orthodoxy ever since:

Following the Holy Fathers, we all with one voice teach that it should be confessed that our Lord Jesus Christ is one and the same Son, the Same complete in godhead, the Same complete in humanity, truly God, and truly man, the Same of a rational soul and body, of one substance with the Father as touching his godhead, and of one substance with us as touching his humanity, in all respects like us sin alone excepted, begotten of the Father before the ages as touching his godhead, and, in the last days, the Same, for us men and for our salvation, of Mary the Virgin the Mother of God as to his humanity, one and the same Christ, Son, Lord, Only Begotten, made known in two natures without confusion, without change, without division, without separation, the difference of the natures having been in no way taken away by reason of the union, but rather the properties of each being preserved, and both concurring into the one person and substance, not divided or parted into two persons and substances . . .

Even this definition did not silence controversy. The crucial reading 'made known in two natures' is uncertain. Originally the text was probably 'made known in two natures and from two natures'. At any rate after the Council the Monophysite schism developed, which claimed substantial parts of the Eastern Church, holding that 'out of two natures' Christ incarnate had only one nature.

In order fully to understand the history of the doctrine which underlies this definition it is necessary to know the nuances of the Latin and Greek terms which were used; *substantia* and *persona* in Latin, and *prosopon, ousia* and *hypostasis* in Greek. Thus *persona* never means what we mean today by 'person': it refers to status or character or part or function. *Hypostasis* is a word with more than one meaning: it can designate simply being, but it came to mean existence in a particular mode (i.e. *persona* as it was then understood). The whole Christological controversy was conducted in metaphysical terms, far removed from the personal categories in which we think today, and very distant from the language and the concerns of the Gospels.

This ancient Definition, for all the authority that it carries, is no longer credible as it stands in today's world, with our more sophisticated linguistic analysis, and our more personalist thinking. In a famous phrase, it was remarked that it represents 'the bankruptcy of Greek patristic theology'.[9] As a foremost patristic scholar wrote: 'Jesus Christ disappears in the smokescreen of a two-nature philosophy. Formalism triumphs, and the living figure of the Evangelical redeemer is desiccated to a logical mummy.'[10] In any case Chalcedon did not *solve* the Christological problem: it merely *stated* the elements that must be included if a solution were possible in those metaphysical terms. It gave rise to what seem today as absurdities, such as the assumption by God the Son of an '*impersonal*' manhood (i.e. manhood without a hypostasis, or existing in a particular mode), in order to preserve the divine nature as directing the one person Jesus Christ. In the light of modern understanding of humanity, this idea of 'impersonal' manhood no longer makes sense. Again, the Chalcedonian Definition, in order to avoid division of the two natures, required what was called *communicatio idiomatum*: although the two natures were distinct, there had to be a mutual sharing of the personal characteristics of each if the unity of the person was to preserved.

According to the orthodox doctrine of the Incarnation, the 'impersonal' human nature of Jesus is united with the divine nature of the Second Person of the Trinity in an indissoluble union, so that there were two natures and one substance. This served well the metaphysical thinking of the early Church. But today it leads us into a morass.

It must be respected because it preserved in its day the kernel of the Gospel. But we can no longer accept it as an explanation of the mystery of

Jesus' person which rings true for us today. In the first place Being itself –
the infinite God – cannot coexist in indissoluble union with a finite
human being: they are of a different order. If God is regarded as
incapable of suffering, as he is according to the orthodox doctrine, he
could not be united to a human nature which suffers and is put to death
on a cross. An impassible God could not himself suffer God-forsakenness,
as Jesus did on Calvary. If the divine nature were united with human
nature, God would have to own all Jesus' beliefs as his own, and they
could not be in error: but some of them we know were erroneous, for
example, the imminence of the world's end. If God were united with man
in this way, the resultant God-man could not sin, and therefore he could
not be tempted to sin as we are. Yet we have in the Gospels evidence
(which could hardly have been fabricated) that Jesus was frequently
tempted (Luke 4.13). Under the orthodox formulation Jesus could have
had a human will, but not the same freedom of choice that we have,
because he was not able to choose what is sinful: he would have had no
option but to be aligned to his Father's will. Even more importantly, the
orthodox doctrine is arid. It does not speak to us of God's loving
relationship to a human being, but of his metaphysical union with an
'impersonal' human nature. It does not spell out God's freely given grace
and help to one who seeks to do his will, but it implies rather that such a
person had no option but to do it. It requires a belief in Jesus' divine
perfection which seems inconsistent with every human being's inevitable
conditioning by the culture of his age. It demands omniscience and
omnipotence which are incompatible with humanity. Jesus was certainly
in some sense unique, yet the orthodox doctrine makes the humanity of
Jesus so different from our humanity that it is not easy to regard him as
our representative before God. It even gives us a distorted view of
divinity, suggesting that God's action in the Incarnation must have been
different in kind to all his other actions towards his creation. Modern
apologists have tried to resolve these antinomies, but without success.

Post-Enlightenment thinking

Since the Enlightenment many attempts have been made to reinterpret
Jesus. Some of these have stemmed from presuppositions which minimize
his status or reject his divinity. In our own times Jesus has been
portrayed in roles as different as that of a revolutionary or a magician, a
Gnostic or a Hasidic holy man. Christian interpretations have tended to
reflect the key categories of their authors or their *Zeitgeist*. George Tyrrell,

the Catholic modernist, wrote of the Protestant Harnack's search for Christian origins as one who looked down the deep well of history and saw there the reflection of his own face; and the same remark could be applied to many others besides Harnack. For Hegel, the idea was the regulative category, and for him Christ was divine because he was the complete expression of the divine human idea; but this was to put idealism before reality. Ritschl, who believed in the primacy of value judgements, believed Jesus was God because of the complete moral union between him and God, whereas in fact Jesus spoke more about God's love than he did about morality. For Schleiermacher, for whom feeling was the key category, Christ was divine because he was supremely God-conscious and the source of God-consciousness to believers, despite the fact that our knowledge of Jesus' own inner feelings and religious experience is minimal.

Is it possible to keep the kernel of the orthodox doctrine of Incarnation, but to express it in such a way that it avoids the difficulties enumerated above about its traditional metaphysical expression? There have been many attempts to do this.[11] Most have rightly taken a diminished view of Jesus' omnipotence and omniscience. Here in Britain we should note two particular ways in which this has been attempted. A kenotic Christology,[12] which takes its origin from 2 Corinthians 8.9 and the passage from Philippians quoted above, suggests that the Second Person of the Trinity emptied himself of all his divine attributes in order to become man. Jesus was therefore simply a man, although in essence he was divine, as though his divinity was, as it were, in abeyance. If this were indeed the case, it is difficult to understand how there could be any continuity between the being of the pre-kenotic and kenotic Christ. Nor does the theory explain how (according to orthodox doctrine) Jesus really was Emmanuel, God with us, if the Son had voluntarily (and temporarily) abandoned his divinity *in toto*. Furthermore, since we cannot envisage any division of powers between the Father and the Son, there is no explanation of God's continuing governance of the universe during the time of his temporary theophany on earth. Traditionally the Incarnation has always been understood as the assumption of humanity rather than the divesting of divinity. Kenotic Christology seems to be based on myth rather than metaphysical theory (perhaps this is inevitable when attempting to describe the indescribable). Yet it does highlight the love and humility of God through his voluntary self-restriction in abandoning his divinity in order to disclose himself in human personality. It shows the continuity between the act of Incarnation and the Crucifixion, when he humbled himself still further to suffer the death of a common criminal.

By 'focusing down' God to the status of man, it illustrates how Christ could indeed be for humanity the image of God. Despite all these advantages, kenotic Christology must be deemed an inadequate explanation of the union of human and divine in Jesus, for the reasons enumerated above.

Another category that has been used is that of organic evolution, as understood in the light of our evolving universe.[13] New levels of being appear through emergent evolution, with each level including within itself the earlier levels, and yet producing a new quality of being which is genuinely novel and inexplicable in terms of the earlier levels. On this view Jesus is seen as the culmination of the evolutionary process, the new emergent being in whom God himself is incarnate. This suggests that the Incarnation is an inevitable result of the process of evolution. But it is not clear how the human species could evolve in such a way that it became indissolubly united to Being itself. Indeed, in the original form of this evolutionary Christology, it was held that God did on this one occasion intervene in the process of cosmic evolution. He had planned the evolutionary process so that it reached the stage when, at the Annunciation to Mary, he become incarnate in her womb. If indeed this were the case, then the act of Incarnation has no necessary connection with evolutionary process at all. On the other hand, if the Incarnation was simply an inevitable part of the evolutionary process, it surely would not have happened merely in the case of Jesus. Of course he himself died without issue; but if Incarnation happened once, the same evolutionary pressures which effected it once would have repeated it again. Attractive as the theory may seem in an age which thinks naturally in evolutionary terms, it does not give a satisfactory explanation of the hypostatic union of two natures in Jesus, as required by the orthodox theory. Since Christology lies at the heart of Christianity, a passionate search for Christological truth is required, wherever it may lead.

A different category of interpretation

What is needed is a totally different type of explanation. So far we have been examining attempted explanations in ontological terms of being and nature. The New Testament is not concerned with ontology. 'Jewish Messiahship does not yield a Christology of status in metaphysical terms of "human" or "divine" *origin at all*. That question is quite irrelevant to the Jewish conception. It yields instead a Christology of function in terms of history.'[14] The writer here is somewhat exaggerating, but certainly

Jesus in the New Testament is not described ontologically as God, but under the forms of images and symbols. He is 'the image of the invisible God' (Col 1.15), 'the stamp of God's very being' (Heb 1.3). Paul prefers phrases which describe his divine function: 'God was in Christ reconciling the world to himself' (2 Cor 5.19); 'We have peace with God through our Lord Jesus Christ' (Rom 5.1).

To approach Christology in this way we must return to the New Testament, and begin where it begins, with Jesus as a human being. We must ask ourselves in what way Jesus differs from other human beings in respect of what he did, rather than in respect of who he was. God used the man Jesus in such a way that he becomes for us the visible expression of God, and the medium through which God's nature has been made known to us. How did this happen?

God's action in Jesus was continuous with his other actions in inspiring and guiding men and women to greater commitment to his will and purpose. We must make here a distinction between the stories of Jesus and the actual life of Jesus himself. 'His importance lies in the fact that his life generates, as a communal response to it, a narrative which elaborates and defines a disclosure of God which has come through encounter with him and reflection on his completed life.'[15] We do not know more than the bare outline of his life. There cannot be absolute certainty about the historicity of any of his reported sayings or actions. To be sure, some may seem so probable as to be almost certainly genuine: indeed, if he did not say them himself, the evangelist or his source must have been as great a religious genius as he was! It does not matter that we do not know all the details of Jesus' life or the actual words he spoke in Aramaic, the spoken language of his day. Jesus made such an impact on his followers in the primitive Church that he gave rise to the Gospel stories as we have them. It is in the stories about Jesus and his sayings in the Gospel that he confronts us as the visible expression of God, and it is through the Gospels that his nature has been made known to us.

Grace and spirit

How did God use Jesus so that he has become for us the embodied expression of God himself and the means by which he has made himself known to us? The 'paradox of grace' can help us to understand God's action in and through Jesus.[16] St Paul gave expression to this paradox when he wrote: 'I live, yet no longer I, but Christ liveth in me' (Gal 2.20).

There is nothing irresistible about divine grace. It has been well said that when we ascribe to God the glory for anything good in ourselves, this does not imply any downgrading of ourselves as human personalities, but precisely the reverse: our actions are never more truly free and personal and human, and never more truly our own, than when they are wrought in us by God.

Our experience of grace is only fragmentary, in respect of something good we have said or done or thought. Jesus however was different. His sinlessness (which implies his perfection in obeying God's will) is affirmed in the New Testament. The Gospel stories show us that this was the impact which he made on his followers and which found expression in the primitive Church, and it is congruous with the fact of his resurrection. At the end of his earthly life God vindicated him by raising him from the dead. His 'cry of dereliction' from the Cross shows that he did not experience unbroken communion with his Father, but his perfect alignment with his Father's will shows that he lived life as it was meant to be lived. It could be said of him *par excellence* 'I live, yet no longer I, but my Father in me'. In fact there is a verse in the Fourth Gospel very much like this: 'In truth, in very truth I tell you, the Son can do nothing by himself: he does only what he sees the Father doing: what the Father does, the Son does' (John 5.19).

Our experience of the paradox of grace, whereby God's assistance in no way abolishes our free choice, but actually enhances it, provides an insight into the union of Jesus' will with that of his Father in heaven; a union not compulsorily effected by hypostatic union, but freely given in personal commitment and total obedience. The words of Newman's famous hymn might seem to contradict this – 'a higher gift than grace did flesh and blood refine'. But if our experience of grace is only fitful and fragmentary, and if Jesus' commitment, as we see it in the Gospels, was total and complete, there is a vast qualitative distinction between him and us which does not remove his real humanity and kinship with us.

Another way of expressing this is through the category of spirit.[17] Revelation never originates from the spirit of man or woman: it always comes from the Spirit of God. Yet it is always mediated through the thoughts and feelings of men and women. Jesus is seen to be unique, because in him the incarnate presence of God provoked a full and constant response of the human spirit. Jesus' response was to the Spirit of God, the same Spirit who was and is present in others; but instead of a partial response, the response of Jesus' spirit was total and complete. There was a union of the divine and the human spirit which was fully personal (in the modern sense of the word); that is to say, a union of mind and will. The difference between him and us is that the relationship between God and a human being was, as we read in the Gospels, perfected in him. He was Son of God because his relationship to God was the epitome of all that sonship comprises.

The sinlessness of Jesus

What does it mean to speak of Jesus as making a perfect and total response to God? Does this imply, as the Scriptures tell us, that he was sinless, and if so, how can we know this? Sin, in this connection, means missing the mark through disobedience to God. There is no fact about Jesus better attested in the New Testament than Jesus' sinlessness: it appears in so many totally separate traditions (Heb 4.15; 2 Cor 5.21; 1 Pet 2.22; 1 John 3.5). This must have been the impression that he made on his friends, just as it is the impression that he still gives in reading the Gospels. However, this impression was not gained over the whole of his life. Can we reconstruct what perfection and sinlessness would be like?

A child is incapable of actual sins until the age of moral responsibility is reached. So there is no need to picture the child Jesus as a Little Lord Fauntleroy suppressing reactions which later may have dreadful results. High spirits, good-natured pranks and even occasional disobedience are not evidence of present or future sin. Even inconveniencing his parents at the age of twelve (on the way home from Jerusalem) could not be called a sin. Nonetheless in childhood habits may be laid down which do in adult life lead to sin; and the tradition that Jesus was without sin is a tribute to his remarkable mother and the happy home in which he must have lived as a child.

Of the 'hidden years' of Jesus, when he worked as a carpenter in Nazareth, we know nothing. But the fact that his family thought he was out of his mind when he began his public ministry (Mark 3.21), and that the villagers at Nazareth would not believe in him (Mark 6.2–6), suggest that he had lived an ordinary uneventful life until his public ministry began. 'There is every reason from the gospel evidence, as well as from the Epistle to the Hebrews, to suppose that Jesus was fully a man like ourselves, sharing the same unconscious desires and libido, with a temper and an intolerance, an anxiety and a fear of death, as strong as anyone else's. Like any other human being, he had a dark side as well as a light, what Jung calls "the shadow", the symbol of all those instinctive, "unclubbable" aspects of the personality, dangerous and resistant to moral control, which are repressed and projected onto others.'[18]

The baptism of Jesus was akin in some ways to a conversion, with a sudden and intense awareness of God. His heavenly Father's coming to him was matched by his full and complete turning to God. Elements of Jesus' human personality which had been suppressed, or which had previously existed only in potentiality, were united in a new synthesis. But the conscious self and the unconscious are not immediately integrated as the result of this kind of experience. He must have known that this had not yet fully taken place when he replied to a questioner: 'Why do you call me good? No one is good except God alone' (Mark 10.18). It has been noted that the Gospels show evidence of 'a progressive integration' during the period of his public ministry,[19] until there was no longer any need for repression or projection. This surely is the meaning of perfection. It is part of our human nature that we go on developing. The unacceptable was speedily internalized and absorbed, until Jesus was able, after a panic-stricken struggle in Gethsemane, to accept even his coming death as the will of his heavenly Father. As the author of the Epistle to the Hebrews put it, 'Son though he was, he learned obedience in the school of suffering, and once perfected, became the source of eternal salvation for all who obey him' (Heb 5.9).

Viewed in this way, Jesus was a human being who had totally and fully committed himself to God's will. He was no mere human being who has been rewarded for his holiness with divine status. On the contrary, God chose him for this purpose. God's hand was at work throughout. God's vocation called him. God guided and inspired and upheld him, without interfering with his freedom of choice. To him was given fullness of grace. He was totally infused by God's spirit so that he is for us the Incarnate Lord, God in human form: 'he that has seen me has seen the Father'. He is the paradigm of divine love, the parable of divine wisdom, our icon of God. He is transparent to God. In him we see the moving pattern of divine activity expressed in terms of his own human activity.[20] For this Jesus must have had total integrity, he must have attained full insight and wisdom (which for humans can only come from their learning experiences), he must have had complete freedom from selfishness. Jesus is God expressed in human personality as fully as human personality can express him. Yet in so depicting him, no *ontological* claim of divinity has been made on his behalf.

Jesus the revelation of God

If Jesus reveals God in terms of human personality, then his own character, in so far as it is revealed in the Gospel stories, is of compelling interest. If Jesus gave us a disclosure of the divine nature, we must look for this not in those characteristics which are common to all mankind, nor in those which he shared with the Jews of his time, but in those which were particular to Jesus himself.[21]

One of these is that he did not merely consort with those who were religiously respectable, but in particular with 'outsiders' and the unloved. He made friends with tax gatherers and prostitutes, people despised in his society. He was conceived out of wedlock. During his itinerant public ministry he had, it is reported, nowhere to lay his head. He was crucified between two revolutionaries. If Christians take the 'option for the poor', they are following in the footsteps of Jesus who reveals to us the nature of God who has a special care for those whom the world despises.

Most of Jesus' life was spent in humble obscurity. This suggests a self-effacingness which is evident during the whirlwind years of his public ministry. He chose for himself the enigmatic title of 'the Son of Man', claiming that as such he came not to be served but to serve. In his teaching, he pointed away from himself to his heavenly Father. When he entered for the last time into the capital city of Jerusalem, he rode not on a proud caparisoned horse, but on a humble donkey. This discloses to us something of the nature of God, whose marks in his creation cannot be easily distinguished from the substance of his creatures, whose providence cannot easily be distinguished from the chain of cause and effect, whose grace can hardly be distinguished from human response, and whose Holy Spirit is hard to distinguish from the operation of human personality.

Another characteristic of Jesus was his willingness to put his fate into the hands of others. He did nothing to avert the coming catastrophe in Jerusalem when he came to the city for the last time in the knowledge of what probably lay ahead. He made no attempt to defend himself against arrest or sentence or execution. And yet although he put himself into the hands of others, he remained master of the situation throughout. This reveals to us something of God's nature, who puts himself into our hands, with freedom to accept or reject him; but at the same time always remains master of the situation.

One final characteristic was his acquiescence in suffering. We shall consider the relation of suffering to God in a future chapter when we come to consider the nature of God (see pp. 132f.). Here it may be said that if suffering was so integral to Jesus' vocation, it must reveal to us something of the suffering in God himself.

The risen Christ

If Jesus in his earthly life was the image of God, the expression of God in terms of human personality, what are we to say of the risen Jesus? St Thomas exclaimed of him 'My Lord and my God!' (John 20.28). St Paul said that at the resurrection God bestowed on him the name that is above every name, that at the name of Jesus every knee should bow – and every tongue confess 'Jesus Christ is Lord', to the glory of God the Father (Phil 2.9–11), and the risen Christ is repeatedly called Lord in the New Testament, the word of worship and adoration. St Paul says that at his resurrection Jesus was declared to be Son of God with power (Rom 1.4) and according to Acts on the day of Pentecost Peter proclaimed that at his resurrection God made him both Lord and Messiah (Acts 2.36). The risen Christ is not identified with God – how could he be if 'he is always living to plead' on our behalf (Heb 7.25)? But he is in the closest possible relationship with God, and the Spirit of God and the power of God and the grace of God are mediated through him. This has been the experience of the Church and of countless individual Christians down the ages. We need not involve ourselves with difficult questions concerning the assumption of his 'impersonal manhood' into God. This is to attempt to define what lies beyond our knowledge. If we do not know what our own future existence will be in the world to come, we are even less in a position to define that of the risen and ascended Lord. It is sufficient for us that he who expressed for us on earth God in terms of human personality, after his resurrection is on the right hand of the Father (that is to say, in the closest relationship with him) and that the Holy Spirit and grace and power are mediated to mankind through him; and that in our worship of Christ we are glorifying his heavenly Father.

Mary, the mother of Jesus

Jesus' upbringing must have been very remarkable indeed, for him to grow up in such a way that he was perfectly obedient to the will of his heavenly Father. We now know the enormous influence that a mother plays in enabling the character of a child to blossom, and the way in which early mothering can affect later adult life. Jesus did not suffer from a mother who caused hang-ups in her adult children. Although his encounters with his mother recorded in the Gospels show that, like all grown-up children, he had to break out of any remaining dependent relationship, the blameless character of her son shows that Mary was blessed among women as well as blessed in the fruit of her womb.

There is however nothing to show that Mary was not an ordinary human person. We have already considered the possibility that she conceived Jesus by normal human generation, with Joseph her betrothed as the father; and it must be added that, if that was indeed the case, betrothal in those days was regarded among the Jews as constituting an 'option to marry'. The bond of betrothal was so strong that infidelity by a betrothed woman was regarded as adultery; and marital relations, although not strictly permitted, were known to take place between betrothed couples in Judaea in that period.

We know nothing, or almost nothing, about Mary's character. She was liable to error, as when she, with the rest of the family, thought her son was out of his mind (Mark 3.21). She thought that she could tell her son what to do, but found out that this was not the case (John 2.3f.). Her son refuted the ascription of blessedness to Mary because she was his mother; blessedness consisted in knowing the will of God and doing it (Luke 11.27). Jesus seemed to think that the ties of family, including the ties of his mother, were not so strong as the ties of those who hear the word of God and do it (Mark 3.34). There is no evidence, therefore, which might lead us to suppose that Mary lacked the tendency to error and sin which is our common human inheritance, and which Jesus himself therefore must have inherited. In other words, Mary was not immaculately conceived. Again, there is no evidence in the New Testament that Mary was bodily transported into heaven at her death. That was originally a Gnostic belief, and only later became part of catholic tradition. When the time came for her to die (and she passes out of the New Testament from the time of Pentecost onwards), she came into the nearer presence of God; and Christians rightly honour and venerate her as one of the great saints of God. God had signally honoured her by choosing her to be the mother of Jesus. But there seems no good reason which explains why God might have transported her body to heaven. In the case of Jesus, his resurrection was a clear vindication of his suffering death. But the falling asleep or 'dormition' of Mary was a normal event. The mission of Jesus was quite different from that of Mary: hers was merely to mother and to bring up the Son of God.

Those churches of Christendom which do ascribe to Mary both an immaculate conception and a bodily assumption into heaven are careful to honour her not on her own account, but because she was *theotokos*, the 'Mother of God' who bore the incarnate Son in her womb. Nonetheless Mary has a special position and plays an important part in the spirituality of these churches. For them a purely male image of God (reinforced by an exclusively male priesthood) is complemented by the female symbol of Mary, who has in the past played almost as much part in popular Christianity as her incarnate Son, taking on at times some of the roles of the goddess cults which used to be rife in Mediterranean lands. Protestant churches, which have in the past had an equally male image of God, have sadly lacked any element of femaleness in their conception of the divine. Today our ability to describe God in female as well as male imagery does away with the need of a female figure close to the godhead (see p. 131).

Jesus the Son of God who brings us to the Father

Mary was a fully human being. In our handling of the Christology of her son, we have suggested that Jesus too was a fully human being, and that we read in the Scriptures how he was totally obedient to his heavenly Father, in the closest filial relationship to him, and that he was so filled with the Holy Spirit that he was transparent to God; the son of God, the image of God, the icon of God, the visible expression of God in human personality. Such a way of explaining Jesus' nature is fully in accordance with the witness of the New Testament, while it avoids the contradictions of Chalcedon. Because Jesus as we read him in the Gospels is the expression of God in human personality, he forms the archetype of humanity. He makes known to us uniquely the nature of God and he brings us into his presence. Moreover he continually points us away from himself to God himself. Christian theology has tended to be too Christocentric, focusing attention on a human person, whereas the witness of Jesus himself was undeniably theocentric, focusing attention on his heavenly Father. The Fourth Evangelist, giving us the fruit of his profound reflection upon the life and ministry of Jesus, possibly based on his own personal experience of Jesus, sums up the theocentric nature of Jesus' preaching and teaching when he wrote: 'I come in my Father's name' and 'My Father is greater than I'. It has been said that the Christ of the Fourth Gospel reveals only that he is Revealer of the Father. This is to exaggerate; but nonetheless Christian tradition has hardly observed the biblical perspective, concentrating on Jesus as divine rather than on Jesus who reveals the divine Father.

If we are to return to New Testament categories and have a Christology of function rather than of status, we must ask ourselves what was the function of Jesus in the purpose of God? For this we must turn to the work of Christ.

Notes

1. K. Rahner, 'On the importance of the non-Christian religions for salvation' in *Theological Investigations* 18 (London, 1984), p. 293.

2. For a fuller discussion, see H. Montefiore, *The Womb and the Tomb* (London, 1992), pp. 14–98.

3. *The Nature of Christian Belief: A Statement and Exposition by the House of Bishops of the General Synod of the Church of England* (London, 1986), p. 32.

4. The following is for the most part a summary from D. L. Edwards, *The Real Jesus* (London, 1992), pp. 108-47.

5. For a fuller discussion, see H. Montefiore, *The Womb and the Tomb, op. cit.*, pp. 101–86.

6. J. L. Houlden, *Jesus: A Question of Identity* (London, 1992), p. 64.

7. See M. Barker, *The Great Angel* (London, 1992).

8. See O. Cullmann, *The Christology of the New Testament* (London, 1959), p. 326.

9. W. Temple, *Foundations* (London, 1912), p. 324.

10. G. L. Prestige, *Fathers and Heretics* (London, 1946), p. 146.

11. J. Macquarrie, *Jesus Christ in Modern Thought* (London, 1990).

12. See C. Gore, *Belief in Christ* (London, 1922), pp. 225ff.

13. See L. Thornton, *The Incarnate Lord* (London, 1928).

14. G. Dix, *Jew and Greek* (London, 1953), pp. 79–80.

15. See K. Ward, *A Vision to Pursue* (London, 1992), p. 75, to whom I am greatly indebted in this section.

16. D. M. Baillie, *God Was in Christ* (London, 1948), pp. 112ff.

17. See G. W. H. Lampe, *God as Spirit* (Oxford, 1977), pp. 115–16.

18. J. A. T. Robinson, *The Human Face of God* (London, 1973), p. 85.

19. L. W. Grensted, Appendix on 'The sinlessness of Christ', *The Person of Christ* (London, 1933), p. 279. See also chapter 'The sinlessness of Christ' in H. Montefiore, *Awkward Questions on Christian Love* (London, 1964), pp. 40–68.

20. See W. R. Matthews, *The Problem of God in the Twentieth Century* (London, 1958); H. Montefiore, 'Christology for today' in *Soundings*, ed. A. R. Vidler (Cambridge, 1963).

21. See H. Montefiore, 'Jesus the revelation of God' in *Christ for Us Today*, ed. N. Pittenger (London, 1968), pp. 105–40.

chapter 5

The work of Christ

The flaw in mankind

There is something wrong with humanity. Almost alone among mammals, human beings engage in wars among one another. Many countries are constantly engaged in hostilities: the number of outbreaks of war since the end of World War II is already nearing a hundred. Individuals quarrel and fight with one another. Many people are manifestly unhappy. They seek medication or psychotherapy to ease their mental and emotional problems. A number are so unhappy that they try (many with success) to commit suicide. The reported breaches of the law suggest that a high proportion of the population is involved. Over a third of all marriages in Britain now break down irretrievably and very large numbers of children are brought up in broken homes. There is not only confusion over morality, but personal frustration as well, people finding that they cannot control their instincts or impulses. They are often unable to change their attitudes even when they want to do so. They feel a vacuum in their life, an alienation from themselves and other people and from the Ground of their being. This is not to deny that there is much love and goodness and virtue, nor that many people do experience happiness and creativity, leading peaceful, contented, law-abiding lives. But their good fortune does not alter the fact that there is something wrong with the human race as a whole.

Salvation

In the past the Church has accounted for the origin of this fault in mankind by means of its doctrine of original sin, with an inherited tendency to disobey God's commands, as though his original plan for the human race has gone wrong, with consequent disaster for humanity. In an earlier chapter we have concluded that what we call original sin is in fact a blend of many effects; the entail of our animal past, the influence on us of the past attitudes and actions of humanity, the consequence of our own attitudes in infancy, the nurture we have received since then, the frustrations involved in breaking away from parental dependency and trying to become adults, and the influence on us of the atmosphere of contemporary society (see pp. 64f.).

Psychotic illnesses, involving some gross disorder of perception and thought, are more likely to be mitigated than cured; but neurotic tendencies (which involve maladaptive habits which are resistant to the normal processes of learning) can usually be treated through medication or psychotherapy. Apart from psychoses and neuroses, there seem to be persistent failures on the part of ordinary people to do what they know to be right. While this is in part due to the weakness of the will, the fault lies deeper; and it has been the Christian claim that there is an inherited sickness of the human soul which can be healed through the atoning death of Christ. The Church has never defined one particular theory of the atonement as orthodox, but it has always insisted on the *fact* of atonement. The word means 'at-onement', that is to say a state of being at one with God. The other ills to which mankind is heir, alienation from self and from others, are believed to stem from the basic alienation of mankind from God. Unless this wound is healed, there is no hope for humanity. Mankind needs salvation.

The word salvation requires further definition. A person may be in the process of salvation, or destined for salvation, or already saved. A person may be 'saved from', which is not the same as being 'saved for'. Salvation implies rescue from the alienation in which the human soul naturally finds itself; an alienation from the self, from others and from God. In earlier ages this rescue was described as 'salvation from hell', for humanity was thought to have deserved the wrath of a righteous God whose sentence would be imposed at the Last Judgement at the end of time. This is a paradoxical idea in the faith which, while asserting the righteousness of God, regards his foremost characteristic as pure love. Hell – if it exists – is better understood as eternal separation from the love of God (see pp. 233f.), either as a state of being or through extinction.

Forgiveness

People who are alienated from God risk being perpetually unable to respond to God's love. Such people will then have brought upon themselves such a sentence, to be passed at the Last Judgement. Whether or not it will continue as the permanent state of the soul, this alienation is certainly one which can be experienced in the present, and which a person can be 'saved from' in the present. What is mankind 'saved for'? That is less easy to define succinctly. Perhaps it is best expressed as being saved for the fulfilment of that for which a person was created. But that in itself has little content. Human beings were created to share in God's love, to enjoy his peace and joy and glory, to be with him for ever, and thereby to reach their potential and find a wholeness which is otherwise denied them.

A major factor in the human predicament is guilt, whether openly felt or inwardly suppressed. Excessive guilt may be the result of pathological illness, and it may need treatment on psychiatric lines. But ordinary guilt is endemic in human beings as the normal effect of a bad conscience on someone who has transgressed God's laws (except for those whose 'consciences have been seared with a hot iron' (1 Tim 4.2)). Guilt is well illustrated by many of the myths of ancient Greece. It is the subjective feeling which arises from our consciousness of having done wrong. It is the subjective aspect of the objective fact of sin. Sin we may best understand as missing the mark (its primary meaning in the Greek verb *hamartanein* which is used in the New Testament to signify sin). Sin has many causes, but it is essentially disobedience to the will of God.

Many atonement theories focus on the forgiveness of sins as the outcome of Christ's atoning death. But to confine atonement to this is to diminish what God did through Christ. It was something far deeper than mere forgiveness. When we wrong some other human person, and we wish to receive forgiveness from that person, we tell them what we have done and express our sorrow, and our hope that we will never do this again; and if they are well disposed towards us, we are forgiven. God is well disposed towards us. Whenever we tell him we are sorry that we have disobeyed his will, and express our sorrow and our purpose of amendment, we are forgiven. This simple truth is expressed in the Lord's Prayer, when we ask God to forgive us *providing we also forgive others*. That is the only additional proviso needed. The liturgies of the Church, with their prayers of confession and their declarations of God's forgiveness, witness to this simple but profound truth. We find it very difficult to accept, because the disappearance of our guilt feelings does not always accompany the forgiveness of our sins. But atonement is not just the stilling of our subjective feelings of guilt. These are a pointer to a more profound sickness of the human soul.

Rich diversity of images for atonement

The New Testament Scriptures have many references to the atoning death of Jesus, whereby we are made 'at-one' with God. In the primitive Church, as evidenced by the early speeches in Acts, Jesus' death was not so much interpreted as emphasized, and a special importance was attached to it, e.g. as when Peter tells the Jews: '. . . he has been given up to you, by the deliberate will and plan of God' (Acts 2.23). Paul tells us that according to the Gospel which he had received (and he received it within four or five years of the resurrection), 'Christ died *for our sins*, in accordance with the Scriptures' (1 Cor 15.3). Already his death had been connected with the removal of sins, no doubt through the experience of those early Christians. Further reflection resulted in a series of biblical images by which to elucidate how this happened. In the New Testament the effects of his death are variously described as forgiving, healing, rescuing from the domain of darkness, liberating by payment of a ransom, sealing a pledge, justifying, consecrating, electing, redeeming (as in the Roman custom whereby a freed slave was 'bought back' by a god through money he had paid into the temple treasury'), atoning, expiating, reconciling, cleansing, incorporating into Christ, transforming the personality, bringing life or rebirth, recreating, overcoming the world, illuminating, bestowing the spirit of God and bestowing the glory of God. There was a wealth of imagery to illustrate what was a key fact of Christian experience.

This rich diversity of expression was used to signify the new reality brought through Jesus' atoning death. Images may be jumbled together. Thus Paul writes: 'We have been justified by Christ's sacrificial death' (Rom 5.9); a mixture of forensic and sacrificial metaphors. Paul's literary style in his Epistles is somewhat rhetorical; that is to say, he tends to argue dialectically by a series of contrasts, rather than logically from premises to a conclusion. He was not writing a theological thesis for a doctorate: he was arguing if not with others, then with himself. All the New Testament writers' images of the atonement have an aptness to describe Jesus' atoning death. Like Paul's, they were not intended to give a logical explanation. They were used to proclaim his death and its meaning by images easily comprehended by those to whom they were addressed. These images were not only familiar to their readers, but also likely to touch their hearts and imaginations. There is no logically expressed New Testament theory of atonement which explains just how it was accomplished.

Atonement as sacrifice

The sacrificial imagery used is particularly diverse; at one point Jesus is the means of expiation, at another a Passover sacrifice, at another his death is the sacrifice of the New Covenant, at another an odour of a sweet savour, and at yet another a sin offering. The metaphor of sacrifice is most closely sustained in the Epistle to the Hebrews, which is precisely and rigorously argued.[2] It approximates to a theory of atonement, based on the presuppositions that sacrifice is effective, and that without the shedding of blood there is no forgiveness. Jesus, who is our great high priest after the model of Melchisedek (see Heb 6.20), offers himself in fulfilment of the levitical high priest's sacrifices on the Day of Atonement (Heb 7.1–28). But even here a mixture of sacrifices is involved, for Jesus' death is described not only after the model of the Day of Atonement sacrifice but also as a covenant sacrifice. The typology breaks down in that Jesus is not only the officiating high priest but also the sacrificial victim.

Sacrifice remained an important image in the early Church for describing God's atonement in Christ. To understand the meaning of sacrifice to the Jews, it is necessary to enlarge our popular concept of what it meant.[3] In Jewish tradition, some sacrifices were communion sacrifices in which the participants enjoyed fellowship, and a portion of the animal sacrificed was put aside for God, a practice which later became refined, so that the sacrifice became for God 'an odour of sweet savour'. There were also sacrifices of praise and thanksgiving, and, of course, sin offerings. The latter came into prominence during the post-Exilic period.

All three types of sacrifice were used by the Fathers of the early Church in order to interpret the death of Christ, which shows how apt an image it was by which to communicate the work of Christ. His was a communion sacrifice in which the community participated through eucharistic worship. Participation also involved lives of self-sacrifice on the part of the worshippers. Christ offered to his Father a sacrifice of praise and thanksgiving by his perfect obedience. His was a sin offering in which Christ himself was the victim, a kind of substitute whose death took away the sins of the people. Sacrifice is no longer a potent image for us today, except perhaps when used to describe the death of soldiers dying on behalf of their fellow countrymen in time of war, or the sacrifice parents may make for their children. But in New Testament times it communicated with popular sentiment. All Jews knew about the sacrifices in the Jewish Temple. If they lived in the Holy Land, a journey to the capital had to be made three times a year. If they lived in the Diaspora (meaning 'scattered', i.e. in lands outside Judaea and Galilee), a half shekel had to be paid annually for the maintenance of the Temple sacrifices; and pagan temples would be constantly in evidence throughout the towns of the Hellenic world.

The comparison of Christ's death with a sacrifice implies that he 'died for our sins', and that his death was made on our behalf. That is different from saying that he died in our stead. The concept of substitutionary punishment is generally foreign to the New Testament, and reference to it is found in only a very few texts, one of which, 'a ransom for many', seems likely to come from the lips of Jesus himself. The word translated here 'for' ('a ransom *for* many') is in the Greek *anti*, which means 'instead of'. A similar word for ransom applied to Christ is found in 1 Tim 2.6. The same idea of substitutionary atonement recurs in 1 Peter, where we read: 'In his own person he carried our sins to the gibbet' (1 Peter 2.24). Usually Christ is said in the New Testament to die not 'in our place' but 'on our behalf'. While substitutionary punishment is generally absent, it is common ground that the death of Jesus did for mankind what mankind could not do for itself; and the idea of his death on behalf of mankind is present in all those references in the New Testament to Christ as one of the forms of sin offering.

The idea of substitutionary punishment is morally abhorrent. It is offensive to the conscience. Why should one person be required to pay the penalty for offences committed by others, unless some responsibility had been incurred? It seems to conflict with our concept of justice. Surely wrongdoers should either be forgiven or punished. Why should a third party be introduced to bear the burden, so that their sins could be expiated and God's wrath could be propitiated? Expressed in this way the argument against substitutionary punishment seems unassailable. But one of the early Fathers found here a deeper meaning. If the victim were God, he would be as it were taking the blame on himself. God's love required him to reconcile his creation to himself. Since God is responsible for the creation of sinful humanity, and for the existence of a world in which they are born into an inheritance of sin, he saw it as morally appropriate that *God* should pay the penalty for wrongdoing. So the sacrifice of Christ has been regarded, paradoxically, as 'an act of God performed on himself'.[4] It is a way of marking for human beings divine responsibility for the rampant sinfulness of mankind. Seen in this light, the vicarious punishment inflicted on Christ is no longer morally abhorrent, because it is no longer substitutionary. On the contrary it could be said to be morally appropriate that God should take this kind of action to reconcile mankind to himself.

Ransom imagery

In the writings of the Fathers, the image of Christ's death as a sacrifice co-existed with the image of his death as a ransom. This formed part of what has been called the 'classic idea' of atonement. The combination may seem strange, but there is a connection between the two. If it was appropriate that God should act to show his ultimate responsibility for sin, it was also appropriate that he should act to break its power. To 'redeem' means to buy back. When Paul used the word, he was probably comparing the liberating effect of Christ's death to the freeing of a slave in the Roman world, which required that the owner sell him to the pagan god to whose treasury the slave had earlier made a payment. 'When anybody heard the Greek word *lutron*, "ransom" in the first century, it was natural for him to think of the purchase money for manumitting slaves.'[5] Redemption was also used of a first born child, which belonged to God, but which might be redeemed by the ritual payment of a sum (Num 18.15f.). The image of redemption is not dissimilar to that of a ransom. For nearly a thousand years the ransom theory of the atonement, originally elaborated by Irenaeus, was dominant in the Church. Mankind was in the power of the Devil, but in taking Jesus the Devil overreached himself. He was outwitted by the use of his own tools, being induced to effect the death of Jesus, thinking he was a mortal man, but finding that his captive was the Prince of Life who not only could not be killed but became the source of life to his emancipated subjects. Humanity, it was said, was the bait which the Devil was induced to swallow, but he was caught on the hook of Christ's divinity.[6] This kind of statement, which seems grotesque to us today, is a strange elaboration of Jesus' own words that he gave his life as 'a ransom for many'. The inspired imagery of ransom is important, in as much as it emphasizes the costliness of Jesus' death, and that it achieved for us what we could not do for ourselves. The addition of the words 'for many' gives it a universal application. ('Many' is a Semitism for 'all'.) Its effects were not merely confined to his followers, as was often later thought to be the case. It also points to the universal scope of the atonement so as to include the power of evil.

The worsting of the Devil includes also the conquest of all the 'powers and principalities', which today we might paraphrase by the impersonal evil structures of the world. Conquest is a New Testament image[7] where these powers play an important role, at least in the thinking of St Paul. They infect individuals. Their conquest by Christ points to the profound truth that the power of evil has in principle been broken, although its disappearance awaits the final consummation when God's purpose is complete. These are among the positive values to be found in the imagery of ransom. But once questions are asked as to whom the ransom was paid (to the Devil or to God), the image collapses into a theory, which destroys its power.

The 'ransom' of Christ from the power of the evil powers was just as appropriate an image in the days of the primitive Church as was sacrifice. There was a very widespread belief in the power of evil spirits and demons. The spread of Christianity may be largely explained through people's desperate need to be freed from their power. Ransom was frequent in those days to buy back prisoners of war, just as in our own age it has been connected with the release of hostages. It is said that the classic idea of the atonement, encapsulated in the image of Christ's conquest, through his death, of sin, death and the devil, expresses the fundamental truth that God acted to save mankind. The atonement is not achieved by human conversion, or through some correct legal process, but through the action of God coming to the aid of humanity. It was never worked out into a theory or a doctrine. 'The classic type is characterized by a whole contrast of opposites which defy systematization . . . any attempt to force this conception into a purely rational scheme is bound to fail: it could only succeed by robbing it of its religious depth.'[8]

Satisfaction theory

During the Middle Ages, when social thinking expressed itself in terms of the honour or satisfaction that should be rendered to an overlord in feudal society, another theory grew up, which originated in the thinking of that great Archbishop of Canterbury, St Anselm. His argument was complex. Every rational creature owes to God the debt of perfect obedience to his will. For Anselm sin was the failure to honour God through disobedience of his will. Justice required that sin could not be unjustly forgiven. Either punishment must be involuntarily suffered, or the sinner must voluntarily offer 'satisfaction' as a substitute for what the injured party has lost.

In this case the injured party is God the Father. 'Satisfaction' in those days was required for post-baptismal sin through penances, etc. Anselm took this idea and applied it to relations between the persons of the Trinity. The Son voluntarily offered his life as satisfaction to the Father for the sins of mankind. Mankind's sin, according to Anselm, was infinite; and so infinite satisfaction was required by God. Mankind could only give finite satisfaction. Because he was divine, God the Son alone could give to the Father the infinite satisfaction that was required. He could not be required to do this. But he could voluntarily offer himself to die upon the Cross in satisfaction for the sins of the whole world; and this he did.

Because man had incurred the debt, it must be repaid by man. But no ordinary man was able to do this, because, far from paying God anything extra, mankind had failed to give him the honour that is God's due through obeying his will. Christ however was perfectly obedient to his Father's will. He did not therefore deserve to die, because he had done nothing to deserve punishment. Yet he was man as well as God, so he alone was in a unique position to offer satisfaction. By his voluntary self-offering he acquired infinite merit. Justice required that the Father should meet this infinite merit with an infinite reward. Yet there was nothing that the Father could give the Son that he did not have already. And so he transferred it, as it were, to the account of mankind, and thus humanity was justified. Since the merit was infinite, but God's justification of mankind finite (because there is a finite number of mankind) there is therefore a surplus of merit. And so God the Father had his infinite satisfaction. God the Father was honoured through the death of the Son, and mankind was saved.[9]

It is all too easy to condemn this atonement theory today. It was a signal example of contextual theology, a brilliant attempt by a deep thinker to use the assumptions and presuppositions current in his age to explain how mankind has been reconciled to God through Jesus' death on the Cross. Its flaws, as we see them today, lie in its unquestioned fundamental assumptions; that the satisfaction which a villein had to render to his feudal lord is an appropriate image for the homage that is due to him who is the Lord of lords; that there is a kind of celestial 'treasury of merit' and that God's righteousness has a priority even higher than his love. According to the biblical view, God's righteousness is shown precisely in his love.

The substitutionary death of Jesus which forms part of Anselm's theory is far removed from the thoughts of that early Father that God was engaged in an act which signalled his own responsibility for sinful humanity. It was more a matter of God the Father noting the addition to the already infinite credit balance on the account of his Son, and transferring it to the account of mankind which was overburdened with hopeless debt. This theory has the value of emphasizing that something was done at the Atonement by God to reconcile human beings to himself. It also emphasizes that humanity had to be involved in this reconciliation, in so much as Christ as the Second Adam regained for the rest of mankind what had been lost through the First Adam. Relics of this medieval theory remain in Cranmer's eucharistic liturgy, according to which Christ made a 'full perfect and sufficient sacrifice, oblation and *satisfaction* for the sins of the whole world'; but the theory is far out of line with our presuppositions today.

Justification

At the time of the Reformation Paul's words about God justifying the ungodly through the death of Christ gave rise to another form of the substitutionary theory of atonement. All have sinned, and because all have sinned, they deserve to die. God's righteousness is manifested by his passing judgement on sin. But since God did not wish mankind to die, he provided his Son as victim in their place. His Son died, but was victorious over death, when he was raised again on the third day. By his death he suffered the punishment due to sinners, and they were acquitted. They have righteousness imputed to them; that is to say, although they are not righteous (because they have sinned) they are *accounted* righteous because of the death of Jesus. This theory was popular in the Middle Ages, when the Christian religion was much affected by legalism, and it is still held as one of the fundamentals of the faith by 'fundamentalists' today. It is especially connected with Martin Luther, who espoused it as a result of his own personal experience of freedom through Christ from the impossible demands of law, after a reading of St Paul's Epistle to the Romans.

In opposition to Lutheran teaching Roman Catholics at the Council of Trent insisted that Christians are made righteous by their membership of Christ's body and their participation in him. The ancient disagreement between Lutherans and Roman Catholics on these matters has been recently resolved. In the Report of the Anglican–Roman Catholic

Commission on 'Salvation and the Church', the difference is explained by reference to justification and sanctification which are said to be neither wholly distinct from nor unrelated to one another. Roman Catholic theologians, by translating the verb *dikaioun* 'to make righteous' rather than 'to account righteous', have tended to include within justification elements of salvation which the Reformers regarded as belonging to sanctification.[10] It is unfortunate that the Commission did not, as in their earlier reports, go behind Reformation controversies to the early Church, and indeed to the New Testament Church. Had they done so, they would have found that the Hebrew *tsedeqah* (righteousness) and its correlatives can be used to designate vindication and salvation rather than ethical righteousness.[11] Had they investigated Septuagintal usage they would have found that the verb *dikaioun*, which in classical Greek is used to mean 'to do a person justice' was used in the Septuagint with the meaning 'to redress' or 'to vindicate'. Pauline usage naturally followed the Septuagint rather than classical Greek.[12] And so it follows that in Pauline thought God neither imputed righteousness through the death of Christ, nor did he impart righteousness. Instead he put people 'in the right': he vindicated them. The word refers to the dynamic action that God took to accept mankind through Christ. The doctrine of justification through faith has been well translated into modern idiom as 'accepting acceptance although being unacceptable'.[13] Although this was the basic Pauline meaning of justification, it is hardly surprising that a forensic interpretation was given to it during the period of the Reformation, when ideas of sin as the transgression of law were dominant; and indeed Paul's own thought sometimes topples over into a legalistic interpretation.

Exemplarist theory

Contemporary with Anselm in the Middle Ages was Abelard, whose theology was far more in tune with more recent liberal thinking. Far from endorsing Anselm's theories of satisfaction, Abelard swept away any idea of ransom or substitutionary death. He would have nothing to do with sacrificial expiation, or God's need for infinite satisfaction. He believed that the love manifested in the voluntary self-offering of the Son of God on the Cross has such a moving effect on believers that their shackles fall away. They are no longer slaves to sin: they are restored to the glorious liberty of the children of God. There is no need of an objective sacrifice or propitiation. The subjective effect of Christ's love on the hearts of men and women brings about the reconciliation of God and humanity.[14]

This theory, which was officially disowned by the Church authorities, achieved fresh popularity with the blossoming of liberal theology around the beginning of the twentieth century. A theory based on 'moral influence' seemed appropriate in an age which based education on the premise that humanity only had to see what was good in order to appropriate it. No doubt it could call on such biblical texts as 'I shall draw all men to myself, when I am lifted up from the earth' (John 12.32), and 'God has shined in our hearts to give the light of the knowledge of the glory of God in the face of Jesus Christ' (2 Cor 4.6). But the terrible events of two World Wars, and the monstrous evil of the Holocaust, have dented this central assumption. The theory however, for all its flaws, does have a lasting value in that it does not depict God's attitude to mankind as changing as a result of Christ's death. God is always loving towards his creation. But it suggests a somewhat superficial view of evil. Bad attitudes are far too deep seated in the psyche to be so easily eradicated. It does not seem to take seriously enough the doctrine of sin.

Atonement theory for today

It has been necessary to survey the past history of atonement theories before we can begin to construct one for the present time. It will be apparent how each theory, based on biblical imagery, has drawn on the presuppositions and assumptions of the age in which it was conceived, and in which we no longer share. Today too we have a larger vision of the extent of the universe which God has created, and we have a deeper understanding, so it seems to us, of the motives and working of the human heart. No theory of the atonement based on animal sacrifice, or the manumission of slaves, or a payment made for ransom, or the proceedings of the law court, or the honour of feudal overlord, or the example of moral influence is sufficient for our day. We retain the old imagery to show our continuity with the past, and because it contains important truths; but we cannot believe that these are valid ways of explaining the atonement today.

We find in the New Testament references to the cosmic atonement achieved through Christ (e.g. Col 1.20). This seems inappropriate for the age in which we live.[15] It may be that there is intelligent life which has evolved on other planets in this universe; but it is no longer credible to hold that what happened on this planet nearly two thousand years ago can have any effect on intelligent beings who have no contact whatsoever with us, and who may live many many light-years away in space. No doubt in New Testament times it may have been appropriate to describe the universality of the atonement in such terms; but it has no meaning for us today.

Cosmic atonement can be understood as referring not to people living elsewhere in the universe but to Christ's conquest of supernatural powers of evil. However, what are sometimes perceived as evil spirits molesting human beings may well be the impact of spirits of the dead people which have become earthbound and which are awaiting release. But at times the sense of evil is very strong; and it may be that there are spiritual powers of evil extraneous to mankind which have a malevolent influence on humanity. Those who recall what Christ did on the Cross are impervious to their influence, because through their identification with Christ, they are open to the grace of God which overcomes the power of evil. So evil spirits, if they exist, have no power over them. It is not only the knowledge that evil can be overcome, but also the actual experience of this happening that has brought wonderful relief and a marvellous sense of freedom to millions, especially those who live in a primitive culture. It was after all Christ's power over the demons which caused the Christian faith to spread so rapidly in the ancient world. But it is not so easy to understand how Jesus' death on the Cross could have actually conquered their power: after all, people are still aware of the presence of evil, and its strength. What the Cross effects is not so much ending the power of evil as such, but ending its power to influence human beings who recall the work of Christ.

Any theory of atonement which appears adequate to people living in the modern world, as the twenty-first century after Christ approaches, is likely to be psychological. The imagery of reconciliation is used in the New Testament to describe the work of Christ, suggesting a comparison of the effects of Christ's death with the psychological processes involved in putting right personal relationships. This was not further elaborated, since it was not a category much explored in New Testament times. The imagery can be developed into a theory, although it is as unlikely to hold the whole truth as any previous theory. But at least it will give an explanation of the atonement in categories which are more accessible to twentieth-century hearts and minds.

Here I find I cannot improve on what I wrote nearly thirty years ago:[16]

The death of Jesus can be Atonement precisely because it manifests God involving himself in human calamity and identifying himself with men in their desperate plight. The story of the Cross is a story of injustice and malice, betrayal and beating, denial and despair, forsakenness and desolation, jealousy and envy, spite and rage, taunting and mockery, rejection and condemnation. The Incarnate Son suffered both as subject and as object. As subject he underwent the crushing experience of physical and psychic agony. As object he was the victim of his enemies' rage, his acquaintances' indifference, and his friends' weakness. God Incarnate endured the effects of both the impersonal irregularities which govern human existence and the personal assults upon his dignity inflicted by friend and foe alike. God Incarnate suffered to the full the evils of the world for which God alone is ultimately responsible. He endured the impersonal cruelty of creation (no miracle prevented his physical agony) and the personal cruelty of malice and weakness (doctors suggest that the reason why Jesus remained alive for so short a time upon the Cross was the emotional shock caused by the events of his trial and thereafter). God subjected himself in Christ to the impersonal cruelty of own physical world and to the personal cruelty of his own physical world inflicted by his own creatures . . .

Man can, then, no longer accuse God of being more like a devil than a loving Creator. He can no longer with justice charge God with creating a universe in which he is indifferent to its inevitable sin and suffering, evil and disaster. The death of Jesus shows God caring to the point where he can care no more; that is, by sharing human pain to the point of human death. The death of Jesus shows God Incarnate accepting men even as they inflict upon him the worst that they can do . . . He accepts men even in all their unacceptability and unacceptingness. By so doing (or rather by man's realization of what God has done) he draws the sting of their hate. Man's unconscious grudge against life, against himself, and against God exhausts itself on the crucified figure of the tortured and dying Christ. Here hatred runs out into the sand. As Jesus' death was the gateway to renewal of life through what we call the Resurrection, so also troubled men who pour out their hidden jealousy and spite and rage against God at the foot of the Cross find that at this very point they are standing on the threshold of that new life in Christ of which the New Testament so often and so eloquently speaks . . .

This is why the image of the Crucified is such a potent symbol, and even to make the sign of the cross is to invoke it in our subconscious minds. It is in this subconscious area of our being that we most need deliverance, for few of us are conscious of a grudge against God. The love of God shining through the image of Christ helps to achieve this deliverance.

We are in a state of internal disharmony. The stresses and strains of life may force us back to childhood states without our realizing that this has happened. The calamities of daily existence may cause us to react unconsciously as well as consciously to protect ourselves. As a result of unconscious regression we are often in a state of internal disharmony and out of relationship with our families, our friends and acquaintances. This regression to infantile states usually takes one or other of three main types (although few of us fit neatly into categories).[17] Infantile rage may have caused compulsive attention-seeking behaviour, or it may have been inverted into mordant despair, or it may have resulted in detachment and distrust of social involvement and personal relationships. This suppressed rage, which in infancy was directed against the mother figure, becomes in adults directed against the self, or against those with a claim on our affections, and especially against God, the author and source of our affections.

Our internal disharmony removes from us a sense of self-esteem and worth. We desperately need this self-esteem, and so we try to snatch it from others, through envying them as persons or coveting their possessions. We try to compensate for this lack of self-esteem in ourselves by giving way to the pleasures of greed or lust. We externalize our hatred of ourselves by transferring it to others; and instead of doing violence to ourselves, we tend to inflict it on those who stand in our way. Such are some of the tragic effects of internal disharmony.

It may in part be dispersed by greater self-knowledge, and by the experience of friends' or a spouse's love breaking through into those subconscious parts of the psyche where disharmony lies. Our unconscious self is not only the sink of suppressed feelings which we dare not bring into consciousness; it is also the window of inspiration and the gateway through which the healing flows of divine love and compassion can enter and give us back that sense of worth which we so desperately need. This love is supremely focused in the image of the Crucified, so that divine love ceases to be an ecclesiastical formula or a conscious avowal from which the unconscious revolts. It becomes the expression of an experienced reality. Only when we receive this in faith (for God never forces himself upon us) are we freed by divine love to make a fuller response with our own love. Our internal disharmonies begin to disappear, and the peace of God, which passes all understanding, sweeps over the psyche. We are no longer afraid to be ourselves, because we know that we have been accepted in spite of our unacceptability. We no longer have to protect ourselves from ourselves: we no longer have to regress to infantile states in order to make up for the lack of self-worth which had earlier forced us into those infantile states. We are free to use the given creativities of our human nature so as to become the people that God wants us to be. We are set on the way of salvation.

Such is a psychological model of the atonement. If it rings true for today (and it is unlikely to accord with everyone's inner self-consciousness), that does not mean that it contains the whole truth, any more than the earlier theories which we have considered.

To what extent is such a theory congruous with our earlier rejection of Chalcedonian orthodoxy of the two natures of Christ in one being, and our substitution of a functional and inspirational model (see p. 87)? Christ is for us the icon of God, so that with Thomas we cry out in worship and commitment 'My Lord and my God!' (John 20.28). Jesus did not think up the idea of becoming the Saviour of the world! The initiative came throughout from God. God gave Jesus the vocation to be Messiah. God called him to his public ministry and his atoning death. God chose the man Jesus to be the instrument and expression of himself. God inspired him and empowered him throughout, so that 'He who has seen me has seen the Father' (John 14.9). As the divine instrument of love, Jesus was the Lamb chosen from the foundation of the world, he was the Christ anointed by God's Holy Spirit. In the words of St John's Gospel, 'I do nothing on my own authority, but in all I say, I have been taught by my Father. He who sent me is present with me, and has not left me alone; for I always do what is acceptable to him' (John 8.28b–29). Jesus' words are the human expression of God's words: his love was the full human expression of the divine love, in so far as this can be expressed in human personality. We are therefore justified in using the language of incarnation for Jesus, providing that we do not mean by this that he combined in one person two natures, human and divine. Rather, God was acting through Jesus' humanity to remove the alienation from all humanity.

So God shows his great love towards mankind by the death of Christ. Jesus is obedient to his will, filled by his spirit and upheld by his love, even when all consciousness of that love was removed when he cried out on the Cross: 'My God, my God, why have you forsaken me?' (Mark 15.34). God called Jesus to the vocation of suffering. God suffers with the suffering Christ, showing us that in all our afflictions he is afflicted. The God whom we thought to be impassible has suffered for our sakes with Jesus on the Cross.[18] The image of the crucifix is a valid image of God suffering in his love for his creation.

This model of Christ actually increases the relevance of the Atonement, showing not only that God was in Christ reconciling the world to himself, but God is with us all in all our sufferings, caring for us by sharing with us as he did with Christ. In this sense Christ is, as Pascal said, in agony to the end of the world. And so even within their sufferings human beings can find paradoxically the love of God and a hint of the glory to come. Up to the time of his betrayal, Jesus lived an active life during his whirlwind public ministry, preaching the Kingdom and healing the sick and gathering round him his group of disciples. But from the time of his arrest he 'handed himself over' to the authorities.[19] From that time onwards he reacted passively to the false charges against him. By so doing he showed in a particularly telling way, the amazing humility of God, exactly the same humility with which God shares in all our human sufferings.

We have already made it clear that this is not the only way of looking at the meaning of Christ's work to inaugurate God's kingdom. It has been said that a psychological model of the atonement is essentially exemplarist, and so does not help the multitudes of people who have never heard the Good News of God in Christ. It is true that it does not help them in this life to be reconciled to God. But, as we shall note later (see p. 230), the preaching of the Good News of God's love is not confined to this world. After his death Christ 'in the spirit made his proclamation to the imprisoned spirits' (1 Peter 3.19). The same writer also speaks of the Gospel being preached to those who are dead (1 Peter 4.6), although this may refer to those who had died after they had heard the Good News. In ways unknown to us the love of God and his suffering in and with his creatures may be conveyed to those who die without knowing on earth the Good News of Christ.

Whatever understanding of the Atonement we may have, earlier theories lack credibility today. In the past people thought of God having created all things good, but then the angels fell from heaven, and Adam and Eve by their action entailed sin on the whole human race. So God acted first in creation to make all things good, and then later acted in redemption to bring things back to good after they had gone wrong. Even Irenaeus, with his seemingly modern doctrine of *anakephalaiosis* (the summing up of humanity in Christ) believed this. But we no longer think in this way. If there was a Fall, it was a fall upwards, with our human consciousness of good and evil and our freedom of choice leading to human potentiality for good as well as to the (almost inevitable) probability of evil (see p. 61). So God's work in atonement must be *in continuity* with God's work in creation. It was not Part Two of a cosmic drama when Part One had ended in disaster and confusion, but the continuance of his loving activity in his creation of the universe. Atonement in this sense must be seen as much part of God's eternal purpose for his universe as his creation. There must be a principle which holds them both together.

This principle is the Kingdom of God. We have already seen that the natural world, in obeying the laws of the Creator, manifests his Kingdom according to its mode. His kingly rule has set boundaries, so that the physical constants are fine-tuned to enable matter to develop in such a way that it self-assembles itself quite naturally into more and more complex forms until human beings evolve (see p. 36). This whole creative process testifies to his kingly rule. In the stories of Jesus of Nazareth his kingly rule is manifested in a different mode, personally in Jesus through his total obedience to his heavenly Father's will. During his ministry the Kingdom of God was foreshadowed among his disciples: it was present as it were by anticipation. Jesus himself insisted that his task was to be both the announcer and the bearer of his Father's Kingdom. From the time of the New Testament epistles onwards, Christian theology has tended to divorce its theology of redemption from Jesus' own priority of the Kingdom. Christ's death and resurrection must be seen as inaugurating the Kingdom as much as attesting the King. We have already noted the tendency of Christianity to become more Christocentric than Christ was himself (see p. 95). Jesus himself always insisted that his work was to point towards his Heavenly Father. It has been the fault of catholic and evangelical theology that it tends to attest the King without the Kingdom, just as liberal theology has tended to affirm the Kingdom without the King. We need the one as much as the other. God's act of 'at-oning' through Christ must be understood in a way that inaugurates God's Kingdom for human beings, just as God's process of creation in his universe must be understood in a way that attests not only the freedom given to that process but also the kingly rule of God who gave it that freedom throughout its almost unimaginably vast extent. As we shall see, the Church is a sign and symbol of the coming Kingdom, and Christian spirituality aims at realizing the Kingdom in an individual, in imitation of Christ and in the power of the Spirit.

Thus the idea of God's Kingdom, on which Jesus centred his own message, binds together in a single whole both Creation and Atonement, and reaches out to include both ecclesiology and spirituality. As a unitive concept it has been largely ignored by theologians; and it deserves to be reinstated to its central position in Christian theology.

Notes

1. See A. Deissman, *Light from the Ancient East* (London, 1910), pp. 322–34.

2. See H. Montefiore, *Commentary on the Epistle to the Hebrews* (London, 1964), Introduction.

3. See F. M. Young, *Sacrifice and the Death of Christ* (London, 1975), Part 1.

4. *Ibid.*, p. 95.

5. A. Deissman, *op. cit.*, pp. 331–2.

6. For references, see Hastings Rashdall, *The Idea of Atonement* (London, 1919), pp. 247–8.

7. See R. Leivestad, *Christ the Conquerer* (London, 1954).

8. See G. Aulen, *Christus Victor*, tr. G. Herbert (London, 1934), pp. 172 3.

9. Anselm, *Cur Deus Homo*, Book 2, c. XIX.

10. ARCIC II, *Salvation and the Church* (London, 1987), para. 14.

11. N. Snaith, *The Distinctive Ideas of the Old Testament* (London, 1944), p. 87.

12. C. H. Dodd, *The Bible and the Greeks* (London, 1935), pp. 42–59.

13. P. Tillich, *Courage to Be* (London, 1952), p. 156.

14. Abelard's Latin texts may be found in Hastings Rashdall, *op. cit.*, p. 362.

15. To criticize 'cosmic redemption' does not mean that the effects of redemption should be confined to humanity. 'To accept God as Saviour is to work out our own salvation and so to do our part in restoring and recreating what by our frailty and folly we have defaced or destroyed': H. Montefiore (ed.), *Man and Nature* (London, 1975), p. 77.

16. H. Montefiore, *Awkward Questions on Christian Love* (London, 1964), pp. 84–5.

17. See H. Montefiore, 'Christology for today' in *Soundings*, ed. A. R. Vidler (Cambridge, 1963), p. 168.

18. See J. Moltmann, *The Crucified God* (London, 1974), p. 275.

19. See W. H. Vanstone, *The Stature of Waiting* (London, 1982).

chapter 6

The doctrine of God

The Holy Spirit in the Bible

The word 'spirit' has as many nuances in English as it does in Greek.

In English it can mean what is immaterial, in contrast to the materiality of matter. It can describe supernatural essence or power. Or it can denote a common mind and outlook held by groups of people. It can designate a direction or vision. Or it can refer to the character of an individual. It is a flexible word with many nuances and meanings. It is the same in Greek, the language in which the New Testament was written. It is used there both of the spirit of man and of the Spirit of God.

In the Old Testament there are two words for spirit. There is *nephesh*, God's breath which gives life, and which comes to mean in later writings 'inner consciousness' or even a person's character. There is also the more important word *ruach*, wind, which sustains the whole natural world, and invades men and women, giving strength, leadership, wisdom, ecstasy, the inspiration of prophecy. It is prophesied in the Old Testament that spirit will be the characteristic of the Last Days, of the Messiah, and of the resurrection of the nation.[1] 'Spirit in the Old Testament is not a person or a definable object or substance. It is a mode of describing how the holy God is active in the world which he has created and especially in the persons in which his purpose is fulfilled.'[2] In later Jewish writings, such as the Wisdom of Solomon (written in Egypt during the early New Testament period), spirit was equated with the figure of wisdom. Spirit here has a cosmic function, as it had in Stoic thinking. 'The spirit of the Lord has filled the world' (Wisdom 1.7).

The New Testament opens with the word for 'spirit' used in the same way as in the Old. Jesus was conceived by the power of the Holy Spirit, and he also received the gift of the Spirit at his baptism. He applied to himself the text: 'The spirit of the Lord is upon me' (Luke 4.18). At his death the words translated 'gave up the ghost' may be better translated 'handed back the spirit' (Mark 15.37). He himself is recorded as referring very seldom to his reception of the Spirit, which may perhaps be explained by his natural self-effacingness.[3]

During his life, the Spirit was in him among men and women: after his death and resurrection the Spirit was in men and women from him. This gift of the Spirit, described as inspiring the primitive Church from Pentecost onwards, was the *arrabon* or pledge of its full arrival at the Last Day. (*Arrabon* is properly the down payment on a hire purchase!) The Spirit is described in terms that are either invasive from without, or filling a person from within. This invasive power of the Spirit probably expresses the impact of God on the unconscious, which gives the impression of a power from without as it breaks into the conscious, whereas the fulfilling power of the Spirit expresses the impact of God on the conscious mind and feelings. The Spirit when it fills a person may result in the gifts of order and peace, or when it appears to come from without it may give rise to ecstatic phenomena (which again bear the marks of a breakthrough from the unconscious). It is bestowed on the whole Church, and within the Church on individual men and women. The Spirit is described in personal terms and called the Paraclete (Counsellor and Comforter). The Spirit is always to be understood as coming from Jesus as the result of his death and resurrection. There is no real distinction to be made between the Spirit of God and the Spirit of Jesus. To be in the Spirit is the same as to be in Christ.

The Holy Spirit in the early Fathers

The use of 'the Spirit' in the Bible is very varied, and it does not suggest any clear-cut doctrine. The early Fathers were not at first concerned with the doctrine of the Spirit; and we find among many of them differences of emphasis, especially during the Arian controversy over the status of the Son. The orthodox doctrine of the Holy Spirit as an eternal Person of the godhead was anticipated in thinkers such as Tertullian in the West, and Origen and Athanasius in the East. The solution of the Arian controversy meant that there was a need officially to define the status of the Holy Spirit. In AD 362, at the Council of Alexandria, it was unanimously agreed that 'the Holy Spirit is not a creature, not foreign but proper to, and inseparable from, the essence of the Father and the Son'. It remained for Basil and his younger brother Gregory to give substance to the doctrine by the treatises on the Holy Spirit which they both wrote.

Thus Christendom developed its orthodox doctrine of the Trinity, 'three persons and one God'.

The Holy Spirit and the created world

Can we determine the scope of the Holy Spirit's work? The New Testament is a Christ-intoxicated collection of books, and therefore it is not to be expected that the Spirit will be thought to act except in connection with the Christ event. Is this same Spirit to be found in the natural world? Does it explain the diffused goodness in the world? Does it lie in some sense behind the inspiration to be found in the great world religions? These questions are not even asked in the New Testament; but nowadays they impinge upon us, forcing us to consider them.

God interacts with his created world. He is always present within it, if only we had eyes to see him. He is present in an immaterial way, and so we speak of his presence as Spirit; and because God is holy, we usually designate this as the Holy Spirit. God's Spirit does not normally interfere with his own natural laws (although we are ignorant of the full effect that Spirit may have on spirit or on material things). God is always at work in the openness of natural systems, guiding the process from within towards order and unity and increasing complexity. 'As a believer in the Creator Spirit I would say that deep within the fabric of the universe, the Spirit is present as the Go-Between who confronts each isolated spontaneous particle with the beckoning reality of the larger whole and so compels it to be related to others in a particular way; and it is he who at every stage lures the inert organisms by giving an inner awareness and recognition of the unattained.'[4]

Similarly the Spirit of God inspires all that is good and noble and beautiful and true, both in the world religions, and in individual men and women.[5] As we have seen, it may appear to be invasive from without, when there is a breakthrough from the unconscious to the conscious, or it may appear an internal fulfilment, when God's Spirit informs the judgements and thoughts of men and women. It is not easy to write at length about the Spirit, because this is the sphere where God is experienced rather than described, and because this experience (like all experience) is often emotionally coloured rather than susceptible of cool logical analysis. However, it can be said with assurance that it is the experience of the Holy Spirit which makes our faith a living reality instead of a merely intellectual conviction. The Holy Spirit brings us religious experience, inspires us with what is true and good and beautiful, and enriches us with the grace of God and brings us together in fellowship. Without the Holy Spirit there would be no creativity: faith would be cold and the Church would be dead.

The Spirit and the Son

In the New Testament the Holy Spirit is equated with the Spirit of Christ. This is to be explained by the New Testament belief that it is through Christ that all things came to be, and so the Spirit of God let loose in the world must be the Spirit of Christ. As theological reflection proceeded, the Spirit was believed to proceed from the Father: the word 'proceed' is first used in this connection in St John's Gospel. Although there 'procession' describes the coming of the Spirit into the world, this was also believed to be the mode of the Spirit's origin. 'Procession' of the Spirit is in contrast to the generation of the Son, although the difference between the two is not easy to define. It suggests the difference between asexual and sexual reproduction, although neither metaphor is suited to the eternal creativity of God within himself.

In the West the words of the Creed were expanded from 'proceeding from the Father' to 'proceeding from the Father and the Son'; first by Latin writers in the fourth century and by Augustine in the fifth, and then by the Council of Toledo in AD 589. In many places in the West the addition was made to the Nicene Creed itself (which the Church had agreed in AD 431 was the only creed to be used). Around the end of the first millennium it was introduced into the Roman liturgy, and shortly afterwards Pope Benedict VIII formally approved the addition. This was the occasion of the schism between the Catholic and the Orthodox Church. These precise definitions apply only to those attempting to define the 'essential Trinity', God as he is in himself, which involves the attempt to exceed the scope of human knowledge.[6]

These definitions go far beyond what is revealed in the New Testament. There the Holy Spirit is best understood in a similar sense to that in the Old Testament; God in action (and because Christ's actions were God's, also Christ in action). In the words of a scholar who has deeply pondered the evidence:

We are using the word 'Spirit' to speak of God as active and as related to human beings, which is the only way in which we can speak of God, since this is how he discloses himself to us and we can know nothing about God which he does not reveal. There was much dispute in the early Church as to whether the Holy Spirit is to be regarded as an anhypostatic operation of God (*energeia*) or as a substance or entity (*ousia*). In speaking now of God as Spirit we are not referring to an impersonal influence, an energy transmitted by God but distinct from himself. Nor are we indicating a divine entity or hypostasis which is a third person of the Godhead. We are speaking of God himself, his personal presence, as active and related.[7]

The doctrine of the Blessed Trinity

However, the Church opted for a doctrine of three 'persons' and one God, the dogma of the Blessed Trinity; according to the ecumenical Council of Constantinople (AD 381): 'One and the same Godhead in the hypostasis of three Persons of equal honour and equal power; namely the Father, Son and the Holy Spirit'. In direct reaction to this Trinitarian formula we read in the Qur'an: 'Those certainly are disbelievers who say: Allah is the third of three. There is no one worthy of worship but the One God' (5.74), and later in Maimonides' thirteenth Fundamental Principle of the Jewish Faith: 'I believe with a perfect faith, that the Creator, blessed be his name, is a Unity, and that there is no unity in any manner whatsoever like unto him, that he alone is our God, who was, and is, and ever will be.'

The English words which translate the Greek and Latin formula of the Blessed Trinity here are somewhat misleading. In neither language do they designate either three Gods or one God with three different personalities! 'Person' represents the Latin *persona* and the Greek *hypostasis*. The words as we have seen (see p. 84) mean something very different from the English 'person'. Since there is only one God with these three roles or concrete expressions, they cannot pull in different directions. There was developed the doctrine of *perichoresis*, coinherence, according to which the three 'persons' of the Trinity coinhere with one another, so that there is no difference of function between them. In Augustine's words, *opera Trinitatis ad extra indivisa sunt*, the works of the Trinity, seen from without, are indivisible. What therefore distinguishes them? Only that the Father has no origin, the Son is begotten from the Father, and the Holy Spirit proceeds from the Father (and the Son?). Even though the Church was searching into the deepest and most arcane mysteries of God, it is strange that it should have decided on such obscure and almost unintelligible dogma.

The doctrine of the Blessed and Undivided Trinity remained a front rank doctrine until the early nineteenth century, when it was relegated to an appendix by Schleiermacher in his book on the Christian faith.[8] Biblical criticism developed, and revelation was no longer believed to be in the form of biblical propositions, and a 'lower' Christology became acceptable. In the light of this, Trinitarian doctrine became increasingly neglected. It seemed a dry intellectual formulation compared with the concrete self-revelation of God in Jesus. Christianity tended in Liberal Protestant circles to become monarchian rather than trinitarian. In the more recent past however there has been some reaction, initiated by Barth's commentary on the Epistle to the Romans. The doctrine has been subject to renewed study, and as a result it has tended to regain its place in the forefront of Christian theology.

Two main analogies lie at hand in any attempt to explain the Trinity. One is 'the social analogy', based on the relationship between three human persons. An advantage of the social analogy is that the godhead can be shown to be involved in an eternal activity of love between the 'persons' of the Trinity. Among Augustine's many analogies, that of the lover, the beloved and the love which passes between them both, particularly appeals to the imagination. (Augustine wrote thirteen books in a work on the Trinity 'lest nothing be said'.) Organic unity is far more complex than mere mathematical unity.[9] But as Being itself, God's nature is not complex but simple, and why should his unity correspond to organic unity? We readily attribute to God the personal attributes of Will, Wisdom and Love; but these are in no sense *personae* or *hypostaseis* of his One Substance: they are simply elements which constitute the complex unity of human personality, but we cannot argue from the nature of humanity to the inner nature of God. Yet this form of argument is not uncommon. It has been said that:

> . . . if God is Personal at all; and if Will and Wisdom and Love are elements in the conception of Personality; it follows, from analysis of the necessary meaning and implications, even of the inchoate personality of which we ourselves are conscious in ourselves, that Divine Personality cannot mean a sole and unrelated unity. There must be to Itself both subject and object; and moreover a mutual relation of subject and object; that is to say, a mutually personal relation. There must be mutuality of contemplation, mutuality of Love. . . . and mutuality is the one thing which I can see to be an intellectual necessity in my thought of Divine Personality – so necessary that Divine Personality cannot even be thought without it.[10]

It is true that human beings find their being through their relationships, so that one might say 'I relate, therefore I am'. But we cannot argue by analogy in this way from humanity to God. We rightly affirm that there is personality in God, but that is not to say that the Divine Being suffers from the same restrictions as human personality imposes upon us.

In fact the objections to the social analogy outweigh the advantages. The human analogue is three human persons, and so it tends towards tritheism, as is apparent from the famous fifteenth-century Russian Orthodox icon of the Trinity by Rublev under the form of three persons communing. Why three, we may ask? Why not two, or even four? Of course it may be said in reply that that is how God is, and we know that God is thus because he has revealed it. But the doctrine of the Blessed Trinity, whether or not it represents the truth about God, can hardly be called a revealed doctrine, except on the authority of the Church Councils which formulated it. It is a human construct made from the New Testament revelation on the basis of Hellenistic metaphysics. It is hard enough to prove, on the basis of New Testament evidence, that the Father eternally begets the Son throughout eternity (and even more difficult to explain what this means). The New Testament evidence certainly does not attest the person of the Holy Spirit eternally proceeding from the Father (and perhaps the Son). If the Church had not been beholden to Greek metaphysical and Roman legal thinking the doctrine of the Trinity would never have been formulated in terms which seem to make the social analogy appropriate.

More attractive is the modal analogy. God discloses himself as Father, Son and Holy Spirit. He reveals himself to us in the three modes of creating, reconciling and sanctifying; and these modes, although distinct, are all interconnected. The difficulty about this modalist analogy is that it tends towards unitarianism. The early Fathers were terrified of 'Sabellianism', that God displays different characters at different times, so that the Father can turn into the Son, who may turn into the Holy Spirit. Modalism however can equally portray God in three eternal modes of being, or in three permanent modes of self-disclosure. This 'modal' view of the Trinity gives rise to the question: if there are not three 'persons' of the godhead, what did the one God do before the creation of the universe? There could hardly have been an exchange of love within the godhead of the kind postulated by the 'social analogy'. So did God spend eternity contemplating his own beatitude, after the Aristotelian model? We simply do not know the answer to any question concerning the mystery of God's being throughout eternity, nor is this question framed in such a way that any answer could be given. There was no 'before the creation of the universe', because time did not exist until the universe was created. For all we know, God is eternally creating and reconciling and sanctifying.

As for what God is in himself, that is beyond our comprehension. We know only the outskirts of his ways. We cannot even say that God is a person, for that would place him in a category with others, and it would imply constraints on his being; but, because he cannot be less than the persons he has created, we must content ourselves with saying that there is personality in God. God is Being itself dwelling in the eternal present, and his internal life must ever remain unknowable to human beings. We do not and cannot know the inner life of God himself. This is to penetrate further than is possible for frail and finite humanity. What God is in himself must remain an impenetrable mystery. We must resolutely affirm the apophatic nature of this mystery. Christians down the centuries have been far too inclined to define the indefinable, with a certitude that is sometimes breathtaking. There is much that we do not know and cannot know. We would do better to believe more about less! In so far as the doctrine of the Trinity purports to go beyond what can be known and attempts to define the mutual inner relationships of the three Persons of the Trinity, it is attempting to define something which is beyond our knowledge. Even the Scriptures hardly speak of these inner relationships.

An objection to this view, which restricts our field of enquiry to the 'economic Trinity' (that is, God in relation to the universe), is sometimes raised on the grounds that God's self-disclosure is always a true disclosure of who he is. If he reveals himself to us in three modes, then he must exist in three modes throughout all eternity. Of course we must grant that God's self-disclosure is always truthful. It would be unthinkable that he should reveal himself otherwise than as he is. But all revelation has to be accommodated to the capacity of a person to receive it (according to the medieval tag, *omnis revelatio secundum modum recipientis*); otherwise nothing is revealed. It is in order to reveal himself to us in our human condition that God discloses himself in the three modes of creating and reconciling and sanctifying. This does not necessarily mean that these are eternal characteristics of his nature and permanent modes of his being.

A doctrine of the 'economic trinity' flows naturally from our earlier conclusions about the nature of creation, the status of Jesus and the work of the Holy Spirit. God's Spirit is active in the creation and evolution of the universe. God's Spirit was active in the person of Jesus, guiding and inspiring him and upholding him so that he was the Son of God, God's icon. God's Spirit is active in helping others to conform to the image of Christ, and in inspiring all that is good and beautiful and true. God's Spirit is active in all three modes, in so far as he relates to his universe; creating, redeeming, sanctifying. The One God acts towards us in these three modes rather than eternally existing in three persons linked in mutual love. We may of course continue to use the ancient formulas of the Church, to show our continuity of faith and life, for we are trying to reinterpret doctrine in a way which does full justice to his divine self-disclosure through Christ, and which is also credible to us today. Later ages may find this explanation unsatisfactory. But in our present age we do need to explain to others as well as to ourselves just what we do really believe if our faith is to be credible to us and to them; and we also need to avoid occasions of stumbling in our relations with other faiths.

The relation of God to his universe

We have spoken of God as active and related to his universe. We must discuss how God could relate to it. How can the impassible relate to the suffering of the world? How can 'necessary being' relate to what is contingent? How can he who is changeless relate to a world of change and flux? How can Perfect Being be affected by anything or anyone?

Very different doctrines of God have been held by theologians. There are those who believe in a divine Being whose only contact with the universe was in his creation of it. Such a God would be a kind of cosmic engineer who has designed and constructed a vast and elaborate mechanism, or an infinitely unfolding organism, and who then leaves it alone to let it take its own course. He himself would have nothing to do with it. He would live in beatitude unimaginable, remote from the cares and concerns of humanity. This was a popular view of God when the laws of nature were being discovered, and when God was thought of, as Paley thought of him, as a kind of Divine Watchmaker. It was a belief typical of an age which was sceptical about the supernatural. Such a view of God is so remote from his self-disclosure found in the Scriptures, as well as from our own religious experience, that it may safely be regarded as an aberration.

Other thinkers (like Spinoza) have equated God and his universe. God is identified with nature. This view can be found in some forms of Eastern religions, notably Hinduism. There is a resurgence of this view in some New Age theologies. In its favour are some forms of nature mysticism, and the feeling of kinship with the natural world which is a common human experience. But this could equally well be explained by the Divine Spirit which fills the world and brings us into communion with itself and with one another and the world of nature. Pantheism is alien to the revealed nature of God in the Scriptures. It is inconsistent with the contingent nature of the universe. It cannot explain its own existence. Nor can it explain the existence of evil. It is repulsive to the human spirit to regard evil itself as part of God. There is what might be called a secular form of pantheism current among some contemporary scientists, the concept of an evolving God within the universe, with intelligent life (or even machine life) perhaps fusing with other such intelligences, and gradually extending control over matter and energy until all nature is subjugated and it becomes indistinguishable from nature itself. Such a faith is either a fantasy of megalomania, or the product of unwarrantable overconfidence in the potentiality of the power to be gained through the natural sciences.

Transcendence and immanence

According to traditional theism, God is both transcendent over the world, and immanent within it. It has been reduced to what is tantamount to a simultaneous equation:[11]

The world − God = 0
God − the world = God.

God is other than his universe, and he is not to be equated with it. But his universe does not exist apart from him. 'In him we live, and move, and have our being' (Acts 17.28). His spirit is immanent within it. God is infinite, and no finite universe can make him more than he is. God is God whether the universe had been created or not. This universe exists within God, without adding to God. God is pure Being, and the universe exists by participating in his being according to its created mode.

If we look for human analogies whereby the relation of the universe may be imagined, two present themselves. A mother bearing a child is transcendent over the baby in her womb. She is other than the baby, and has existed without it, and when it is born she will again exist without it. At the same time the baby is part of her, even though it is an organism complete in itself. It is nourished by her body, and it contains her genes: it is part of herself. She is immanent within the baby and at the same time transcendent over it.

A closer analogy is that of poets or dramatists who create books or plays. They create a whole world out of nothing. Without their imagination and application, this world would not have come into being. They create people, and the people have characters of their own, indeed lives of their own, and the authors cannot make them do things out of keeping with their characters (or, if they do, they are bad writers). They not only create people, they create the world in which their people live. They are transcendent over their world. Yet although the people they create have lives of their own, at the same time there is something of the author in them all. It is in their authors' imagination that they live and move and have their being. Although the people 'do their own thing' in the drama or the story, the authors exercise an overall control. They only exist, as it were, within their authors' providential care; and if things seem to be getting out of hand, so that the plot is becoming disrupted, the authors introduce some way of bringing it back to where it should be. So authors are not only transcendent over their creation, but also in some sense immanent within it.

Panentheism

These two analogies fall far short of the reality of God's transcendence and immanence; but they do convey some impression of the relationship of him who is transcendent to his creation and yet immanent within it. There are some aspects of this traditional view, however, which seem to fit ill with the doctrine of God revealed in the Scriptures and reinforced by our own experience. We have already seen that the Christian Church borrowed from the Hellenistic world many of its concepts in its attempts to define the person of Christ, the Holy Spirit and the Blessed Trinity. Inevitably it was deeply influenced in its doctrine of God by the culture in which it was placed. This gave rise to what is known as the *via negativa*, that is to say, an approach to God not by affirming his likeness to us, but by emphasizing the differences, and in particular by insisting that God is unaffected by time or change. (This is different from affirming that there are many aspects of God about which we must remain agnostic: it is positively affirming what he is not.)

According to this traditional view God is perfect, omniscient and omnipotent. He is unchanging, unaffected by human beings, and incapable of suffering. In him there is the fullness of beatitude, beauty and joy. But such a God seems to have little in common with God as he is revealed in the Old and New Testaments. The chasm between divine transcendence and immanence was bridged by the Church's doctrine of Incarnation, but as we have seen, only paradoxically, by claiming that Christ suffered although his Divine Nature was totally unaffected by this suffering (see p. 85). According to the traditional view God remains strangely unaffected by whatever has happened, happens and will happen in the universe which he has created. Such a view has been challenged by theologians who espouse what is called 'panentheism'. This is a form of theism which criticizes traditional theism for depicting the world as external to God and for his being totally unaffected by it.

Traditional theism affirms that the perfection of God consists in his divine absoluteness, eternity and independence. Panentheism also affirms these attributes, so that panentheists can happily sing the well-known hymn (based on 1 Tim 1.17):

Immortal, invisible, God only wise,
in light inaccessible hid from our eyes,
most blessèd, most glorious, the ancient of days,
almighty, victorious, thy great name we praise.

Unresting, unhasting, and silent as light,
nor wanting, nor wasting, thou rulest in might; . . .

But as well as these characteristics, panentheists add to them perfect relationality, mutability or responsiveness, perfect temporality and dependence. Process theologians are convinced that God is affected by the processes of the universe. 'Since God includes the world, God's experience is related to the world, altered by the changes of the world, involved in time, and dependent on what happens in the world.'[12] Originally immutability, before its meaning was overlaid by Greek metaphysics, represented reliability, whereas mutability was the character of pagan deities, who were fickle (Virgil also called the female sex *semper mutabile*, always fickle). In this sense God is indeed immutable, eternal and independent. God's character remains unchanged by everything that happens. But he reacts to humanity's pains and joys. He shares them and sympathizes. Such a God both knows and loves the world. He acts within it and participates in the joys and sorrows of its creatures. He was involved in the Crucifixion by sharing the suffering of Christ on the Cross. In the same way he is present and shares in all our human sadnesses and sufferings, as well as in our joys and happinesses.

This is an attractive way of thinking about God which should be endorsed. More questionable, however, is the suggestion by some process theologians of the mind–body or mind–brain analogy for conceiving God's relation to the world; but this does at least suggest that what happens in the world contributes to the experience of God, who nonetheless transcends, both quantitively and qualitatively, the experience of the world.

Such a view of God, freed from the negativism of Greek thought, certainly seems more in accord with the biblical revelation, and it also accords with our own religious experience. God is with us in our joys and in our sorrows. He is afflicted in our afflictions, and he rejoices in our joys. He is above and beyond us, and yet is also with us and in us. God is unchanging in the sense that his character is eternal, and his love is everlasting; but he is not unchanging in the sense that he is unaffected by anything which we think or say or do or suffer. God is impassible in the sense that we can never make him different from what he is or from who he is, and we can never alter his nature of joy and beatitude,[13] but he is passible in the sense that he responds to us and shares with us our sufferings; but these are subsumed within the totality of his love. Just as individual people are not so much changed by a relationship as able to find their true selves within it, so God, according to his mode, enjoys his relationship with us, which is an overspill from his eternal Being. God is eternal, and so beyond time; and yet he also enters into time, so makes himself known within our space–time continuum.

The nature of God

It is very unusual for belief in God to be the result of logical reasoning: we approach him through faith. Faith is not of our making, it is the gift of God; but it is received through the person as a whole rather than through humanity's rational deliberations. God willed it to be thus. So his existence cannot be proved. But it may reasonably be inferred. Our faith, if it is to be accepted with integrity, needs to be a reasonable faith. It is a reasonable question to ask why there is something rather than nothing; and if the question has an answer, it can only be that God has created it. This gives rise to the further question: who made God? If God is said to be self-existent, would it not be simpler to regard the universe as self-existent? There are however several strong indications, as we shall see, that it is not self-existent, but that it betrays signs of order and purpose and signals of transcendence, while the concept of self-existent 'necessary' being who created and upholds it is not self-contradictory.

Although the argument from design in its old-fashioned form is now rightly discarded, the amazing coincidences in the evolution of the cosmos and of the planet can hardly have happened accidentally: they suggest a goal and a purpose, although it always remains possible that they are only 'lucky chances', especially if there is an infinite ensemble of universes. Beauty and goodness, truth and love are not just subjective qualities: they have an absolute value; and absolute values suggest the need for an absolute being to validate them. Religious experience is very widespread; and although it is by its nature only fully convincing for the person who experiences it, nonetheless it is not easy to explain it all away on psychological grounds. None of these reasons for believing in God provide knockdown arguments; but taken together they make it entirely reasonable to believe in God and to entrust one's life to him.[14]

In addition to these, there are what have been called 'signals of transcendence'.[15] Among these is humanity's innate propensity for order, deprived of which the individual and the group are reduced to terror, and which corresponds to the divine order underlying the universe. Without this faith in order, there can be no maturation among children. Play too constitutes a 'signal of transcendence', for it is a joyful activity which brings liberation and peace and in which the time structure of ordinary life is suspended, pointing towards the quality of eternity. Humanity also is inherently hopeful: mankind has an unconquerable propensity to hope for the future, pointing towards the conquest of death. The fact that some deeds strike us as monstrously evil, brooking no excuse and deserving total condemnation, seems to point to the existence of an absolute standard; and our sense of humour, based on humanity's incongruity with the universe, is a pointer towards the imprisonment of the human spirit within the confines of the world. None of these are more than 'signals of transcendence', but they form a cumulative addition for the reasonableness of faith, an 'illative sense' of the existence of God.

Nor does the list end here. 'The psyche in open-ended desiring; the spirit in its transparency to truth, the *zoon logicon* or "speech-using animal" who finds the language of perfection on his or her lips; the sense of the fragility of beings; the witness of mystical encounter; the inner contradictions of the human being that call for a resolution from beyond themselves; the imperiousness of conscience; the existential demands of becoming a self . . . Are these merely facts about the human condition, or are they significant facts, facts which, when interpreted in terms of each other, become signs of, pointers to the reality of God?'[16] The analysis of the human condition leads inevitably, it has been claimed, to an 'orientation towards mystery' when we reflect on our freedom and sense of responsibility, or the nature of unconditioned love. Awareness of this mystery need not necessarily be in intellectual terms, but present as a kind of 'unthematic awareness'. Corresponding to this orientation towards mystery there is always the divine gift of self-communication, in which God reveals himself to all within the human condition. It is rather as though there is a God-sized blank in every human being which is complemented by the offer of a God-sized gift to fill it.[17]

Belief in God from the natural world, however, tells us that he is, not who he is. We see only his footsteps, and not himself. We are like Moses who hid in a cleft of the rock until the glory of the Lord passed by, so that we see only his back parts, not his face (Exod 33.22f.). How do we know what he is like, his character, his nature? We cannot know anything about him, unless he reveals it to us. How do we know that what is alleged to be revealed to us truly discloses the nature of God? We can rely to a large extent on the judgement of the Church in its Scriptures and in its tradition, but it will not ring true for us individually unless we find in it the disclosure of what is for us of supreme value.

We may at least determine what are our basic human values. These have been described as happiness, wisdom, knowledge, freedom, and justice.[18] (Love is strangely missing from this list.) Does this mean that these are the values which we attribute to God? No doubt it describes the values which we would *like* to attribute to God: but we are only justified in attributing to him those values which he has revealed to us as inherent in his nature.

Adherents of the various world religions are likely to find within them what they perceive to be of supreme value (see pp. 151–8). Christians affirm that they find supreme value for themselves in God's self-disclosure in the person of Jesus Christ as depicted in the Christian Gospels. Hence the well known saying: 'God is Christlike, and in him is no unChristlikeness at all.'[19] In the stories of Jesus, Christians find that they are face to face with the Ultimate in value. It is therefore worthwhile examining in greater detail the character of Jesus in the Gospels to discover what are his particular characteristics, apart from those which he shared with the people of his culture and times (see p. 92).

Gender and God

One obvious characteristic, however, which Jesus shared with nearly half the human race, ought first to be considered. Jesus was a male. He spoke of God as his Father, and (if the Fourth Gospel may be trusted) of himself as God's Son. Certainly his followers use these terms both of Christ and of God. Does this mean that God is male? The very question verges on the absurd. Sex is a characteristic of the majority of living organisms because the admixture of genes in sexual reproduction produces novel combinations which can result in progeny fitter to survive. Inevitably this has resulted in differences between the sexes; differences in body shapes and differences in the 'wiring' of their brains so as to facilitate those characteristics most needed in each gender (males are stronger and better at motor activities such as catching balls; women tend to be reconciling by nature (except when their offspring are threatened), with their bodies shaped for the bearing and nurture of offspring). God exists eternally, and in the eternal sphere there is no sexual differentiation, *God has no gender.* He is neither male nor female; and we rightly predicate of him those qualities which we admire in both sexes, as well as those which they have in common. (The fact that we use the masculine pronoun in referring to him points to the inadequacy of our language, not to the maleness of God; see p. 3.)

Some theologians however have held that the fact that in Christianity God is known as Father, and that Jesus is known as his Son, inescapably gives to God a male image, and attributes to him a male stereotype. They therefore find the Christian faith fatally flawed, because it has an incorrect image of God.[20] But it was inevitable that God should be described in male terms during that period of human history in which males were dominant. With the coming of the sexual revolution the situation is already changing. For example, in the Inclusive Language Lectionary produced through the initiative of the US National Council of Churches, Jesus' word for God, *Abba*, is changed from 'Father' to 'Father and Mother', and the word for Christ's relationship to God altered from 'son' to 'child'.[21] In 1992 the Methodist Church in Great Britain at its annual conference concluded that 'the use of female imagery is compatible with faithfulness to Scripture – indeed Scripture itself points in this direction, and also gives us examples of that imagery'. It recommended that to avoid distortion in our image of God, female as well as male images should be used for him.[22] Even the Church of England, while not going so far as this, has made some suggestions for inclusive language. No doubt such measures are as yet in their infancy. Teaching will in future focus on the filial relationship of Jesus to God rather than on his sonship, and on our dependence on God and on his love and care for us, rather than on his Fatherhood. If we are to address God in personal terms, we have to address him in either the male or the female gender, and either term alone is equally misleading. Therefore *any* form of theism could be described as 'fatally flawed'. In fact, if sufficient care is taken, the flaw may be avoided as indicated above.

The differentiating characteristics of Jesus

We must now consider those characteristics of Jesus which marked him out from his fellows.[23] In the first place, he seems to have been extraordinarily self-effacing for one who inspired a mass movement among the people, and who is worshipped as the icon of God. For most of his life he lived in a small village an uneventful life in a large family. Even during his public ministry he pointed away from himself to his heavenly Father. He chose for himself the enigmatic title 'Son of Man'. At the most crucial moments, when he was on trial for his life, he kept silent. (We find this same self-effacing character in what we call the working of the Holy Spirit, so that it is difficult to distinguish his influence from our own endeavours.) This points to the self-effacing nature of God himself, seldom disclosing himself with power, but reliant on inner persuasion or the good sense of people to decide for themselves. God's nature is to 'let be' rather than to interfere.

Secondly, Jesus seems to have taken sides with the outsiders. He made friends with the publicans and sinners, who were shunned by respectable religious people. By whatever means, he was conceived out of wedlock, and he was put to death by the most ignominious kind of execution alongside revolutionaries. During his ministry he risked obloquy by his open friendship with women. At times during his public ministry, he had nowhere to lay his head, even, according to the birth stories, at the time of his birth. He mixed not only with respected people (as when he accepted hospitality from a Pharisee), but also with ordinary poor folk. If Jesus is the icon of God this suggests that God's nature is to side with the poor and those who are deprived or held low in public esteem.

Thirdly, he was willing to put his fate in the hands of other people. Clearly he did not stick his neck out so that he would have been arrested before he had had time to say what he had to say. But when he journeyed to Jerusalem for the last time, he seemed to be aware of a coming disaster which he did nothing to avert. When his time had come, Jesus made no attempt to defend himself against arrest, sentence or execution. He 'handed himself over' to the authorities. And yet at the same time, even though he put himself in the hands of others, he remained master of events. Here again we have a disclosure of God. Divine providence is often imagined as a supernatural overruling of men's wills. But the story of Jesus leads us to the conclusion that in fact God puts himself into our hands: man makes his own providence and yet God reveals himself as master of events (see p. 92).

The chief activities of Jesus during his public ministry were teaching and the performance of mighty works. His healings suggest that God is opposed to our suffering and sickness and works towards wholeness and health (see p. 199). His teaching carried immense authority, but he refused to disclose his credentials. He never gave a hand-out, preferring to appeal to the natural instincts and responses of his hearers. He preferred concrete situations to abstract reasoning, but he was clearly a person of wisdom and justice and knowledge. Here again he gives insights into the nature of God, who gives us freedom to make up our own minds and convinces us not by a show of authoritativeness but his own intrinsic authority.

The chief characteristic of Jesus is his total concentration on doing his Father's will, and this points to God's utter constancy and concentration on his goals, from which he will not be deflected. The Gospels as a whole, and in particular the story of the Passion, show Jesus' loving obedience to his heavenly Father and his caring love for his fellow men and women. This love is interpreted in the Epistles as God coming to the aid of mankind.

In fact the love of God manifested by Jesus in the Gospels is very different from what is commonly supposed. It included a certain ruthlessness in his care and concern, a willingness to condemn not individuals but classes, a hatred of bigotry and pretence. This again points to the fact that the love of God is quite unsentimental and more ruthless than the kind of love which we usually imagine. It corresponds to the apparent ruthlessness which we see in the world of nature. Jesus' love is one that goes to all lengths, and which is prepared to suffer obloquy and stress and pain in order to respond in love and obedience to his heavenly Father. This shows us God's love which involves him in union with suffering humanity, as it were paying the penalty for all the ills to which humanity is heir and for which he as Creator is ultimately responsible. In the story of the Passion we are face to face with archetypal love, Ultimate Value, authenticating divine revelation in Jesus through its own intrinsic authority.

God does not only disclose himself through Jesus Christ. He does this also in the story of his People which precedes the coming of Jesus, and other religions are not without witness to his nature. But in the story of Jesus Christians claim they are face to face with Ultimate Value, and from this they know, through the mirror of human personality, the essential character of God.

God and evil

Yet there is still one vital subject to be considered before we can have any real assurance about the nature of God. How can we be sure that God is love and not evilly disposed towards us? For it is a fact of life that there is much suffering in the world, for which God must be held ultimately responsible. In the world of nature there is suffering, especially through predation, although we tend to judge the suffering of animals in the light of our own capacity to feel suffering. Nonetheless God must be seen as responsible for the evolution of species through the survival of the fittest, which involves not only predation of other species, but also the ruthlessness of the 'selfish gene' in its struggle for survival within its own species. There is suffering too through natural calamity and there is suffering through the foolishness or thoughtlessness or malice of mankind. There are people who are evil, and it seems as though at times we may be in the presence of non-human forces of evil. How is this compatible with God whose nature is absolute love?[24]

It is easy to treat the 'problem of evil' merely as an intellectual exercise. It is only when people have experienced extreme suffering in their own lives, or when they have been close to someone greatly beloved who has had to endure terrible experiences involving loss of personal dignity and the disintegration of the ego, that suffering and evil cease to be problems and begin to take on the character of personal agonies. The appearance on television of famine involving hundreds, perhaps thousands of starving people, can be literally unbearable; but while the listener can always switch off the set, nothing stops the agonies of starvation for those who have to endure them. Again, the horror of large-scale massacres and wholesale torture, when portrayed on television, is a visual reminder of the potentialities of the terrible wickedness inherent in humanity. The question recurs with redoubled force: 'How can the God of love create a world like this?' Is God indifferent to the human condition? Does God actually take pleasure in our sufferings? Or is God impotent to prevent them?

Some arguments which attempt to explain away the seriousness of the objection seem trite. Thus it is said that suffering in the world is justified if human creativity can find ways of overcoming it. But it is little consolation for those who suffer to feel that they are affording a challenge to their fellow humans; and it does not help those who have to endure suffering before any remedy for it can be found. Again, it is said that, such are the conditions of our planet, earthquakes and drought and ice ages and hurricanes are inevitable; and if God were to take extreme steps to prevent these hurting human beings, he would be disrupting the ordered world on which we all depend, and thus causing worse ills than those we already suffer. But we cannot resolve the problem of evil on this kind of cost–benefit analysis. Nor can we resolve it on a quantitative basis.[25] As Ivan asked Alyosha in Dostoevsky's *The Brothers Karamazov*:[26]

I appeal to you – answer me: imagine that it is you yourself who are erecting the edifice of human destiny with the aim of making men happy in the end, of giving them peace and contentment at last, but to do that it is absolutely necessary, and indeed quite inevitable, to torture to death only one tiny creature, the little girl who beat her breast with her little fist, and to found the edifice on her unavenged tears – would you consent to be the architect in these conditions? Tell me and do not lie.

Attempts to answer on behalf of God by claiming that pain and suffering are deserved, or that they are useful in warning us of danger, or that they constitute a way of learning truths that cannot be learnt in any other way, evade the challenge that evil and suffering present, even if the premises on which they depend are true. Nor does it help to say that, just as human beings have their shadow side, so too does God; for the God we see mirrored in Jesus Christ has no shadow side of this kind: he is the God of absolute love.

The truth of the matter is that we cannot explain evil and suffering. It remains a cruel surd sticking out like a sore thumb. The most that we can do is to see some pointers towards reconciling it with the God of absolute love in which we believe.

In the first place, we simply do not know the options open to God in his creation of the world. We do not know what kind of alternatives were open to him, if he had the aim of an evolving universe in which creatures would emerge capable of freely responding to his love. Free response must include the possibility of refusal. Freedom to do good must also include freedom to do evil. If we are not free, we cannot freely respond to God's love and commit our lives to him. It seems that God puts tremendous value on freedom of choice, and that he has given mankind a greater freedom than we usually seem to accord our fellow men and women. If creatures are to emerge capable of free choice, freedom has to be built into the universe as a whole, and this freedom to evolve results in famines and floods, earthquakes and hurricanes, ice ages and prolonged heat spells. It means freedom for nature to evolve red in tooth and claw. It means freedom to live by aggression and predation. It means freedom to do evil as well as to do good. 'Let us say that God would never have allowed evils to subsist in his creation, were it not that he might find in them the occasion to produce good things unique in kind, and dependent for their unique character on the character of the evils in question.'[27] Another writer has put the same point in different terms: 'God has ordained a world which contains evil – real evil – as a means to the creation of the infinite good of a Kingdom of Heaven within which His creatures will have come as perfected persons to love and serve him, through a process in which their own free insight and response have been an essential element.'[28]

Even so, such freedom seems too high a price to pay for all the suffering and pain and evil in the world. We still cry out: 'How can God allow it to go on?' There is only one answer that can satisfy us. God himself is involved in the suffering and the pain and the evil. We see his involvement in the Passion of Jesus Christ; and this is a pointer towards his involvement in all suffering and all pain and all evil. Only if God suffers the pain of his own creation is its moral stigma removed. Only if he is involved in the suffering of mankind is he justified in permitting a structure of life which makes suffering inevitable. Just because at the very heart of its message the Christian Gospel proclaims that God is involved in pain and suffering and points to the Cross to validate this, it alone can not only satisfy the religious aspirations of humanity, but also silence the moral accusation against God and turn our outrage against God into heartfelt worship and love:

See from his head, his hands, his feet,
    sorrow and love flow mingled down;
did e'er such love and sorrow meet,
    or thorns compose so rich a crown? . . .

Were the whole realm of nature mine,
    that were an offering far too small;
love so amazing, so divine,
    demands my soul, my life, my all.

Notes

1. E. Schweitzer, *Spirit of God* (London, 1960), pp. 1–2.

2. A. M. Ramsey, *Holy Spirit* (London, 1977), p. 10.

3. C. K. Barrett, *The Holy Spirit and Gospel Tradition* (London, 1947), p. 158.

4. J. V. Taylor, *The Go-Between God* (London, 1972), p. 31.

5. C. E. Raven, *Creator Spirit* (London, 1928), p. 273.

6. See *Spirit of God, Spirit of Christ*, ed. L. Fischer (London/Geneva, 1981); also H. Montefiore, 'And the Son?', *Theology* (1982), pp. 417–22.

7. G. W. H. Lampe, *God as Spirit* (London, 1977), p. 208.

8. C. Welch, *The Trinity in Contemporary Theology* (London, 1953), pp. 3–4.

9. L. Hodgson, *The Doctrine of the Trinity* (London, 1943), p. 91.

10. R. C. Moberly, *Atonement and Personality* (London, 1909), p. 164.

11. W. Temple, *Nature, Man and God* (London, 1934), p. 435.

12. J. Cobb, 'Panentheism' in *A New Dictionary of Christian Theology*, ed. A. Richardson and J. Bowden (London, 1983), p. 432.

13. Herein lies the fault in F. von Hügel's paper on 'Suffering and God' in his *Essays and Addresses*, second series (London, 1930). He wrongly assumes that divine passibility would change God's essential nature of joy and beatitude.

14. See H. Montefiore, *Reclaiming the High Ground* (London, 1990), p. 137–41.

15. See P. Berger, *A Rumour of Angels* (London, 1967), pp. 71–96.

16. See A. Nichols, *A Grammar of Consent* (Edinburgh, 1991), p. 173.

17. K. Rahner, 'On the importance of the non-Christian religions for salvation' in *Theological Investigations 18* (London, 1984), pp. 293–4. Cf. also M. Wiles, *Christian Theology and Inter-Religious Dialogue* (London, 1992), pp. 48–51.

18. K. Ward, *A Vision to Pursue* (London, 1991), pp. 181–2.

19. A. M. Ramsey, *God, Christ and the Word* (London, 1969), p. 98.

20. D. Hampson, *Theology and Feminism* (Oxford, 1990).

21. See R. R. Reuther, 'Feminism and Jewish–Christian dialogue' in *The Myth of Christian Uniqueness*, ed. J. Hick and P. Knitter (London, 1988), p. 144.

22. The Methodist Faith and Order Commission, *Inclusive Language and Imagery about God* (Peterborough, 1992).

23. See H. Montefiore, 'Jesus the revelation of God' in *Christ For Us Today*, ed. N. Pittenger (London, 1968), pp. 108ff.

24. See H. Montefiore, *Awkward Questions About Christian Love* (London, 1964), pp. 9–39; *Reclaiming the High Ground, op. cit.*, pp. 135–7.

25. R. Swinburne, *The Existence of God* (Oxford, 1979), pp. 218–21.

26. F. Dostoevsky, *The Brothers Karamazov* (London, 1982 edn), p. 287.

27. A. M. Farrer, *Love Almighty and Ills Unlimited* (London, 1962), p. 163.

28. J. Hick, *Evil and the God of Love* (London, 1966), p. 399.

chapter 7

The Christian mission

Anyone who, like the present writer, has been converted from one mainstream faith to another is bound to be concerned with the relations between the different faiths and with questions of mission and evangelism, especially as he retains a great affection for the Jewish faith and believes that it contains aspects of truth and practice from which Christianity could benefit. Although in his case conversion was not the result of evangelistic effort, he is aware how threatened his brothers and sisters after the flesh feel by the renewal of evangelistic activity targeted at members of their faith. Again these same questions about mission and evangelism are bound to press upon someone who, like the present writer, has had experience of being the bishop of a huge city like Birmingham, where there are very large numbers of people with a religious vacuum in their lives, and where there is also a big multi-ethnic population adhering to non-Christian religions whose leaders appealed to the bishop for assistance (e.g. over the requirement of wearing hospital uniforms which conflict with certain religious traditions), while at the same time certain groups of Christians were targeting members of those same faiths with their evangelism. In order to see these matters in perspective, it is necessary to look at them in their historical context and in the light of the churches' missionary and evangelistic history.

Missionary paradigms in the history of Christianity

These matters seem of such importance today that it is strange to find that the theology of mission has not generally been regarded as an essential element of Christian dogmatics, despite the fact that it is both central to New Testament Christianity, and has often been at the forefront of Christian activity. It has been for the most part ignored by theologians and left to missiologists with practical experience of Christian missions overseas. Although it is in process of being rehabilitated, there is still a big vacuum so far as the theology of religions is concerned.

It has been suggested that during its history Christianity has been expressed in various paradigms.[1] A paradigm is understood as more than a mere model of belief, but rather as the entire constellation of beliefs, values, and methodologies shared by members of a community.[2] When the paradigm theory (which originally applied to developments in the natural sciences) was applied to Christianity, six major paradigms were suggested: the apocalyptic paradigm of primitive Christianity, the Hellenistic paradigm of the patristic period, the medieval Roman Catholic paradigm, the Protestant paradigm of the Reformation, the paradigm which followed the Enlightenment, and the emerging contemporary paradigm. The earlier ones have been superseded but have not disappeared. Traces of the apocalyptic paradigm are found among fundamentalist Evangelicals. The Hellenistic paradigm is developed and refined in Eastern Orthodox theology. The Protestant paradigm is still found in some Reformed churches, while the medieval Roman Catholic paradigm can be traced in hardline pre-Vatican II theology.

It has also been suggested that each paradigm contains its own theology of mission.[3] The New Testament bears witness to the apocalyptic paradigm, with its imminent expectation of the Parousia, or 'Second Coming' of Christ. (The word *parousia* was used of a state visit.) The first coming of Jesus Christ had already set in motion the beginning of the Last Things. Eschatology however did not dampen zeal to spread the Gospel. On the contrary, there was no time to be lost; the Gospel was to be preached throughout the entire world (which meant in all parts of the Roman Empire) before the Day of the Lord took place. In some circles it was even held that the End (which was eagerly if mistakenly awaited) could not come until the Gospel had been preached throughout the world. The only exception to post-Resurrection mission was perhaps St Mark's Gospel, whose abrupt ending suggests that there was no time even for this: the Last Things were imminent. The Great Commission at the end of St Matthew's Gospel attests the missionary imperative in that work. While the perspective lengthens in St Luke's Gospel, 'the period of the Church' is a time of missionary expansion until the Lord returns. In the Fourth Gospel the emphasis is on 'realized eschatology' (that is, the belief that the Last Things had already arrived with the coming of Christ), but belief in the future Last Day is certainly not lacking in that Gospel. The whole Pauline corpus is evidence of Paul's almost frenetic determination to speed the coming of the Kingdom by taking the Gospel to all parts of the known world without trespassing on another's territory.

The Hellenistic paradigm

As the Church grew in the Diaspora, it was inevitable that the Gospel became Hellenized. Competing among many religions, it was easy to see it as the fulfilment of pagan myths. Originally popular among the least privileged classes, it quickly spread among the educated, so that Christianity, instead of being opposed to Hellenistic culture, became its bearer. There was a tendency to intellectualize the faith under the impact of Greek philosophy. Systematic theology, quite uncharacteristic of the earliest paradigm, began to make its appearance. Eschatology tended to be replaced by metaphysics. By AD 300 half the urban populations of the big cities of the Roman Empire were Christians. The Edict of Toleration (AD 313) paved the way for the supremacy of Christianity under Constantine, leading in AD 380 to the suppression of other faiths within the Empire (except for Judaism, which was put under great constraints). The Church became the ecclesiastical face of the State: each supported the other's unity, leading to a doctrine of the Church in Eastern Orthodox theology in which mission and unity go hand in hand.

How did this remarkable turnabout in the fortunes of Christianity come about, from a persecuted sect to the religion of the Roman Empire? There was an odour of decay in the old pagan religions of the Empire, but the ancient world saw love in action in the lives of ordinary citizens giving meaning to their existence, and a special quality which was otherwise lacking. People in the countryside were impressed by the monastic movement. It was also seen that Christian belief was intellectually respectable as well as personally satisfying and communally strengthening.

The medieval paradigm

The Roman Catholic medieval paradigm was quite different. The Eastern tradition focused on the birth of Christ, incorporating humanity through the Church into a union with Christ which led to ever closer identification, even to *theosis* (divinization); while the Western tradition concentrated on the death of Christ and the restoration of fallen humanity. Humanity as the West saw it needed not divinization but redemption. The world was fallen; but the individual could find salvation through, and only through, the Catholic Church. The Pelagian heresy (that human beings, by their own efforts, take the initial and fundamental steps towards salvation) led to the belief that the irresistible grace of God was needed in order to lay hold of the redemption already achieved by

Christ. The Donatist schism (caused by the allegation that a bishop who had betrayed the faith during persecution rendered void his subsequent acts of consecration) led to the insistence that to depart from the Catholic Church was to be alienated from God. Baptism implanted an indelible character on the baptized. There was no salvation outside the Church (see p. 232). By 1305 a Bull declared that for salvation it was necessary to be subject to the Roman pontiff, and the Council of Florence (1302) stated that Jews, heretics and schismatics have no share in eternal life.

It follows from this that Christian mission involved baptizing people into the Roman Catholic Church, and forcing back those who had left the Church in order that they might find salvation. The close relationship in Europe between the Church and the State (with a claim to superiority by the Church) involved the State in fighting wars on behalf of the Church, at first indirectly and later directly. This later led to the State using its influence to spread Christianity among the indigenous peoples of its colonies overseas. At the same time the Christian mission was also carried out effectively in a gentler style through the monastic movement.

The Protestant paradigm

The Protestant paradigm is less clear cut, with differences between Lutherans and Calvinists, and a strong contrast between their intellectualism and the warm subjectivity of Pietism. Whereas Rome insisted on the legal and the institutional, Protestantism insisted on sound doctrine. Lutherans only wanted to reform Rome, not to demolish Roman Catholicism (unlike Anabaptists, for whom all Europe was a mission field). At first under the Reformers missionary activity ceased. It was believed that the Great Commission had been completed by the Apostles. In any case under the principle *cujus regio ejus religio*, the religion of a region was decided by the religion of its ruler. Missionary initiative, it was held, is in the hands of God and not of Christian men and women. The Pietists, however, changed all that, making Germany the leading missionary country, with many humble folk venturing overseas. They were concerned with the body as well as the soul, but not with planting Churches. They regarded conversion as a private matter, and converts were free to join the Church of their choice. Calvinism by contrast with its theocratic features emphasized the rule of Christ in society as a whole.

The post-Enlightenment paradigm

The Enlightenment inevitably affected the Church's view of mission, just as it affected everything else. There has in the nineteenth and twentieth centuries been a huge increase in missionary activity. The key concepts of the Enlightenment – the supremacy of reason, the confidence that there are answers to every problem, the ideal of emancipated autonomous individuals – these were all assumed. Although obedience to the Great Commission predominated, there were many motifs: 'The glory of God, a sense of urgency because of the imminent millennium, the love of Christ, compassion for those considered eternally lost, a sense of duty, the awareness of cultural superiority, and competition with Catholic missionary efforts – had blended together to form a mosaic. Now, however, there was no pattern of thought and practice.'[4] The author quoted was writing about Protestant missionaries, mostly Evangelicals; but there were also many devoted and heroic Roman Catholic missionaries who dedicated their lives to mission and evangelism in 'foreign parts'. Most of them, Evangelicals and Catholics, would have been opposed to many Enlightenment presuppositions; but nonetheless they were influenced by them.

It has been suggested[5] that if texts are used to express the understanding of mission in the successive paradigms which the Church adopted, John 3.16 would encapsulate the patristic understanding: 'God loved the world so much that he gave his only Son that everyone who has faith in him should not die but have eternal life.' In the medieval Roman Catholic paradigm the text would be Luke 14.23: 'Go out on to the highways and along the hedgerows and make them come in', while the Reformation text would of course be the one which meant so much to Luther: 'the Gospel . . . is the saving power for everyone who has faith – the Jew first, but the Greek also – because here is revealed God's way of righting wrong, a way that starts from faith and ends in faith; as Scripture says "he shall gain life who is justified through faith" ' (Rom 1.16f.). For the post-Enlightenment paradigm the text must surely be Matt 28.19 which had such force with missionaries: 'Go forth therefore and make all nations my disciples; baptize men everywhere in the name of the Father and the Son and the Holy Spirit, and teach them to observe all that I have commanded you.'

A new emerging paradigm?

What about the new paradigm of Christianity that is emerging? The position is too confused to discern it clearly as yet. Nor it is possible to discern the new missionary paradigm, except that it will certainly be ecumenical. The change in the attitude of the Roman Catholic Church since the Second Vatican Council is most marked, as well as that in the Protestant Churches towards the Roman Catholic Church. There is a concern too with a mission to culture as well as a mission to individuals.[6] The threat to the environment necessitates a rethinking of some traditional aspects of the post-Enlightenment paradigm. Despite the contrasts, there is a recognition of an intimate link between the Church and the world of humanity, as well as an insight into the Church as a sign and pointer of the Kingdom but certainly not the Kingdom itself (see p. 168). The importance of social, political and economic conditions is increasingly recognized, as well as the need for individuals to re-orient themselves towards God.

The meaning of mission

Mission is an integral part of the Gospel. The word means in origin a 'being sent', and was originally used of the Trinity: The Father 'sent' the Son into the world, and the Spirit too was 'sent' into the world. Sending is therefore integral to the Gospel. Christians are members of the Church sent into the world to do God's will. To deny mission is therefore to deny the Good News of the Gospel which they bring. What mission consists of and how it is actually accomplished are more complex matters. Mission includes all forms of Christian service in the world; among these the healing ministry, the personal acts of service which Christians render to non-Christians, as well as social action at a corporate level undertaken by Christians as a way of serving their fellow men and women (for example, the provisions of schools for children or hospices for the dying, and the provisions of wells and clean water in developing countries). Even this does not exhaust Christian mission. Christians are sent into the world to be, as well as to act. The very presence of Christian men and women, leading the Christian life and showing love and kindness to their fellow men and women, forms an important aspect of mission.

One vital aspect of mission is evangelism, which is the sharing of the Good News of Christ with others, and especially with those who have no lively faith in God. There are many ways of evangelism (in the sense of sharing the Christian faith). This must be distinguished from proselytism, which involves manipulating people into the Christian faith and which is an offence against their integrity. In some situations, the liturgy is a powerful form of evangelism. There are situations (e.g. towards the Jewish people) where evangelism is better accomplished not by naming the name of Christ but simply by manifesting the love of God through personal life-style. Despite the fact that in the popular mind evangelism is connected with crusade meetings, and although in some church circles it is often thought of in terms of 'church planting' or 'church growth', in fact it is at the personal level, through perhaps the unconscious witness of an individual to the Good News of the Gospel, that evangelism is most authentic. The content of the Good News has been discussed earlier (see p. 144). In essence it is about the love of God and how he has acted to help the world of humanity. Those who have received this love naturally want to share it with others. They need to show it in their lives, and they think it selfish to keep it to themselves. Evangelism therefore is a part of mission, and however it may be carried out it is an integral part of the Gospel.

Evangelism and conversion

The psychological phenomena of conversion must be distinguished from the fact of conversion. The latter means the turning of a person to God to accept the Good News of the Gospel; and the means by which this happens are diverse. In all cases there is formed a new psychological sentiment, that is to say, a change of beliefs and convictions tinged by emotions, both consciously and below the level of consciousness. Sometimes this takes place in a dramatic and sudden fashion, with apparently auditory and visual accompaniments, as happened in the case of the present writer; and this is usually followed by feelings of intense happiness and joy. In such cases there is breakthrough from the subconscious areas of the psyche: the normal restraints of consciousness are no longer able to contain acknowledgement of the grace of God which has been mediated in many ways. In fact such a conversion is no better (and no worse) than the gradual dawning of belief through the influence of friends (whose impact is greater than they know), through the words of Scripture (as in the case of Luther), through worship and the sacraments (the only form of evangelism that was open to the Russian Orthodox Church in the USSR) or through the promptings of moral consciousness.

It is possible to 'condition' people into conversion.[7] If sufficient emotional stress is applied, especially the fear of hell, transmarginal abreaction takes place, causing agonies or writhing, and almost a trancelike condition; and when people emerge from this state, behaviour patterns are reversed. (Some people reacted like this to Wesley's preaching.) To use such methods deliberately is to negate the freedom of the will, which is God's great gift to each individual. It is to be distinguished from the sort of mass evangelism associated with e.g. Dr Billy Graham, when permissible persuasive techniques are used in communicating the Good News, including soft music, warm words of invitation and mass emotions, but where a person's freedom of choice is left inviolate. Many people who want the spiritual vacuum in their lives to be filled seem unable to achieve this without the stimulus of such an occasion. Even so, such techniques show no lasting results unless they are immediately followed by counselling and induction into a Christian community.

Christianity and other faiths

The 1988 Lambeth Report, in its section on Mission and Ministry, speaks of mission to the unreached peoples and those who have become alienated from the Christian faith, the lapsed, the young people, the rural poor, refugees, the urban poor and the marginalized. It mentions other faiths, but goes into no details.[8] This is hardly surprising, because Christianity has only lately been in contact with the other great mainstream religions of the world. Christians in the past have tended to encounter Buddhism and Hinduism, and to meet their adherents, as members of a master race during a colonial era. Where there were indigenous Christian minorities in predominantly Muslim or Hindu communities, these made little impression on their non-Christian neighbours, and they were mostly concerned with the maintenance of their own rights. As for the Jews, the atmosphere had been poisoned by centuries of Christian persecution, and when dialogue did happen, it did not really take place on a level playing field.[9]

Only during the second half of the twentieth century has real dialogue seemed possible. The Christian conscience had been stirred by the appalling details of the Holocaust (which Jews speak of as the *shoah*); and this stimulated the desire for genuine and sympathetic dialogue between Christians and Jews. The immigration into Britain of large numbers of members of other faiths from the 'New Commonwealth' has meant that many lay men and women in Britain daily meet people of Eastern religions, whose naturally strong faith is often increased by their minority status in these islands. The dialogue to which this should give rise has hardly begun; and when the long history of these mainstream religions is borne in mind, the brief period during which they have begun to listen to one another is too short to be able to predict what the eventual outcome of dialogue will be.

Christians generally speaking have adopted greatly differing attitudes to other religions, ranging from at one end the belief that they are inspired by the Devil (which is thought to account for any apparent similarities that exist between them and Christianity) all the way across the spectrum to the belief that all may be regarded as equally valid approaches to God.

Negative attitudes to other faiths

The very idea that other faiths are Devil-inspired is so alien to contemporary pluralism that it comes as something of a shock to realize that this view was held little more than half a century ago. (It seems somewhat akin to the Victorian belief that the Devil had planted fossils in order to mislead people into accepting a theory of evolutionary development.) Yet a Professor of Missions wrote in 1937: 'On one side stand God's words and acts; on the other, the demonic impulse to picture God in one's own image . . . Any attempts to make links with them would be to make links with lies and deception.'[10] This viewpoint, like all the others, claims to find some authority from the Bible, in such texts as that of 1 John 4.2–3: 'Every spirit that acknowledges that Jesus Christ is come in the flesh is from God, and every spirit which does not thus acknowledge Christ is not from God. This is what is meant by "Antichrist".' It finds expression in Heber's famous missionary hymn 'From Greenland's icy mountains . . .' (still to be found in old copies of *Hymns Ancient and Modern* but absent from the 1983 edition):

In vain with lavish kindness
  The gifts of God are strown;
The heathen in his blindness
  Bows down to wood and stone.

Somewhat akin to this is the Barthian view of radical discontinuity between divine revelation in Christ and man's striving after God. It is maintained that the Christian revelation is in its essence so entirely different from all other religions that there is no point of contact between them. 'When Christianity as a total religious system approaches the non-Christian religions as total religious systems, there is only difference and antithesis. It follows from this that non-Christian religions are simply irrelevant to salvation or bringing any genuine knowledge of God to mankind.'[11] Here again resort may be had to the Scriptures: 'When anyone is united to Christ, there is a new world; the old order has gone, and a new order has already begun' (2 Cor 5.17).

Christianity as the fulfilment of other faiths

The position of 'radical discontinuity' developed partly in reaction against liberalizing notions that Christ is the fulfilment of other faiths. This found expression in various ways. According to one line of thinking, the partial truths found in these are all thought to be comprehended in Christ, by whom their errors are purged and the truths that they lack supplied. The full radiance of Christ fulfils the scattered lights in other faiths. Such a viewpoint encourages the genuine study of other faiths but retains the finality of Christ, and seeks to bring all mankind to the full knowledge of the truth. A favourite text of the proponents of this view is Matthew 5.17: 'I did not come to abolish, but to complete'. Sometimes this viewpoint finds expression in terms of implicit revelation, as in the phrase 'the unknown Christ of Hinduism'.[12] Sometimes it is expressed in the form that adherents of other faiths, because they are recipients of supernatural grace which has been given to human beings through Christ, are thereby 'anonymous Christians',[13] a phrase which they not unnaturally themselves reject. (The phrase is somewhat unfortunate. Of course non-Christians are in receipt of God's grace, for God wills all to be saved. The Roman Catholic doctrine expressed in Vatican II asserts salvation of non-Christians 'in ways known only to God', as though it is a truth which must be held, since God wills all to be saved, without any adequate explanation of how their salvation is effected.) This way of thinking is more congenial to Eastern Orthodox and Catholic belief, where it finds a basis in the doctrine of analogy between things human and divine; but it has found less favour in Protestant circles, where emphasis is usually put upon the need for personal faith in the atoning sacrifice of Christ.

In order to relate the Christian faith to the great Eastern religions, it is necessary not only to know from within the Christian tradition and the Christian experience that underlies it, but also to have experienced at first hand the Eastern religions not only as systems of thought but also as living faiths. A few attempts have been made to do this. There has been a longer tradition of dialogue between Christianity and Hinduism than with other faiths.[14]

There has been one particularly striking attempt to bring together Western science, Eastern mysticism and the Christian faith into a synthesis.[15] In modern physics, it is claimed, the universe is conceived as a field of energies which is structured by an organizing power, and this field of energies is described as a 'dynamic web of interdependent relationships'. The whole cannot be understood in terms of its parts, nor can the parts be understood apart from the whole. As for human consciousness, it is now possible to go below our present level of rational consciousness to various levels of preconscious life, both to the primordial undifferentiated state before rational consciousness developed and to a state of superconsciousness where there is an attainment of total being. What the physicists have come to understand as a result of their observations, the mystics had already discovered in their experience. There is, it is claimed, a *philosophia perennis* among the great mainstream religions, including Christianity, in which Godhead is beyond word and thought. This universal wisdom comes down from ancient times and was formulated in India, China, the Arab world and in Christianity, and it corresponds to the divine mystery behind human life: 'At the Renaissance, and particularly with the rise of modern science and philosophy, it was largely lost in the West. Only very recently have we in the West come to realize the existence of this universal wisdom and only now are we beginning to recover some of it.'[16]

Despite this claim of convergence in belief about the unknowable Godhead and his relations with the world, there is also a real difference, in that the Christian faith asserts that the infinite was manifest in Jesus Christ. As the early Apologists (second-century writers who attempted a reasoned explanation of the Christian faith to outsiders) had claimed, the Word of God (of which St John writes in the prologue of his Gospel), while universally present in all religions, was incarnate in Jesus. To use Eastern terminology, the Word appeared in the flesh in his 'gross body' (incarnate, as we would say); after his resurrection he appeared in his 'subtle body' (which we call his resurrection body); and at the ascension he passed beyond space and time in his spiritual body into the eternal order of being which transcends this world. 'The time–space world is an appearance, determined by a particular mode of consciousness, of the one infinite and eternal reality, which manifests itself under these conditions.'[17]

This claim that in Jesus the infinite was manifest within this finite world is quite alien to the other mainstream faiths, and marks the chief differentiation of Christianity, even though it is claimed that the Logos which was incarnate in Jesus can be found, under different forms of expression, in other faiths. Here is an attractive synthesis, in which the redemptive presence of the Spirit and his redeeming power are seen to be universal, but at the same time these are focused in Jesus and the community he establishes, which are at the centre of the regeneration of mankind; while the destiny of mankind is seen in that eternal order that transcends our existence in the space–time continuum.

Pluralism and Christianity

Despite Christian triumphalism voices were not entirely lacking before the present post-modern era which maintained that there were truths to be found in Oriental faiths which Christianity could with benefit incorporate into its thinking, and that other faiths are different languages in which God has spoken to mankind in different cultures. St Peter could be subpoenaed, for he is reported to have said that 'God has no favourites and that in every nation the man who is godfearing and does what is right is acceptable to him' (Acts 10.35). But the manifest differences between the great world religions make it impossible to believe that they are all saying the same thing in different cultural settings, and the claim that each is an equally valid way of ascending the Mountain of God breaks down because of these differences unless they can be reconciled or explained away.

Recently an attempt has been made to explain them away by philosophical argument, and so validate the view that all religions have equal worth, and that differences are due to different cultural expressions of belief, none of which are absolutely true, although each true to their believers.[18] The basis of this view is the Kantian theory of knowledge, according to which humanity cannot know anything at all about things as they are in themselves (*noumena*). We experience *phenomena*, 'the manifold' of experience, a kind of outer skin of reality impinging on the human organs of sense which gives us no insight into things-in-themselves, and which the regulative categories of the mind (common to all humanity) order, interpret and render into intelligible form. In the same kind of way it is claimed that we know nothing whatsoever about God as he is in himself: indeed we do not know even enough to call him God, as this implies personal divinity, and so we should content ourselves with speaking of Reality. The various religions of the world give differing cultural expression to faith in and experience of Reality. No one faith therefore is better than another: it is simply a different cultural expression of Someone or Something that is wholly unknowable. (We must say Someone or Something because we cannot even know whether or not this Reality is personal or impersonal.) Such a view is superficially attractive; but it breaks down at many crucial points. Not everyone would hold a Kantian view of perception, according to which we know Reality as an object rather than relate to Reality as a person. An epistemology based on acquaintance is preferable. Even if Kantian epistemology were to be true, there is no particular reason why it should apply in a completely different field. To apply an argument about perception to an argument about theology is to alter the whole shape of the argument; a *metabasis eis allo genos*, that is to say, leaping from one category into another that is entirely different; and there is no reason why the two should be connected. Finally, a theory of Reality which is equally applicable to an impersonal view of God as it is to a view in which there is personality in God is not of much ultimate value. If God is as unknowable as that, it is hard to give much truth value to any religious viewpoint, however useful it may be in psychological or sociological terms.

The Kingdom of God and the world religions

It has been the thesis of this book that the Kingdom of God is the key category for Christian theology. In the natural world the elements and constants all obey the laws of nature, and thereby witness to God's Kingdom in so much as they obey his sovereignty as inanimate objects. When *homo sapiens* evolved, his will was not fully under rational control, but at the behest of feelings and instincts. Frailty, folly and deliberate wilfulness combine with unconscious factors to mar humanity's witness to God's sovereignty and prevent the manifestation of his Kingdom in human society and in individual lives. This changed with the coming of Jesus. He preached the imminent coming of the Kingdom and since his own response to his heavenly Father was complete and unconditional, he revealed the Kingdom of God among us in his own person. By his death and resurrection he inaugurated the Kingdom on earth, initiating a community which was and is a pointer and sign of the fullness of the Kingdom, and enabling individual people in union with him to share in it. Christian ethics are the ethics of the Kingdom, and show the moral imperatives which constitute acknowledgement of the sovereignty of God. Love is the keynote of the Kingdom; the love of God for his creation, and the love for God and for all creation on the part of his children. The Kingdom of God cannot be complete among men and women of flesh and blood. It awaits its fullness in the future Kingdom of God in the eternal world. In a following chapter, we shall argue that Christian spirituality is concerned with spiritual growth in the life of individuals, so that they may approximate more closely to the person of Jesus and the Kingdom of God may be more clearly manifested in the person of that individual.

It follows therefore that the Kingdom of God (focused on this love) is the touchstone whereby Christians tend to evaluate other religions. Looking at other faiths from the perspective of Christianity, we may ask whether their adherents through participation in these religions are brought in any meaningful sense within the Kingdom of God.

First, however, there need to be considered those people who, enjoying an inheritance enriched by earlier centuries of faith, but not committed to the practice of any particular religion, nonetheless hold a high set of personal values and manifest in the quality of their lives a personal integrity and authenticity. In what sense are such persons within the Kingdom of God? They may not explicitly confess to belief in God, and so it cannot be said that they align themselves as God's children within his Kingdom. But Jesus, when a Roman centurion without any explicit mention of religious faith asked him to heal his pain-racked son, replied that nowhere, not even in Israel, had he found such faith, and he went on to warn: 'Many, I tell you, will come from east and west to feast with Abraham, Isaac and Jacob in the kingdom of Heaven. But those who were born to the kingdom will be driven out into the dark, the place of wailing and grinding of teeth' (Matt 8.11f.). This suggests some future surprises. Again, when a lawyer commented on Jesus' teaching about the two great commandments by saying that they were far more important than any sacrificial rituals, Jesus answered by saying 'You are not far from the Kingdom of God'. According to Vatican II, 'Divine Providence does not deny the help necessary for salvation to those who, without blame on their part, have not yet arrived at an explicit knowledge of God, but who strive to lead a good life, thanks to his grace. Whatever goodness or truth is found for the Gospel.'[19] All acknowledgement of truth and beauty and goodness is a partial acknowledgement of him who creates them. It is better to be not far from the Kingdom of God than to think that one is within the Kingdom, only to find oneself driven into the dark.

1: Judaism

The Jewish faith is that which is closest to the Christian faith. Indeed the Christian Church began as a sect within Judaism; and at that point probably the only difference between Jews and the disciples of Jesus was that the former believed that the Messiah was yet to come, while the latter were clear that he had already come in the person of Jesus the Christ. Later the relationship of Jews and Christians worsened. Christians became *aposunagogoi*, no longer welcome in the synagogue, and in modern parlance excommunicate. To the Eighteen Benedictions was added a nineteenth, cursing the *Minim*, among whom must be included Christians, against whom this additional clause was aimed. Christians on their part accused the Jews of deicide by the crucifixion of Jesus, despite the fact that he was actually put to death by the Romans. Already there is apparent in St Matthew's Gospel the condemnation of all future members of the Jewish race, and not merely those who clamoured for Jesus' death, in the words attributed to them: 'His blood be on us, and on our children' (Matt 27.25). Although there were some attempts at dialogue in the past, these were heavily weighted against Jews.[20] With increasing misunderstanding on both sides, there was little chance of mutual reconciliation, and a proper evaluation of the relation between Judaism and Christianity. It is only in the recent past that this has become possible.

The Vatican Council, to which reference has been made above, pays tribute to the Jewish people, and rejects all antisemitism.[21] (The World Council of Churches has also done this, but in these statements neither apologized explicitly for the wrongs they have inflicted on the Jews in the past.) After recalling that in the mystery of God's design, the beginnings of the Church's faith and her election can be traced back to the Patriarchs, and after quoting Paul on the 'adoption as sons, the glory, the covenant, the legislation, and the worship and the promises' which God has given to the Jewish people, the Declaration about the Jewish people goes on to state that 'according to the Apostle, the Jews still remain most dear to God because of their fathers, for he does not repent of the gifts he makes nor of the calls he issues'.

It is sometimes alleged that the constraints of legalism in Judaism are in direct contrast to the freedom of grace which Christians enjoy in the Christian Gospel.[22] Research into rabbinic sources show that St Paul's strictures on this subject, with his contrast between Law and Gospel, may have been justified for some Jews, but that they were unrepresentative of contemporary Jewish thinking in general. There are, of course, non-legalistic forms of Judaism. In fact, legalism is a curse of most religions. It is found among Brahmins in Hinduism. It is certainly found in some forms of Christianity. Christians may have denounced Jewish legalism but some of them professed an equally legalistic Christianity.

While there are some differences, Jews and Christians share to a great extent a common ethic – indeed Christians have derived theirs from Judaism. For example, the commandments to love God and to love our neighbours as ourselves are derived from the Jewish Old Testament. (Most of the absolutism of the Sermon on the Mount can be paralleled in rabbinic sources, although not expressed in such striking form.) The Beatitudes, which are unique to Christianity, are not ethical injunctions, but recipes for happiness (see pp. 240f.). Jesus himself said that to love God with heart and mind and strength, and to love one's neighbour as oneself are the two Great Commandments on which hang that Law and the prophets: that is to say, they include all God's imperatives for mankind. As for worship, much Christian liturgy ultimately derives from Hebrew liturgy. The continuing persecution and suffering of the Jewish race, and its subsequent resurrections to new beginnings suggests a kinship with Jesus the Jew who died and rose again from the dead. The Jews have not forfeited their election as God's people, nor does God change his mind. The faithful Jew earnestly desires to live under God's sovereignty both as an individual and within the Jewish community (although not necessarily in Israel, for Israel is a secular state). Beyond doubt faithful Jews, committed to the God who calls them, are within the Kingdom of God. There is much that many Christian people could learn from their committedness, their goodness and their spirituality.

At the same time they are not Christians. They believe that God forgives sins, and the Day of Atonement is set aside to reinforce their penitence and to assure them of forgiveness. But the horror of the *shoah* confuses and confounds their doctrine of God. How could God permit such genocide of his chosen people? Could it be punishment for unfaithfulness, or 'divine interruption' of providence, as though God had for a time ceased his providential care of his chosen people?[23] How can it otherwise be reconciled with their divine election? Neither the emergence of the State of Israel, nor the eminence of individual Jews can justify a massacre on a hitherto unknown scale. As we have seen, suffering is a terrible mystery (see p. 135), but Christians claim that, if they cannot fully explain it, at least they can find a meaning in it through Jesus Christ the Jew who suffered an unjust death at the hands of his persecutors and was vindicated at his resurrection by his heavenly Father. This faith, of course, is not held by the Jewish people to which Jesus himself belonged, and so it is hard for them to have that sense of self-worth that comes from the knowledge that God suffers alongside them and with them and for them, which belief in Jesus the Christ would bring them. Jews who are also Christians have found the fulfilment of their faith in Christ, and this gives added meaning to their Jewish inheritance.

2: Islam

If Judaism is the parent from which Christianity has grown, Islam belongs to the next generation. There is profound respect for the Christian faith in Islam, and again there is much in the commitment of its members and in the devotional habits of its adherents from which Christians can learn. The very word Islam means obedience and submission – obedience and submission to the will of God. All life is to be brought under the sovereignty of God; personal life and communal life. No one can say that Muslims do not live under the sovereignty of God. As the Vatican II statement puts it:

Upon the Muslims, too, the Church looks with esteem. They adore one God, living and enduring, merciful and all-powerful, Maker of heaven and earth, and Speaker to men. They strive to submit wholeheartedly even to his inscrutable decrees, just as did Abraham, with which the Muslim religion is pleased to associate itself. Though they do not acknowledge Jesus as God, they revere him as a prophet. They also honour Mary, his virgin mother; at times they call on her, too, with devotion. In addition they await the day of judgement when God will give each man his due after raising him up. Consequently, they prize the moral life and give worship to God especially through prayer, almsgiving and fasting.[24]

Muslims, Christians and Jews, all belong to the same family of religions. While there are many similarities between them, there are also many differences, deepened by their own characteristic traditions and ethos, and, alas, exacerbated by religious wars in past centuries and again today. It is not appropriate here to enter into a detailed analysis of these differences (including the verbal inspiration of the Qur'an), but two of the most important may be distinguished. For Muslims, Jesus is a prophet, while for Christians he is the Son of God. However, this phrase needs further explanation. The kind of Christology adumbrated earlier (see pp. 187f.), while insisting on the uniqueness of Jesus and emphasizing that he is the image and icon of God, at the same time equally insists that he was not God in human form, but a man so totally filled with the Spirit of God that he was transparent to God, and that God acted through him. Viewed in this way, one of the main obstacles between Christianity and Islam (shared also with Judaism) might be overcome in a reconciliation which keeps intact the convictions of all three faiths.

The second basic difference between Islam and Christianity seems more difficult to overcome. While Christians insist that there is a finality about Christ, in as much as there could not be a revelation of God expressed in human personality which could surpass that of Jesus, Muslims insist that Muhammad is the final prophet, for whom the coming of Jesus was a preparation. It follows therefore that while Muslims are within the Kingdom of God, and for them God is compassionate and all merciful, they like the Jews are unable to find renewal in Christ, nor are they able through him to be assured of the forgiveness of their sins, and to know the love of God for every person on earth.

3. Hinduism

It is customary to speak of Hinduism as a religion, but in fact it is an amalgam of religions practised on the continent of India, ranging from pure philosophical monotheism to popular cults associated with sexual practices. It is therefore difficult to speak generally of Hinduism. The Vatican Declaration confines itself to a very general statement: 'In Hinduism men contemplate the divine mystery and express it through an unspent fruitfulness of myths and through searching philosophical enquiry. They seek release from the anguish of our condition through ascetical practices or deep meditation or a loving, trusting flight towards God.'[25] The Vatican Declaration does not doubt the reality either of Hindu religious experience or of the Hindu search for God. Those who speak of a 'universal wisdom' see a convergence in Hindu and Christian concepts of God as ultimate Reality, and in forms of Christian mysticism and Hindu (as well as Buddhist) experience of meditation, as well as in ideas about a Cosmic Person.

The Declaration hints at but does not make explicit the great divide between Christianity and Eastern faiths, corresponding to the tendency towards activism in the West and passivity in the East. It is the Good News of Christianity that God comes to the help in this world of the human beings whom he has created, and that those who have known the regeneration that faith in his saving acts has brought to their lives are under an obligation to work in the world to make it more consonant with his purposes. On the other hand in Eastern religions there is a tendency not to work for the betterment of the world (which is the sphere of illusion), but to escape from it into the spheres of psychological self-knowledge and into expansion of self-consciousness in the psychic and spiritual realms, returning finally to the world in a spirit of compassion for the sufferings of mankind. This divide between Eastern and Western faiths however is not absolute. Christian Churches in the East have absorbed some of these attitudes without losing their hold on the Good News of Christianity, while the Christian mystical tradition has, as we have noted above, elements very similar to those found in Hindu and Buddhist traditions.

Again, the Vatican Declaration hints at but does not make explicit the tendency towards pantheistic belief in some strands of Hinduism, manifested in the pantheon of gods and goddesses who are the object of worship in its various cults. These seem to be the personification of powers of the inner psyche and of the psychic realm which can assist either integration or disintegration. They may perhaps be compared with the Christian belief in angels, which also may be benevolent or maleficent. Although in philosophical Hinduism *Atman* (ultimate reality) is seen as transcendent as well as immanent, in popular Hinduism it is these gods and goddesses which capture popular devotion. (A similar tendency may be seen in some cults of the saints in popular Christianity.) In much philosophical Hinduism the emphasis is on the world spirit which contains all things within itself, again a pantheistic notion. In examining the Christian doctrine of God (see p. 125) we have given a proper place to divine immanence, for God's presence is everywhere, and in him we live and move and have our being. But at the same time he is transcendent over everything and everyone. This paradox is not always clear in Hindu theology; and, although there are certainly forms of Hinduism in which God is personalized, it is not always clear that in strict Hindu theology God could be properly called 'personal' in the sense that Christians hold that there is personality in God. Even *avatars* do not really provide analogies to Incarnation.

A further important distinction between Christianity and Hinduism (and Buddhism) is found in the notion of *karma*, the doctrine that a person gets his deserts for the life that he leads, and this can be exemplified in their doctrines of reincarnation, in which the nature of a person's conduct and attitudes in this life determines the nature of the next reincarnation. By contrast, it is of the essence of Christian belief that if we turn to God in faith we do not get our deserts. God accepts us as we are despite the fact that we are unacceptable (see p. 107). Paul certainly wrote: 'Make no mistake about this: God is not to be fooled; a man reaps what he sows' (Gal 6.7), and in the second chapter of his Epistle to the Romans he elaborated the theme. Yet this does not conflict with 'justification through faith'. Faith in what God has done for us through Christ places us in a right relationship with God even though we do not deserve it.

Hinduism has a tendency to swallow up other religions in the sense that it can accept Christianity as a form of cultus while denying its finality or exclusiveness. What has Christianity to say about Hinduism?

As we have noted, there are those who find the 'unknown Christ' within it. There are others who have rejected it as heathenism. It certainly cannot be said that all Hindus understand themselves as personally or communally living under the sovereignty of God. Of course in all Eastern religions, as in the religions of the West, it is not possible to generalize about their adherents. Nonetheless in Hindu religions the practice of religious faith is not usually closely allied to moral behaviour: ascetical practices seem often to be employed as a way of gaining access to profound religious experience (including the expansion of self-consciousness) rather than as a form of obedience to the divine will. Yet Hindus are frequently deeply religious. There have been Hindus of great profundity and sanctity who centred their lives on the love of God and who have devoted themselves to the welfare of their fellow human beings and even suffered martyrdom for their beliefs. Mahatma Gandhi is an obvious example. 'God himself is not far distant from those who in shadows and images seek the unknown God, for it is he who gives to all men life and breath and every other gift.'[26] The plan of salvation certainly brings, through the grace of God, the future goal of eternal life to those who, not far from the Kingdom, seek while they are in this world the experience of eternity beyond this world.

4: Buddhism

Although Buddhism has marks of resemblance to Christianity, it also has fundamental differences from it. As in Hinduism, its tenets require adherents to seek to escape from the illusions of this world (and to release themselves from the otherwise endless suffering of reincarnation) by an expansion of their self-consciousness; and they finally hope to obtain Nirvana, the bliss that arises from the cessation of all desire.

There is within Buddhism a great divide, between those who are theists (believers in a personal God) and those who are agnostic and even atheist. Among theistic Buddhists, Gautama Buddha is a kind of incarnation, an icon and an image of the invisible God; while among agnostic Buddhists, he is the exemplar, the perfect man whose attitudes and life-style are a pattern for all his followers. In this sense he is parallel to Jesus Christ, who is all these things for Christian adherents. The Buddha is set above the gods and goddesses of his contemporary world, as Jesus is set above all powers and principalities. The Buddha, though a human being, is also the expression of the transcendent, as is Jesus Christ for Christians. The Buddha brings salvation through enlightenment, as Christ brings salvation through his life of total love. The Buddha liberates us from the world of illusion: the Christ liberates us from ourselves and from the powers of darkness. Although there are great differences between the two, very similar claims are made on behalf of them both.[27]

To decide between the two, it is necessary to consider the doctrine of Creation. According to Christian doctrine, it is good (see p. 24). According to Buddhist belief, it is the sphere of illusion. In a sense, the differences between Buddhism and Christianity all stem from this basic fact. The doctrine of Creation determines the doctrine of salvation. There is no reason to doubt the common sense of many of the Buddha's teachings, or to deny his spiritual insight into human nature with its deep-seated desires, or to question the expansion of self-consciousness that the Buddhist life of meditation can bring. If we wanted to escape from this world, he would be the person to follow. But if this world is created good by God, it is to be savoured and enjoyed and its sufferings are to be endured; and salvation is to be found not out of this world but within it.

A Buddhist would not regard himself as within the Kingdom of God: indeed he might well deny the reality of God, so that there is no Kingdom of God. But Buddhism teaches compassion, and their peace of soul means that Buddhists show some of the fruit of the Spirit and that they are not far from the Kingdom within. As with Hinduism the plan of salvation certainly brings, through the grace of God, the future goal of eternal life to those who, not far from the Kingdom, seek while they are in this world the experience of eternity beyond this world.

Dialogue and commitment

These remarks about other faiths are not made as a result of listening to their adherents: they spring out of judgements made intellectually without any first-hand knowledge or experience of these faiths (other than Judaism). They must therefore appear superficial to believers in other faiths and must be regarded as provisional. Dialogue between the great religions of mankind has barely begun. It is very tempting to agree with the International Missionary Council statement of 1928: 'We recognize as part of the one Truth that sense of the Majesty of God and the consequent reverence in worship, which are conspicuous in Islam, the deep sympathy for the world's sorrow and unselfish search for the way of escape, which are at the heart of Buddhism, the desire for contact with ultimate reality conceived as spiritual, which is prominent in Hinduism; the belief in a moral order of the universe and consequent insistence on moral conduct, which are inculcated by Confucianism.'[28]

The 'one Truth' in the statement is of course Christianity; and the statement presupposes that Christianity fulfils the other religions. But this must only be a provisional judgement, because most Christians know so little about the other faiths, as do their adherents about the Christian faith; and no one as yet has adequate criteria for a theology of religions. Meanwhile serious dialogue between religious institutions must begin. But dialogue can only take place within the context of commitment. We must want to listen to the beliefs and experience of others who are committed to their faiths, just as they must want to hear ours. What the outcome will be we cannot know. But that in no way prevents us from making provisional judgements so long as we recognize them as provisional, and it in no way dampens commitment on the part of all participants for the claims and truths of their own faiths. Christians however would not be true to the basic attitudes of Christianity unless they entered such dialogue in a spirit of vulnerability and humility.

Notes

1. H. Küng, *Paradigm Change in Christianity* (New York, 1989), quoted by D. Bosch, *Transforming Mission* (New York, 1991), p. 181.

2. T. Kuhn, *The Structure of Scientific Revolutions* (Chicago, 1970).

3. D. Bosch, *op. cit.*, p. 185. I have drawn heavily on this work in the first part of this chapter.

4. *Ibid.*, p. 342.

5. *Ibid.*, p. 339.

6. *Evangelii Nuntiandi*, para. 18.

7. G. W. Sargant, *Battle for the Mind* (London, 1957), pp. 72ff.

8. *The Truth Shall Make You Free* (London, 1988), pp. 32ff.

9. See H. J. Schoeps, *The Jewish–Christian Argument* (London, 1965).

10. E. Schlink, *International Review of Missions* (July 1938), pp. 465, 470, quoted by E. C. Dewick, *The Christian Attitudes to Other Religions* (Cambridge, 1953), p. 41.

11. H. Kraemer, *The Christian Message in a Non-Christian World* (London, 1938), p. 300.

12. The title of a book by R. Pannikkar (London, 1964).

13. See K. Rahner, 'Observations on the problem of the anonymous Christian' in *Theological Investigations 14* (London, 1976), pp. 280–94.

14. E.g. the Hindu writers S. Aurobindo and S. Vivekananda, or the Christian writers A. J. Appasamy and R. H. S. Boyd. See J. A. T. Robinson, *Truth is Twin-Eyed*

(London, 1979). For a defence of Hindu thinking, see C. Badrinoth, *Dharma, India and the World Order* (Edinburgh/Bonn, 1993).

15. B. Griffiths, *A New Vision of Reality* (London, 1989).

16. *Ibid.*, p. 227.

17. *Ibid.*, p. 226.

18. J. Hick, *An Interpretation of Religion* (London, 1989). See criticism by C. Gunton, 'Knowledge and culture: towards an epistemology of the concrete' in *The Gospel and Contemporary Culture*, ed. H. Montefiore (London, 1992), pp. 86–95.

19. *Lumen Gentium*, para. 16.

20. See H. J. Schoeps, *The Jewish–Christian Argument* (London, 1965).

21. *Declaration on the Relation of the Church to Non-Christian Religions*, para. 4.

22. See H. Küng, *Judaism* (London, 1992), p. 109.

23. See *The Holocaust as Interruption*, ed. H. Fiorenza and D. Tracy (Edinburgh, 1984).

24. *Declaration*, para. 3.

25. *Ibid.*, para. 2.

26. *Ibid.*

27. A. Pieris, 'The Buddha and the Christ in liberation' in *The Myth of Christian Uniqueness*, ed. J. Hick and P. Knitter (London, 1987), pp. 169–75.

28. *The Christian Life and Message in Relation to Non-Christian Systems: Report of the Jerusalem Meeting of the International Missionary Council* (Oxford, 1928), p. 491.

chapter 8

The Christian community

Church beginnings

Did Jesus intend to found the Church? This seems a strange question to ask in the light of nearly two thousand years of the Church's existence. But the only mention of *ekklesia* (church) in the Gospels is to be found in two Matthaean passages (Matt 16.18; 18.17). Both passages are very ecclesiastical in tone, and their wording, if indeed based on the words of Jesus, is likely to have been altered by subsequent ecclesiastical interests. For Jesus preached the imminent coming of the Kingdom, not the establishment of the Church after his death. If Paul wrote to the Corinthians that there was no point in getting married if the end of the world was just round the corner, would not the same argument apply *a fortiori* to the establishment of the Christian Church?

However, Jesus' ethical teaching suggests a community in which it could be practised. He gathered around him a group of friends to form the nucleus of a purified Israel, and at his Last Supper gave them a common meal by which to remember him. His perspective seems to have lengthened about the imminence of the End (we find the same with St Paul). When Jesus sent out his disciples on their preaching ministry, he told them that they would not have gone round the cities of Israel before the Kingdom had come in power (Matt 10.23); and this surely refers to the End rather than to the inauguration of the Kingdom after his death and resurrection. It was only later that he admitted – and surely such an admission must be genuine, for no one would have dared to make it up – that he did not know the time of its coming (Mark 13.32). He must therefore have admitted the possibility that it would take some time to come, and that his movement would continue after he had left them.[1] Indeed, Matthew records that after his resurrection he gave them 'the Great Commission' to spread the Gospel to all nations (Matt 28.19f.).

What is clear is that Jesus left no clear instructions during his lifetime about what his disciples were to do if he departed before the End came. He did not write a book and he did not inaugurate an organization. He only promised them that they would eat and drink at his table in his Kingdom (Luke 22.30) – but that was at the Messianic banquet at the end of all time. Meanwhile Peter was to strengthen the fellowship (Luke 22.32). After the Resurrection, the disciples were given some marching orders, but in the vaguest of terms: Christ's sheep were to be fed, the disciples were to proclaim forgiveness of sins to all nations, they were to make all nations his disciples, new disciples were to be immersed in water in his name. There was nothing about an organized Church. And then unexpectedly at Pentecost they were filled with the Spirit – whether this was the only occasion, or as Acts suggests, the first among others (Acts 4.31). After his departure, the Church 'took off'. It began as a fellowship of disciples convinced that Jesus was alive from the dead, who met to break bread together and to worship in the Jerusalem Temple courts and to tell others of his presence and his power. His followers formed an 'interim body' before the End arrived; and that is what the Church is, an eschatological body, living 'between the times' of his first coming and the End of all things; and their enabling and empowering experience of the Spirit was a foretaste of what was to come.

From the New Testament Church to the Church catholic

As we have said (p. 161) the early Christians saw themselves as members of a purified Israel. The word used for the congregation of Israel in their wilderness wanderings in the Old Testament is *q'ahal*.[2] One of the Greek words corresponding to that was *ekklesia*. As yet the word had few of the connotations which we associate with the word church. The *q'ahal* was the pilgrim People of God, on its way to the Promised Land of God's Kingdom. As the number of disciples grew, and as the movement spread to other centres as well as Jerusalem, more rules became necessary, especially when Gentiles as well as Jews were welcomed. Jews who lived in the Diaspora outside Judaea and Galilee (a larger number than those in their home country) paid the Temple tax towards its upkeep, and in the same kind of way Christians outside the mother Church of Jerusalem made voluntary offerings for the relief of poor Christians living there. Later, when Christians were *aposunagogoi* (banned from the Jewish synagogues) the Christian way ceased to be a Jewish sect and began to be a movement on its own. After the fall of Jerusalem in AD 70 the centre of gravity of the movement moved from Judaea to the Diaspora. Already the Church was in being, with its officers, its distinctive worship, its codes of behaviour, its relief organization. Out of the primitive Church the catholic Church was being formed. All this was a logical consequence of Jesus' ministry, and of his death and resurrection. But most of its characteristics were not ordained by him: its codes of behaviour, the threefold ministry, the New Testament canon of Scripture.

The small groups of Christian fellowship which grew up so quickly in many parts of the Middle East as a result of missionary preaching were intense, inward-looking groups, separating themselves from a world which was often hostile to them and which held very different values. This was necessary for their survival; but in some ways their emphasis was different from that of Jesus himself. For example, Jesus defined loving one's neighbour in terms of a hated Samaritan coming to the aid of a Jew in distress, whereas in the primitive Church mutual love was to be shown first of all to those within the fellowship of the Church (Gal 6.10). The early Church felt free to adapt its ethos to the requirements of its situation. So the Church in later centuries, if it is to be faithful to the teaching of Jesus, is free in some respects to diverge from the practices of the primitive Church.

The early Church was described in many different ways and under many different images. St Paul preferred the images of the body, the building (or temple) and the bride, which he applied both to individual Churches and to the Church as a whole. Much has been made of his preferred image of the body, and it became at one point the basic tenet of a theology of the Church. There was the physical body of his flesh, his resurrection body, his glorified and ascended body, his mystical body (the Church) and his sacramental body in the eucharist. Pope Pius XII in his encyclical *Mystici Corporis Christi* (1943) wrote that the doctrine of the mystical body 'has a surpassing splendour which commends it to the meditation of all who are moved by the divine Spirit'. And in a later encyclical *Humani Generis* (1950) the mystical body was identified with 'the Catholic Church in communion with Rome'. (This claim is examined later, see p. 177). It is said that the Church is Christ's body because it is his present means of expression and the instrument of his will, and the way in which he may be identified in today's world. It may be one way of carrying out his will, and one way of identifying him in the world; but not the only one. He himself told the parable of the sheep and the goats in which he said of those in need: 'Anything you did for one of these, however humble, you did for me' (Matt 25.40).

It is doubtful whether Paul intended the phrase 'body of Christ' as a fact (Christians as Christ's literal embodiment in the world) or, more fact (Christians as Christ's literal embodiment in the world) or, more probably, as a metaphor.[3] What matters is that the image of the body and the building (or temple) is corporate (because Christians belong to one another in Christ) and dynamic (so that the building may even be described as 'increasing'), while the image of the bride emphasizes the love of Christ for his Church. These characteristics are also to be found in other images for the Church used by New Testament writers. Is it possible to sum up the effect of all these images?

Although *koinonia* [communion or fellowship] is never equated with 'Church' in the New Testament, it is the term which most aptly conveys the mystery underlying the various New Testament images of the Church. When for example the Church is called the people of the new covenant or the bride of Christ, the context is primarily that of communion. Although such images as the Temple, the new Jerusalem, or the royal priesthood may carry institutional overtones, their primary purpose is to depict the Church's experience as a partaking in the salvation of Christ. When the Church is described as the body of Christ, the household of God, or the holy nation, the emphasis is upon the relationships among its members as well as upon their relationship with Christ the Head.[4]

The Spirit was given to the Church as a whole, and individuals share in it. Christians belong to one another because they belong to Christ. They need one another's support within the Church as well as the strength of Christ and the power of his Spirit. St Paul had a glorious view of the Church as it should be and a clear grip on the realities of what it was. He had a vision of the whole Church of God in addition to the various congregations or churches which comprised it. Already in the New Testament Church there is no such entity as 'the invisible Church'. Christians, and Paul (like the author of the Fourth Gospel) was insistent on the necessity for apostolic authority to resolve these problems and the paramount necessity of retaining unity within the Church. In the New Testament Church there is no such entity as 'the invisible Church'. Whether speaking of the Church or the churches, the writers are referring to visible men, women and children who comprise its membership.

In the early Church details of organization were comparatively unimportant. Paramount was the Church as the body within which men and women were incorporated into Christ and joined in faith-union with him, and in which they shared spiritually in his dying and rising again. In the Church they shared in the Spirit; they were justified, saved, and given a glimpse of the glory to come. They were in the process of becoming what in principle they already were. Within the Church the divisions of sex, race and class were to drop away. It was the focus of faith, hope and love. It was a sign and symbol of the glory to come.

It has been necessary to look in some detail at the early years of the Church because these have been formative and in many ways normative for its future development. The various vicissitudes through which the Church has lived from these earliest days until now have helped to develop its doctrines further. The admission of Gentiles enabled it to be liberated from a purely Jewish ethos, so that Christianity could become a world faith. The need for order helped it to develop the threefold ministry of bishops, priests and deacons. The battle with Marcionites (whose Bible had no Old Testament and a truncated New Testament) made necessary a scriptural canon which could be regarded as authoritative. Its confrontation with the Gnostics (who regarded themselves as an élite possessing secret and authentic knowledge about God) helped the Church to keep its feet firmly on the ground, and to guard its first principles against the spirit of the age. The aftermath of persecutions helped it to define its attitude to rigorism. The establishment of the Church under Constantine raised afresh its relationship to the State, just as later on the fall of Rome forced it to reconsider this. The growing power of Rome in matters of jurisdiction raised questions about the authority of the Bishop of Rome. The schism with the Eastern Church raised questions about the basis of its unity. The excessive preoccupation with law in the medieval Church caused fresh thinking about the relation between grace and law, and led to the Reformation. The further schisms within the Protestant Reformed Churches have led to a reconsideration of doctrines concerning unity and authority. The missionary outreach of the Church gave rise to the ecumenical movement. Dialogue with other world faiths is leading to a renewed consideration of their standing in God's eyes.

Sociology and the churches

The Church can be considered under two aspects; as an organism and as an organization. As an organism it claims to be divine, in the sense that it is upheld by God, obscured though this is by the sinfulness of its members. But the Church must also exist as an organization because continuity is required, and without organization, organisms wither and die. But all organized bodies tend by their nature towards deterioration and malpractice: that is why *ecclesia semper reformanda* (the Church is always in need of reform). The organized Church is open to the same sociological critique as any other human organization.[5] Both these two aspects of organism and organization interact with each other. Thus in the episcopal churches the ministry of bishops is a matter of doctrine and plays a crucial role in the church as an organism; but in terms of organization the autocratic rule of bishops in the past had evident connections with a hierarchical view of society ('No bishop, no king'). The inclusion of lay men and women in Anglican and other synods is obviously not unconnected with the growing tendency of member-participation in secular organizations under democratic influence, but it also involves a positive theology of the laity. The organization of the largest church in Christendom has been run entirely by elderly celibate priests, so it is hardly surprising that church discipline about sex has tended to be negative.

Social psychologists analyse empirical findings about religion from social surveys, field studies, etc., and use these findings to test psychological and sociological theories about the origins, functions and effects of religious behaviour.[6] These are relevant for our knowledge about the Church. Sociologists investigate the attitudes and habits of believers, and the class structures of the church organizations to which they belong. For example, there was in the last century generally speaking a class distinction between members of the Established Church of England, the Methodist Church, and independent Chapels. Contrary to what might be expected, churches tend to grow at times of national prosperity, and to contract in times of national retrenchment. In the Church of England at national level, clergy and laity share in a distinctive 'élite ecclesiastical subculture' which disposes them to embrace political positions to the left of local church activists.[7] Clearly there are many non-theological factors affecting the dynamics, life and make-up of Christian churches.

Sociologists make a distinction between ecclesial bodies which function as sects or as churches. A sect may have many different classifications;[8] but generally speaking it is a gathered group of believers determined on the purity of its doctrine and practice, with strict rules for its members, and generating among them great commitment and enthusiasm for its own internal life, and attracting outsiders by its certitudes and earnestness. A church is a more open body, with a mixed membership, including a large range of beliefs and practice, a more relaxed attitude towards its own life and that of its members, interacting with society and concerned about society's structures and life-styles. At a time when society is less friendly to the church, the latter naturally tends to take on more of the characteristics of a sect; and during a period when membership of the church is static or contracting, the temptation to become a sect is all the greater.

The New Testament Church could be described, in this sense of the term, as a sect, so that fundamentalists have only to appeal to Scripture to point out that theirs is the truly scriptural form of ecclesial body. But the situation in most Western countries today has vastly changed since New Testament times, and the literal application of these scriptural texts is no longer appropriate. Arising out of the days when a country could be properly called a Christian society, there is still a diffused consciousness of Christian values (although this is now changing). This gives rise to what has been called 'the latent church'.[9] The difference between a Christian and a non-Christian in terms of life-style is still not as marked as it was in New Testament times. The life of the Church is not set apart from the rest of the country, but the local church seeks to build up the local community and foster its welfare for the common good. While sects may grow in size by attracting those who warm to their ethos, they will have no influence, other than a negative one, on the values of the country as a whole, or on the lives of people as a whole. Because sects find it difficult to adapt themselves to a changing situation, they are likely to be short-lived. If the ideal of the sect has much in common with the Christian fellowship of New Testament times, the more open approach of the church has much more in common with the style of Jesus himself in his preaching of the Kingdom, when he mixed with the common people and attended public worship without respect of persons.

The Church of God

If the Church as a human organization is open to secular scrutiny, the Church as an organism has its origins in the dying and rising of Christ in which it participates; and it is upheld by the continuing grace of God. The Church is eschatological: that is to say, it stands between the coming of Christ in whom was realized the Kingdom of God, and the full coming of God's Kingdom at the end of time, when God's universal kingship is acknowledged and holds sway all over men. There is a mystery about the Church, with its human and divine natures. Some writers write about it with perhaps too much enthusiasm. 'In this sense [as divine organism] she is entirely holy and unfailing. The Bride of Christ cannot be degraded: pure and uncorrupted, she knows one dwelling alone and keeps in chastity and modesty the sanctity of one hearth. Her doctrine remains perpetually pure and the spring of her sacraments fresh.'[10] The Vatican II document is more circumspect: 'She becomes on earth the initial budding forth of that kingdom. While she slowly grows, the Church strains towards the consummation of the kingdom and, with all her strength, hopes and desires to be united in glory with her King.'[11] This budding forth, however, must not be identified with the Kingdom itself. There has been too much sinfulness within the Church for that. And although it is true that worldwide the Church is still growing, it would be hard to establish that it is actually growing in commitment, faith and holiness of life.

Nonetheless the Church is a real sign of and pointer towards the Kingdom. The Church is divine in origin and could not continue, in the face of all its shortcomings, without the spiritual renewal which comes alone from God. It is said that a Jew once arrived at Rome amid all its medieval corruptions and asked for baptism. When asked why ever he had done this, he replied that only a body which was divine could continue to flourish despite its manifold sinfulness.

The dimensions of the Church

1: Unity

From its earliest beginnings there has been an insistence on the unity of the Church:

What is the nature and meaning of this unity? It is deeper than convenience, organization, human brotherhood. It is less formally expounded than tacitly assumed. There is no Christian community which has not behind it some authority responsible for the larger whole, and there is no letter in the New Testament (except the Epistle to Philemon) which does not show that the local society owes obedience to someone who addresses it in the name of the larger whole. Not of convenience alone, this unity is connected with the truth about Christ himself. It is the unity of his own body, springing from the unity of God . . .[12]

According to St John's Gospel, Jesus prayed to his Father for unity, 'may they all be one, as thou, Father, art in me and I in thee, so also may they be in us, that the world may believe that thou didst send me' (John 17.20–21). Paul wrote of 'one Lord, one faith, one baptism; one God and Father of all' (Eph 4.5). The unity of the Church is an expression of the unity of God. The local churches do not together comprise a united church: on the contrary, each is the local embodiment of the whole Church of God. Within local churches, all members are dependent on one another under Christ who is their head. In this sense the unity of the Church is not a goal at which its members should aim: it is the very meaning and condition of its existence. The unity of the Church has as its corollary the need for the recognition of ministries within the Church: this will be investigated later (see p. 208).

How can this requirement of unity be correlated with the evident disunity of the Church? For the Roman Catholic Church Cyprian's principle of *scindi non potest* (unity cannot be broken) is taken to its logical conclusion.[13] The Roman Catholic Church is united under its Supreme Pontiff. Those Christians and those Churches who do not belong to that Communion do not belong to the Church in the same way. According to Vatican II, 'this Church, constituted and organized in the world as a society, subsists in the Catholic Church, which is governed by the successor of Peter and by the bishops in union with his successor, although many elements of sanctification and truth can be found outside of her visible structure'.[14] ('Subsists in' is an ambiguous phrase; but at the very least it gives a certain priority to the Roman Catholic Church.) Members of other ecclesial bodies may show a true religious zeal and have strong links with the Catholic Church, and yet the Church subsists in the Roman Catholic Church and not in any other body. The Eastern Orthodox Churches, which express their beliefs in less legal forms than the Roman Catholic Church, have a similar view about their identity with the true Church. Although there can be friendly relations with some other churches, the Eastern Orthodox regard themselves as the true Church, and hold that other churches (including the Roman Catholic Church) have departed in some measure from the truth.

This is not the only possible view of the Church's unity. Some Protestant churches are completely autonomous, and the local church, while it is in communion with other similar churches, runs its own affairs in accordance with its traditions. This appears to disregard the larger view of the Church found in the New Testament.

The 'branch theory' used to be popular in Anglican and Free Church circles in Britain.[15] It is not strictly speaking biblical, since in St John's Gospel the 'branches of the vine' with which Christ identifies himself refer to individuals, not churches. According to this theory, the Church is one, like a tree, and the various churches comprise branches of the tree. Some branches are larger than others, but all belong together to form an organic whole which is the Church of God. The difficulty with the theory is that the Chuch is prior to the various divided churches, whereas according to the branch theory the divided churches comprise the Church of God. The analogy also breaks down in so far as it hardly allows different branches to unite (as in England the Presbyterian Church, most Congregationalist churches and most of the Churches of Christ have done to form the United Reformed Church in Britain). Nonetheless the united Church of South India holds the 'branch theory' about the parent churches of those churches which united to form this new church.[16]

Most churches have embraced the ecumenical movement and are members of the World Council of Churches, one of·whose objects is to facilitate reunion. But very few churches are willing to give up their own cherished traditions or to compromise over what they regard as essential in order to unite with other churches. Doctrines of divided churches, although they may be trying to express the same truths in different ways, often seem directly opposed to one another. 'The separated churches have taken an interest in each other's theology. A greater exchange of subject matter, viewpoints, methods, etc. has been and is being achieved. But when we enquire into the end-product of this ecumenical dialogue so far as the unification of the churches is concerned, we have to admit this end-product is very slight.'[17] The ministry has been a particular sticking point; and formulas in reunion proposals which, in order to be acceptable to both sides, are capable of more than one interpretation are denounced as a fudge. The ecumenical movement which started with very high hopes has, so far as institutional churches are concerned, run out into the sand. 'Despite all ecumenical resolves the real frontiers remain stiff and immovable.'[18]

At the same time, paradoxical as it may seem, individual Christians (both ordained and lay) have often come very close indeed to their fellow Christians in churches which are not in communion with theirs; and there is a tendency among them to take the law into their own hands so far as communion is concerned, even when their actions are contrary to ecclesiastical law. At the individual level the ecumenical movement has far outstripped progress at the ecclesiastical level.

This prompts a fresh look at the unity which we seek. According to the Scriptures, the unity of the Church is based on the unity between the Father and the Son. However, this unity, as we have already seen, is obscure and mysterious (see p. 81). If this is the case, it is hardly likely that the unity of the Churches will be a simple mathematical unity. At the same time the Spirit is bringing together Christians of very different traditions into a very real spiritual union. This suggests that spiritual unity is more important than structural unity, however desirable the latter may be. The word 'federal' has been heavily criticized in matters of church reunion; but it deserves re-examination. It means 'covenantal'. The various churches of Christendom which have been divided for so long will not easily desert their own cherished doctrines, liturgies, traditions and life-styles. The visible organic unity of the Church, while admirable as a goal, seems unlikely to be achieved in this world, at least in the foreseeable future. At a time when life is increasingly dominated by large structures, Christians are naturally fearful that their church will be engulfed in some huge new structural entity.

At the same time what churches hold in common is far greater than that which holds them apart. The Eastern Orthodox Churches hold to the maxim 'Unity in things necessary, liberty in things doubtful, in all things love'. Providing that 'things necessary' is interpreted in such a way as to include mainstream churches (and the World Council of Churches would seem to have shown that this can be done without sacrificing essentials), this would seem an excellent principle by which divided churches could covenant to recognize one another if not as 'branches' of the one Church, at least as incomplete but real local embodiments of that Church. This would be a form of federal union.[19] In this way the spiritual unity which individuals are already enjoying could be shared among all members of different churches. All join the one visible Church at baptism (see p. 188). The priority of the Church over the churches would not be jeopardized, because it is not *from* the One Church but *within* the One Church that schisms occur. A family does not cease to be a family because its members have quarrelled and differed, and a family can reunite in love without its members agreeing unanimously so long as they are agreed on the essential ethos of the family. The divided churches could act together far more than they do. They could act on the doctrine enunciated at the World Council of Churches' conference at Lund that the churches should do together all that they do not have to do apart.

What of intercommunion between churches which are not united? It is said that intercommunion requires recognition of one another's ministries, and that this is the crown of the reunion process rather than a means of grace which may strengthen and hasten it. It is further said that the pain and distress caused by being present at a eucharist celebrated by another church but being unable to receive communion is a spur to the process of reunion. But this has not noticeably been the case. The tendency to restrict communion is not merely a characteristic of the Roman Catholic and Eastern Orthodox Churches. The Calvinist churches also used to 'fence the Table' and prevent all those from participating who did not accept Calvinist doctrine.

There has been a tendency in Christendom to exaggerate the claims of doctrine over the claims of Christian fellowship in Christ. Jesus did not require any statement of faith from his disciples before he shared with them his Last Supper: indeed he knowingly included one who would betray him. The communion table does not belong to a church denomination: it belongs to Christ, and it is a pity that the churches do not follow their Lord in this respect. In fact many Protestant churches do issue an invitation at a celebration of communion to 'all who love the Lord Jesus'; and the Church of England now welcomes to the altar all those who believe in the Blessed Trinity. Federal union would require the practice of occasional intercommunion in order to strengthen this form of unity between churches: it would only be occasional because Christians would naturally communicate normally in the places where they usually worship. But they would be enriched by sharing in the traditions and liturgy of other churches, they would be united together sacramentally in Christ, and the spiritual unity which this form of unity would foster, while falling short of full reunion, would be deepened by such practice.

2: Holiness

The Church has often betrayed its title deeds. No mention of the sinfulness of the Church is to be found in Vatican II's renowned Constitution on the Church, or in ARCIC I's much acclaimed reports on the Church. Nonetheless the record is horrendous. The various confrontations of the early Church often resulted in *odium theologicum* and character defamation, with opponents all too easily accusing their enemies of being inspired by the Devil. The writings of heretics were usually destroyed, so that we only hear of them through the biased refutations of their orthodox opponents. The power given to the Church under the Constantinian establishment resulted in progressive discrimination against the Jews, which continued through the Middle Ages and only ended at the Enlightenment. (All the Nazi secular calumnies against the Jews are to be found in an ecclesiastical form in Christian writings, and even the Holocaust was the secular version of the divine judgement against the Jews which the Church left to God to carry out.[20]) Forcible baptisms were not uncommon. The Crusades, whatever idealism they may have engendered, resulted in massacres of Jews and religious wars against Muslims. Particular churches enforced their authority against dissidents, even to the extent of executing or burning opponents. The Church on occasions has used the civil power to enforce its authority, whether the Roman Catholic Inquisition in Roman Catholic countries, or the magistrates in Reformed countries or the penal laws in Britain.

Religious wars were sanctioned. Legalism was substituted for the freedom of the Gospel. The oppression of colonialism was justified on the grounds of the mission of the Church. Those who have a high doctrine of the Church must reckon with the grim reality of its actual history.

The horror of its shortcomings must not detract from the fact that the Church and all its members are called to holiness. In God's great mercy past sins, however horrendous, when truly repented of, are forgiven. And there is another very different record as well; the holiness and heroic sanctity it has engendered, the self-sacrifice and altruism it has evoked, the faith and love it has encouraged, the passionate desire for truth among some of its thinkers, its encouragement of high standards of personal behaviour, the burning desire of missionaries to share their Good News with those who had not heard it, the good works that have been accomplished in healing, education, caring for the poor and outcast and in many other ways. Just as moving is the holiness of unknown men and women living out the Gospel faithfully in their lives. Each of the great churches of Christendom has evolved its own tradition of holiness.[21] 'The saints are lifegivers to their fellow-men, because they themselves have received life from the Lord and giver of life who dwells within them. All men are called to be saints, called to give and receive life, to accept their life as a gift from God, and to offer it back to him in thanksgiving and praise.'[22]

Has the Church done more harm than good? That is a question which cannot be answered, because these matters cannot be quantified. The good that it has done testifies to the inspiration of Christ which undergirds it; while the evil that it has done is the sum of the sinfulness, errors and follies of its members down the centuries. Whether or not the Church measures up to its calling, it is called to holiness. The holiness is not its own, but that of Christ with whom its members identify themselves. In so far as they put on Christ, they put on holiness. The Church, although part of the world, is set apart from the world to follow the example of Christ and to be transparent to his glory. 'It is *God* who distinguishes the Church, sets it apart, marks it out for his own and makes it holy, by winning power over the hearts of men through his Holy Spirit, by establishing his reign, by justifying and sanctifying the sinner and thereby founding the communion of saints. This is why we do not simply believe *in* the holy Church, but believe in God who makes the Church holy.'[23]

3: Catholicity

The word 'catholic' has been hijacked by one part of the Church so that it now has a meaning totally different from its original signification. Derived from a Greek word meaning 'universal', it described the local church as a local embodiment of the universal Church. But when controversies arose, it was used to describe the consensus of the faithful in contrast to the opinions of individuals; and from this grew up the modern meaning of catholic as describing traditional orthodoxy. The classical description of catholic in its original sense was given by St Cyril of Jerusalem:

The Church is spread throughout the whole of the inhabited world, from end to end of the earth; it teaches, without deficiency of any kind, all the doctrines which men ought to know, about things visible and invisible, celestial and terrestrial. It brings the whole of the human race into obedience to godliness and true religion, rulers and those they rule, learned and ignorant alike. It heals and cures every kind of sin of soul and body, and possesses every description of virtue in word and deed, and all varieties of spiritual gifts. It calls and collects all, that they may hear the words of God and learn to fear him and make confession to him and to praise his name.[24]

No doubt this describes the direction of the Church rather than its actual achievements, but the universality of its scope is plain.

The question arises: which interpretation of the word 'catholic' is to be preferred? Should the Church be restricted to those who accept particular traditional doctrines of orthodox belief and practice and the strict disciplines of a particular church body, or should the boundaries be drawn as widely as possible? The benefits of rigorism are evident. Everyone knows just where they stand. The beliefs of a particular church among its members are publicly safeguarded, whatever be the convictions of their hearts. There is no danger of official dilution of required belief and practice.

At the opposite extreme there may be extreme latitude, and doubtless some forms of latitudinarianism are so lax that there are no discernible boundaries at all. But there are other forms of broad churchmanship which enable people with differing degrees of commitment and different structures of belief to share together in Christian fellowship and in loving communion. This is surely preferable. Anglican churches are of this kind. Christians can kneel side by side to receive communion and be strengthened by the sacrament and united sacramentally in Christ, even though they may hold very different opinions about the meaning and significance of the rite. Although such latitude is often rejected on the grounds of incoherent or muddled theology, in fact it gives love and charity a higher priority than doctrinal differences. Thus the life of the Church flows within channels of very broad extent, marked by easily recognizable buoys (the acceptance of the Bible, the Creeds, the two Gospel Sacraments and Episcopal Order [as set forth in the 'Appeal to All Christian People' by the 1921 Lambeth Conference]). The minimum affirmations required of lay people can be found in the questions required of parents and godparents on behalf of an infant to be baptized according to the Alternative Service Book of the Church of England. They comprise turning to Christ and turning from evil and repentance for past sins, as well as expressing belief and trust in God the Creator, Redeemer and Sanctifier.

In the Church of England as established by law, however, all who live within a parish have rights in their parish church (whether they are baptized or not), and can be married there. Can this be justified? A relic of the days when all were assumed to be Christians, it stands today for the outreach of the Church to the whole nation, however nominal this claim may have become. It acknowledges the 'latent church', the many uncommitted people who would acknowledge God and honour Christ without committing themselves to the active practice of the Christian religion. This can hardly be a permanent arrangement. The same applies to the very idea of an established religion in an ecumenical age and in a country where active Christians form a small minority. Special privileges granted to an established church should be reduced: those remaining should be met by requiring special responsibilities from such a church. The situation can only be justified on the grounds that disestablishment would be regarded as the disavowal of the Christian religion by the state. But if the state demands control of the church, or forbids it to do what it has decided through its own synodical procedures that it should do, then it must demand disestablishment. Furthermore, its privileged status makes it imperative that it should feel especially free to criticize the state for any of its decisions if need be.

There is a particular danger in a national church for the Gospel to be confused with patriotism or national sentiment. It is therefore crucial for any church which is confined within national boundaries to belong to a wider international fellowship. The Roman Catholic Church, while centred in its Roman bureaucracy, clearly exists on an international level. Most other churches belong to an international denominational body; the Church of England, for example, to the Anglican Communion.

4: Apostolicity

The Church is founded upon the Apostles and prophets, Jesus Christ himself as the chief foundation (Eph 2.20). The twelve Apostles were chosen by Jesus and, as the word implies, sent by him as his emissaries to proclaim the Good News of the Kingdom of God. Apostleship was confined to those who had seen the Lord, and so, after the admission of someone to take the place of the traitor Judas, and apart from the exceptional case of the Apostle Paul, there was no continuation of the Twelve. But there were apostolic men, sometimes called 'Apostles', one of whom, if the name Junia is correct, may have been a woman (Rom 16.7). The Church as a whole was apostolic in so far as it followed in the footsteps of the original Apostles. The Apostles' ministry was continued in the Church as a whole.

Apostolicity involves faithfulness to the Apostles' ministry and mission and to their teaching and practice. In so far as ministry is concerned, the apostolic ministry involved faithfulness in preaching and in pastoral care. The question of presiding at the eucharist does not seem to have been raised in the earliest days. Apostolicity in the early Church required continuity of bishops in their sees, and later the Church developed the doctrine of apostolic succession, in the sense of continuity of the laying on of hands in ordination from the Apostles onwards (see p. 207).

As for faithfulness to the apostolic mission, this involves the Gospel command to make disciples of all nations, and to proclaim repentance and the remission of sins to all mankind. Today mission is usually understood in a wider sense to include corporate and personal service to help to meet the needs of the world and of individuals, while evangelism is used to describe personal witness and public preaching of the Gospel. The impact of pluralism on the preaching of Christianity has been discussed in a earlier chapter concerning other religions (see p. 145). Those who have received Good News naturally want to share it with others. According to the Evangelicals' Lausanne Covenant 'to evangelize is to spread the good news that Jesus died for our sins and was raised from the dead according to the Scriptures, and that as the reigning Lord he now offers forgiveness of sins and the liberating gift of the Spirit to all who repent and believe'. However scriptural this may be, it breathes a very different air from the preaching of Jesus himself.

Jesus proclaimed the coming of God's Kingdom, for which we need only two things; faith, to open ourselves to God, and repentance to reorient ourselves and our lives. Healing, light, deliverance and freedom are the words which he himself used to describe this Good News (Luke

4.18ff.). We have signs of this Kingdom of which Jesus spoke wherever men and women affirm God's sovereignty and experience something of God's love and joy, justice and righteousness, forgiveness and a fresh start. The Kingdom was dawning in the public ministry of Jesus, and it came after his death and resurrection, when the Holy Spirit was poured out on the Church. Of course the Kingdom has not yet fully come. That awaits the final consummation when God's purposes are fulfilled. But now the Kingdom is an open secret, already present in hidden glory. We must not equate the Church with the Kingdom, because the Church falls so far short of what it should be, but the Church is a real sign and a pointer of the Kingdom which God established through Jesus, and which will finally come when God's purposes are completed. The apostolic mission is to make this Good News known.

So far as faithfulness in apostolic teaching and preaching is concerned, this involves preaching the same essential message and giving the same essential teaching as the Apostles. However there is no record to the effect that these men were endowed with infallibility, and the Church was expressly told that the Holy Spirit would lead them into all the truth which they were unable to accept at the original time (John 16.13). What then are the criteria by which apostolic truth can be recognized? This leads us immediately to the question of authority in the Church.

Authority in the Church

There are two differing concepts of authority in the Church. One, which is held by the Roman Catholic and Orthodox Churches, is essentially hierarchical. According to the Roman view, supreme authority is vested in the Bishop of Rome, as the Supreme Pontiff, who exercises it in union with the bishops who are in communion with him. He has power to define doctrine infallibly in certain circumstances, and all his pronouncements are to be received as authoritative. A Council summoned by him also has power to make infallible definitions of doctrine. He also has universal jurisdiction over the whole Church. (The Eastern Orthodox Churches repudiate the authority of the Bishop of Rome and for them all power is vested in the bishops.) The clergy are the bishop's assistants. The bishops and clergy together comprise the 'teaching church' (*ecclesia docens*) and the laity the 'learning church' (*ecclesia discens*). The role of the laity is to receive these authoritative pronouncements; but their truth does not depend on this reception.

The difficulty with this view is that there is no basis for it in the

Scriptures, and it hardly seems consonant with the teaching of Jesus himself. It seems odd that the Church should require a hierarchical structure of this kind which was foreign to Jesus himself. There is no mention in Scripture of Jesus' commission given to Peter being passed to his successors as Bishops of Rome. The original Apostles spoke with overriding authority; but their office, we have seen, was not continued after their deaths. The picture given in Acts of decision-making in the Jerusalem Church, when the essentials required of Gentile converts were decided, is much more inclusive, comprising the whole body of the Church (Acts 18). A similar picture is given by Paul when passing judgement during his absence from a particular church (1 Cor 5.3f.). The hierarchical structure of the Roman Catholic Church seems even more problematical to those who see no need for and even deny some of the doctrines of faith infallibly defined in that Church; e.g. the immaculate conception of Mary the mother of Jesus, and her bodily assumption into heaven.

There is a different view of authority in the Church according to which it is disseminated throughout the body of the Church. The clearest expression of it is to be found in the Report of the 1948 Lambeth Conference:

Authority, as inherited by the Anglican Communion from the undivided Church of the early centuries of the Christian era, is single in that it is derived from a single Divine source, and reflects within itself the richness and historicity of the divine Revelation, the authority of the eternal Father, the incarnate Son, and the life-giving Spirit. It is distributed among Scripture, Tradition, Creeds, the Ministry of the Word and Sacraments, the witness of the saints, and the *consensus fidelium*, which is the continuing experience of the Holy Spirit through His faithful people in the Church. It is thus a dispersed authority, having many elements which combine, interact with, and check each other; these elements together contributing by a process of mutual support, mutual checking and redressing of errors or exaggerations to the many-sided fullness of the authority which Christ has committed to his Church. Where this authority is to be found mediated not in one mode but in several we recognize in this multiplicity God's loving provision against the temptations to tyranny and the dangers of unchecked power.[25]

In accordance with this doctrine of dispersed authority the bishops in synod, in as much as they have a special teaching authority, may exercise a veto on new teaching, and may determine the form in which it is to be voted on, but nonetheless the Church as a whole, through its bishops, representative clergy and representative laity in synod, makes all the final decisions. The fourfold criteria held within the Anglican Churches of scripture, tradition, reason and experience do not necessarily give a tidy answer when brought to bear on a controversial subject, for they may return divergent answers; but the Church cannot expect always and in every case to have total security and certainty in matters of faith and practice.

Attempts have been made to mediate between these two forms of authority in the two reports on Authority in the Church by the Anglican–Roman Catholic International Commission; but they do not really succeed because the balance is tipped in favour of hierarchical authority, with reduced authority given to lay people, and the further assertion that an ecumenical Council in its decisions on fundamental matters of faith is guaranteed freedom from error, a statement for which there is no adequate scriptural or other authority. A choice is needed between the priority given to each form of authority. Examples of the dangers of unchecked power to which reference is made at the end of the Lambeth Conference report cited above have recently been apparent, both in the appointment of Roman Catholic bishops against the wishes of their dioceses and in the suppression of views contrary to those held by those who hold supreme power. This shows the dangers in purely hierarchical authority. On the other hand, there are some difficulties in a doctrine of disseminated authority which suggest that it needs to be combined with rather than to supersede hierarchical authority. In the first place, humanity is intrinsically hierarchical, a trait evident in almost all mammalian species. Secondly, if disseminated authority is to function, it cannot effectively do this in a worldwide church. This suggests that the doctrine of 'subsidiarity' (that all decision-making should be carried out at the lowest appropriate level) should be an essential feature of church government in world-wide churches. Thirdly, for disseminated authority to function in a church requires a fairly stable secular society within which that church can live.

In a hierarchical church, the faith and practice of that church can be clearly laid down, and people know where they stand. This increases a sense of security on the part of its members and gives them a feeling of assurance. On the other hand a view of dispersed authority rather than strict hierarchical authority is more in keeping with Scripture and the practice of the primitive undivided Church.[26] Truth cannot be imposed. Church leaders carry authority, and theologians may carry respect; but individuals have to make up their own minds for themselves. Truth has to be received within the internal forum of conscience and assimilated. The Holy Spirit moving within a church can produce if not a *consensus fidelium*, at least something approaching it; and safeguards against decisions by simple majority can be built into the system.

A comparable difficulty over the doctrine of dispersed authority arises not in connection with the definition of received doctrine but over the development of doctrine. Development is inevitable. We now live some two thousand years after Christ, and in a very different culture with different ways of thinking and different thought forms. Two thousand years of reflection on the Christian faith are bound to produce some adaptations, some differences, and some additions to it. Except for those few Christians who think that they can live out the faith and practice of the Christian faith exactly as they find it in the Bible (and in order to do that they have to cut themselves off from contemporary civilization), every church and denomination has in some sense developed Christian doctrine. How are we to know whether this development is sound or unsound? A hierarchical form of authority has little difficulty here: a decision comes down from above. A dispersed authority does not enjoy a similar ease of decision-making. Painfully perhaps, and slowly, approval comes from the majority of Christians. For any formal alteration or development a built-in majority (probably two-thirds of a representative assembly) is usually required. Although this may seem an untidy system, it seems to accord more nearly with the way that the Holy Spirit works, inspiring the whole body of Christians, with decision-making embodied in a whole complex of different orders within the church rather than devolved upon one person at the top of the pyramid.

A further problem is caused when autonomous churches belonging to the same communion make opposing decisions. But such divisions are better settled by mutual understanding, and if possible by agreement, rather than by a supreme authority imposing a settlement with which individual churches may disagree. Even if this process is untidy, it must not be presumed that the Holy Spirit is always opposed to a degree of untidiness. Differences can be creative, and, when accepted, they can even deepen fellowship. If the Church is viewed as a mathematical unity, a single person at the top of a pyramid is an excellent symbol of the unity of the whole. But the unity of the Church is in fact more like the organic unity of a family, with great respect being accorded to the older members without according them supreme authority. That authority is disseminated through its different members, traditions and customs.

In the end authority is a mystery, and within the Church it is a sacred mystery. When Jesus was asked by what authority he spoke, he refused to give a direct answer (Mark 11.28f.).

Notes

1. See R. Newton Flew, *Jesus and His Church* (London, 1938), ch. 2.

2. See K. L. Schmidt, *The Church* (London, 1950), pp. 51–2.

3. See for both sides of the argument J. A. T. Robinson, *The Body* (London, 1952); and E. Best, *One Body in Christ* (London, 1955).

4. ARCIC, *The Final Report* (London, 1982), pp. 5–6.

5. See T. O'Dea, *The Sociology of Religion* (Englewood Cliffs, New Jersey, 1966); B. Reed, *The Dynamics of Religion* (London, 1978).

6. See M. Argyle and B. Best-Hallahmi, *The Social Psychology of Religion* (London, 1975).

7. K. N. Medhurst and G. Moyser, *Church and Politics in a Secular Age* (Oxford, 1988), p. 231.

8. B. R. Wilson, 'Religion and social and cultural differentiation' in *Sociology of Religion*, ed. R. Robertson (Harmondsworth, 1972), pp. 364–71.

9. See P. Tillich, *Systematic Theology*, vol. III (London, 1964), pp. 162–3.

10. H. de Lubac, *The Splendour of the Church* (London, 1956), p. 76.

11. *Lumen Gentium*, para. 5.

12. A. M. Ramsey, *The Gospel and the Catholic Church* (London, 1956), p. 46.

13. See *The Nature of the Church*, ed. R. Newton Flew (London, 1952) for the doctrines of the Church held by the mainstream churches.

14. *Lumen Gentium*, para. 8.

15. It is found in the Doctrinal Basis of the Free Church Federal Council.

16. A. M. Hollis, 'The Church of South India' in *The Nature of the Church*, *op. cit.*, p. 223.

17. K. Rahner, 'Contemporary ecumenism' in *Theological Investigations 14* (London, 1976), p. 248.

18. *Ibid.*, p. 246.

19. H. W. Montefiore, 'Federation: a bad word?' in *On the Move to Unity*, ed. J. E. Fison (London, 1962), pp. 44–50.

20. See R. R. Ruether, *Faith and Fratricide* (New York, 1971).

21. See *Man's Concern with Holiness*, ed. M. Chavchavadze (London, no date).

22. A. M. Allchin, 'The Anglican tradition' in *Man's Concern with Holiness*, *op. cit.*, p. 38.

23. H. Küng, *The Church* (London, 1967), p. 325.

24. Cyril of Jerusalem, *Catecheses* 18. 23–8.

25. *1948 Lambeth Conference Report* (London, 1948), pp. 84–5.

26. It also accords with the 'constellation model' of management identified by D. Schon, *Beyond the Stable State* (London, 1971), p. 108.

chapter 9

Word and sacrament

Signs and symbols

We communicate with one another by means of signs and symbols. A sign is only connected with the object that it signifies by convention. Thus a national flag does not actually resemble the nation which it symbolizes; it is only through convention that it signifies that nation. Similarly language (with the exception of onomatopoeic words) does not resemble the concepts and objects which it signifies: it is only by convention that meaning is conveyed, rather than through any likeness between the sound of words and the meaning of words. Symbols however are rather different: they do bear some likeness to that which they symbolize. Thus a symbol on a signpost consisting of an image of a highly stylized bent old couple does bear some resemblance to elderly people crossing a road of whom it is warning drivers to beware.[1]

Apart from telepathy (a comparatively rare phenomenon), we cannot communicate without using some physical means to convey our meaning by means of signs and symbols. We may employ writing to do this or we may use picture symbols. More commonly we use speech or some form of body language. Physical means of some kind are necessary for communication. The outward and material sign or symbol is the medium of inner meaning and signification. Because language is a sign with fairly precise meaning (words have a penumbra of meaning, but when they are put together in the form of a sentence, their meaning is usually fairly precise), language appeals to the mind, and brings a clear message. Symbols on the other hand are less precise: they conjure up pictures and images rather than ideas and concepts. They appeal not so much to the conscious mind as to the unconscious, and they are usually associated with feelings and emotions. Both signs and symbols need to be used in conjunction. In the Church of God they are represented by Word and Sacrament respectively.

The Word of God

God sometimes seems to speak to people in a personal way through an 'inner voice' in their consciousness. They feel under constraint to do this or that, or an idea occurs to them which they can only describe as God-given. Whatever be the source and mode of this inspiration, it is mediated by means of matter, in the sense that it passes through the brain, which is a very material object, and this can be observed indirectly by monitoring its electrical activity. Matter is the bearer of inner meaning. Again, many Christians believe that the Word of God can come to them through the pronouncements of the Church. Whatever be the source of this inspiration, it is mediated by the physical and material. It is the same with Scripture. Many people have experienced what they interpret as God speaking directly to them through reading the words of Scripture. Again, this is a 'mediated immediacy'. It is not the actual words of Scripture themselves which effect this: it is the act of referral of the meaning of a passage of Scripture to the personal or corporate situation of the person concerned. It is therefore inaccurate to describe the actual words of Scripture as the Words of God; but Scripture is the medium of God's Word when anyone appropriates the inner meaning of a passage and applies it to their own life.

Much of Scripture contains historical information, or is in the style of narrative, or in epistolary form. Some of it contains legal enactments, some is imaginative writing (called apocalyptic), some is gnomic (containing proverbs and words of wisdom), some is myth (in the sense that it expresses timeless truths in terms of stories which are not literally true but which are the only way in which these truths can be appropriated). Much of it is inspiring to read: some of it definitely is not.

What then separates Scripture from other writings? The books which comprise the Bible make no claim to inerrancy, and value judgements had to be made to decide which books should be regarded as authoritative. Some writings were included and some were excluded, and the period of selection, so far as the disputed books were concerned, lasted until the fourth century. Until the Council of Trent (1545–63) this was never the subject of a major conciliar decision. However the influence of Jerome and Augustine had already determined its contents in the West.[2] The Church, we have seen, cannot claim infallibility for its decisions (see p. 177). So it is not impossible that one or two wrong judgements may have been made in marginal cases.[3] The canon of Scripture was in fact decided by a growing consensus of opinion within the Church. Its authority is therefore not merely intrinsic but dependent on the Church which recognized it. This does not prevent Scripture from passing judgement on the Church, which it often has to do: indeed this may be regarded as one of its more important functions.

The Church took over the Jewish Bible (which Christians call the Old Testament), although in New Testament times its canon had not yet been firmly fixed. It was taken over because it was the Bible of the Jewish Christians who were the original members of the Church. Without it the New Testament could not be understood, and it contains the record of God's self-disclosure. Its contents contain some very inspiring passages, not least in the prophetic books. The actual reasons by which the Church decided the canon of the New Testament may seem questionable today (concentrating on what was believed to be written by apostolic authorship), but nonetheless churches authorized the New Testament to be read aloud in congregations for worship, because they recognized that its contents contained necessary knowledge about Jesus and the early Church, and that they reflected Christian attitudes, codes of behaviour and beliefs which generally speaking should be normative for the future. In this sense the Scriptures are the Word of God. Nonetheless its contents are not immediately recognizable as such, because our thought forms and assumptions are different from those which were prevalent when the Scriptures were written, and our language today has different nuances. So Scripture needs a hermeneutic, an interpretation. A preacher who interprets the Scriptures for today is attempting to do just that: his address is intended as the spoken Word of God.

Although there are overtones of feeling in the Word of God, it appeals primarily to the mind. Something more symbolic is needed to stir the unconscious, which is the seat of our deepest sentiments and feelings, and which is closest to divine inspiration.

Sacraments

If human beings communicate with one another by symbols as well as signs, it is hardly surprising that God should communicate with them by setting apart particular symbolic acts as his means of grace, and as signifying his relationship to them. This he has done through the institution of particular sacraments. Two are sacraments of the Gospel in as much as the Gospels specifically tell us that they were instituted by Christ. Other sacraments were authorized in his name by the Church. We shall deal here first with the former.

Sacraments have particular value, because they do not depend on the strength of our faith to be efficacious: they function *ex opere operato* (automatically) and only have to be received in faith to be operative. They are outward signs which give a pledge and assurance of God's grace. Just as a woman may not be moved by a spoken assurance of love so much as by an outward sign of affection such as a kiss or a hand squeeze, so human beings are more likely to be assured of God's presence and his help by an outward token rather than by inner conviction or written assurance. (In addition to the Church's sacraments, there are other church rites and customs which are called 'sacramentals' in as much as they operate through the same sacramental principles, but have not been specially set apart by God or authorized by the Church for this purpose.) Sacraments are described in the Church of England catechism as 'an outward and visible sign of an inward and spiritual grace given unto us, ordained by Christ himself, as a means whereby we receive the same, and a pledge to assure us thereof'.

Church buildings are sacramental, outward and visible structures which mediate spiritual and inner meaning. Larger churches are often themselves built in the form of a cross, to symbolize their Christian use. A sacrament points to a universal meaning. 'We need a symbol of the sacred in the midst of the secular to remind us that all is sacred and that we all have souls. The church is a symbol of celebration and joy and leisure and privacy, a sign of transcendence, a pointer of silence and tranquillity: a church is a sacred space, symbolizing to us the sacredness of all space.'[4]

The Church itself is sacramental.[5] As we have seen in the previous chapter, it takes the form of both organism and organization. It has a human and divine nature. Its outward and visible form is essential. There is no Church invisible. The Church consists of visible men and women and children. Yet it is not merely a body with certain external characteristics. It is a means for grace for its members. It has a spiritual nature and meaning. Membership of the Church is a source of assurance for Christian people. The Church is not only itself sacramental but it is also composed of human beings who are sacramental, for, as we have already noted, we use outward and visible means to express inner and spiritual meaning.

The whole universe is sacramental.[6] In any organism the highest and latest principle involved is the distinctive principle of its unity. Thus spirit is distinctive of humanity, because spirit is the highest principle of human personality and gives to it its unity. But the material aspects of the human person are vital if this principle of unity is to operate. A human being is a chemical compound, a biological organism, a living mind and a spirit. Mankind could not exist without each level of being. The lower levels are not abolished by the emergence of a higher level: they are essential aspects of our being. Spirit is expressed by means of the material. The same holds good for the universe as a whole. It is outward and visible and material; and this outward aspect expresses its value and meaning. It is because the universe is sacramental that politics and economics are so important in giving outward and visible expression to meaning and value.

God himself has created the universe so as to express his glory and to carry out his purposes through material means. The Eastern Orthodox Churches understand this sacramental aspect of the world very well, and it forms the basis of their attitude towards the environment: they hold that it must be respected and honoured because it is the outward expression of divine glory and divine purpose.

Baptism, sacrament of initiation

Baptism in the New Testament

Baptism is one of the sacraments of the Gospel, because it was commanded by the risen Jesus, according to the closing words of St Matthew's Gospel. We may perhaps interpret this to mean that the Apostles in the primitive Church felt impelled by the spirit of Christ to resume that practice of baptism which Jesus himself had sanctioned very early in his ministry. Jesus himself was baptized by his cousin John in the river Jordan, and this marked a key point in his earthly life. The report of a dove resting upon him represents the coming on him in a special way of the Spirit of God. He received an inner affirmation of his filial relationship to God as son of his heavenly Father ('Thou art my Son', Ps 2.7) and also of his vocation to be his servant ('in whom I am well pleased' from Isaiah 42.1). The occasion had many of the characteristics of a religious conversion. John's baptism was 'for the remission of sins', and although there is no indication that Jesus felt any personal guilt, as a Jew he would have known the need for corporate repentance on the part of all Jews: 'We do well to conform in this way with all that God requires' (Matt 3.15). It was a moment of deep religious experience of the Divine. It marked a decisive change in his life-style. It communicated to him a strong sense of vocation. When in the primitive Church the practice of Christian baptism began, it was understood as sharing in Christ's baptism. As Paul reminded his readers, and as the 'Nicene' creed maintains, there is only 'one baptism'.[7]

It is reported in the Gospels that John, when he baptized Jesus, affirmed the priority of Jesus over himself and said that he (John) was baptizing with water, but that Jesus would baptize with the Holy Spirit. It is claimed by some charismatics today that this implies that Christian baptism has nothing to do with water, but is a purely spiritual experience, 'the baptism of the Spirit'. This is to misunderstand the meaning of John's words. He himself preached baptism for the forgiveness of sins; but he foresaw that through Jesus baptism would *also* be accompanied by the Holy Spirit, just as Jesus himself had received the Spirit at his baptism. An example of this is given in Acts 19, when the story is told of some converts at Ephesus who had received John's baptism but who had not so much as heard whether there was any Holy Spirit. (It seems likely that John's movement was widespread: certainly its influence was felt outside Judaea and Gaililee.)

After Jesus' own baptism by John, he joined his cousin's holiness movement, but after a time he left him and set up on his own. Some disciples moved from John to Jesus, and (according to St John's Gospel) they continued baptizing people: indeed at one stage they were baptizing more people than John. But we are specifically told that Jesus himself did not baptize, and it seems that after these baptisms at the inauguration of his ministry, the practice died out until after he had died and had been raised from the dead.

The use of water for ritual purposes was common among the Jews.[8] Circumcision for males marked initiation into Judaism, but it was in New Testament times accompanied by a baptismal bath. For women this was the only outward ceremony. Water was also then extensively used for ritual cleansing among Jews, and ritual baths were important in the life of the sect based at Qumran by the Dead Sea whose scrolls were unearthed earlier this century. Water is an obvious symbol of cleansing, hence its use in connection with the forgiveness of sins in prophetic literature; and this forgiveness of sins forms part of its meaning in Christian adult baptism. But the symbolism is much deeper than that. Baptism symbolized death and resurrection. Jesus is recorded as saying that his baptism lay ahead, clearly referring to his coming death. At his own baptism he went down under the water in the river Jordan and rose up again to the surface, which was understood as symbolizing his future death and resurrection. This highlights an important aspect of baptism. It marks the gift of God of a new status which is already given, but not fully realized. The Christian life is a process of 'becoming what you are', and baptism at its sacramental inauguration symbolizes at the start what will be increasingly realized during the Christian life but only fully achieved at the end by actual death and subsequent resurrection. And so Christian baptism is essentially eschatological, with the future brought into the present, but with fulfilment awaiting until the End.

Baptism marks entry into the Christian Church, as Peter's speech at Pentecost makes clear. It is a sacramental incorporation into Christ. Much of the language of the New Testament epistles is baptismal in origin. Indeed it has been claimed that 1 Peter as a whole is a baptismal homily.[9] Many images are used in connection with baptism. It is a washing away of sin. It marks rebirth and regeneration, with the baptismal waters symbolizing the life-giving waters of the womb. It is an anointing, because anointing is itself a symbol for the giving of the Spirit – the word Christ means anointed (with the Holy Spirit). Baptism means entry to the body of Christ. It is 'Christ's way of circumcision', the fulfilment of the 'circumcision of the heart' which marks out the true Jew. As Jews were 'baptized into Moses' so Christians were baptized into Christ. Baptism means 'putting on Christ', just as those who were baptized emerged from the waters to put on new garments. Baptism makes people 'sons of God' by sharing in Christ's sonship. Baptism is a 'sealing' for the day of redemption, a word which is borrowed from the Jewish rite of circumcision, and which shows the eschatological thrust of the sacrament, making its recipients inheritors of the Kingdom of God and heirs of everlasting life.

Baptism is to be regarded as the sacramental expession of 'justification through faith', as was made clear by St Paul when he wrote: 'You were washed, you were justified, you were sanctified', where the words used all belong together. The New Testament doctrine of baptism without doubt implies a sacramental act which functions *ex opere operato* (on its own account). It needs to be received with faith, but it does not depend upon faith: it rests solely on God's free gift mediated through the sacrament.

Infant baptism

The question of personal faith raises both the question of infant baptism, and also that of rigorism. In New Testament times the solidarity of the family was very strong, so that Paul claimed, in the case of mixed marriages, that the faith of one partner sanctified the other. It has been held that so strong was this solidarity that when adults were baptized, children who had been born after their parents' conversion were baptized, but those born earlier did not need the sacrament, but became Christians at their parents' baptism, being regarded as sanctified by them.[10] There is evidence from the second century that the early Church had no doubts on this matter: all infants of Christian families were baptized.

Those who object to infant baptism today believe that a personal profession of faith on the part of every baptizand is a prerequisite. They deplore the splitting of the rite into infant baptism and confirmation. They are not clear what infant baptism is intended to effect.[11] The majority of the churches, however, prefer to follow the example of the primitive Church and to continue to baptize infants. The act symbolizes God coming to the help of humanity before a human being is capable of responding. The infant has no faith of its own: it depends on the faith of its parents as it depends on them for everything else, as well as on the faith of godparents and indeed the whole Church. Most churches, however, agree that, after infant baptism, a further rite is required when the infant grows up and is able to make a personal profession of faith. This is not so in the Eastern Orthodox Churches, which have not split Christian initiation into two. Anointing with chrism forms part of the one rite of initiation, and Holy Communion is administered to a child from the start.

Rigorism

There are those who require more than profession of faith on the part of parents and godparents. They also set minimum requirements, such as attendance at baptismal instruction and/or attendance at church worship in order to qualify for their children's baptism. But God alone knows the secrets of all hearts. Faith cannot be judged by 'good works' of worship or instruction. A minister is not set apart by the Church to make personal judgements about eligibility for membership: only God can do that. Certainly it is a minister's duty to warn with the utmost seriousness those involved that they must not take the name of the Lord in vain. People however are responsible before God for their own actions, and to rebuff parents who wish their children to be baptized seems to them tantamount to telling them that they are not good enough for their child to become 'a member of Christ, a child of God and an inheritor of the kingdom of God' (Church of England catechism). But the Christian Gospel is Good News precisely for those who know that they are not good enough to deserve it.

Baptism and confirmation

In the primitive Church Christian initiation, after a long period of preparation, consisted of total immersion in baptism, laying on of hands and anointing with chrism (blessed oil), carried out in the presence of the bishop. In the contemporary Church, until the recent past, most people were baptized in infancy. The original rite has been split into two. Infant baptism is followed later by the laying on of hands with prayer, when a person has reached the age of discretion and can answer for himself or herself about their Christian commitment. In the Church of England this rite has served as the rite of admission to Holy Communion, but this is not the case in the Roman Catholic Church, and in the Church of England permission may now be given by the bishop for admission to Holy Communion before confirmation. Confirmation is a rite of passage to Christian maturity in which confirmands *confirm* the promises which they made, or which were made for them, at their baptism; and it is also the occasion for a gift of the Holy Spirit for the *confirming* or strengthening of the person being confirmed.

There are however those who hold a different theological view about baptism and confirmation.[12] They understand the former as a preparation for the latter. They hold that it is not until the laying on of hands with prayer that the Holy Spirit is imparted to the believer. Neither Christian experience nor the New Testament nor the witness of the early Church is on their side.[13] Chrism was used for many purposes, and did not necessarily imply a gift of the Spirit. It was employed not only for Christian initiation but also for Christian healing. So too with the laying on of hands, which was also employed for setting apart individuals for a particular ministry. It was also used in the case of the converts in Acts 19 who had not so much as heard of the Holy Spirit. When Paul did lay his hands on them, we are told that they received the Holy Spirit. There is no suggestion that this was normal practice. Special measures were needed in special circumstances. The rite of confirmation grew up because with the advent of infant baptism, some further rite was needed to mark Christian maturity, and the laying on of hands which formed the matter of the sacrament has New Testament precedent and was part of the primitive rite of Christian initiation. The laying on of hands with prayer in Confirmation is a sacrament, but it is not a sacrament of the Gospel because it was not enjoined by Jesus.

The meaning of baptism for today

The meaning of baptism is given in part by the symbolism which accompanies it; washing, dying and rising with Christ, regeneration not in the waters of a mother's womb, but in the womb of mother Church.

This symbolism, however, does not in itself solve all the problems connected with the rite. There are two difficulties which are properly felt. How can the sacrament be understood to function *ex opere operato* (automatically), with spiritual regeneration effected by immersion in (or sprinkling with) water, and the invocation of the threefold name of God? Adults who are baptized have already become 'spiritually regenerate' before their baptism. Baptism for them is an outward sign which marks the final and public step taken to join the Church. (For Jews it is not spiritual regeneration that separates them from the Jewish community, but the final and decisive step of baptism, because that marks formal entry into the Church.) Spiritual regeneration or rebirth seems almost magical if it can be effected not by prior conversion but by the right words being said and the right ritual carried out, even though this is done in faith.

Calvinists reject the efficacy of baptism for a different reason. They believe that God has chosen his elect and that the working of his grace in them is irresistible, so that for them baptism only sets the seal on those predestined to salvation. However Evangelicals in general have a simpler ground for thinking of baptism as a bare symbol rather than an efficacious sign. It is conversion that matters, and it is the grace of God that makes conversion possible; while baptism is the outward act which strengthens and formalizes this new relationship. In fact the truth lies between the two extremes. Baptism is efficacious if it is asked for in faith, in the sense that it enacts sacramentally what has been begun spiritually, and the very fact that it is an outward and visible sign both strengthens the faith of the baptizand and is a public witness to that faith.

The second difficulty specifically concerns infant baptism. How can this be given the same meaning as adult baptism? Baptism according to the New Testament comprises complete Christian initiation. But infant baptism is not the same as the decisive new start of an adult who is baptized, so New Testament doctrine needs to be developed to cover this. We have already seen that there is no 'original sin' to be washed away (see p. 61). God loves all children equally, so how can baptized infants be 'inheritors of the Kingdom of God' in contrast to unbaptized children? What is the difference in status or in reception of grace between a baptized infant and an unbaptized child who share the same loving father and mother? The future life of all baptized infants depends on their upbringing, their parents and many other factors. Infant baptism is only an efficacious sign in as much as on a public occasion parents formally and openly state their faith and promise to give their children a Christian upbringing, and the child, on formally entering the Church, has symbolically and sacramentally died and risen with Christ (although this sacramental symbolism is greatly blurred by the use of sprinkling rather than immersion). The sacrament starts the child on the Christian way. It needs to be completed by a lively faith on the part of the child when it is sufficiently adult to do this. The sacrament is identical for adults and infants; but its meaning needs to be modified in the latter case.

The eucharist

The Last Supper

The Last Supper which Jesus shared with his closest disciples is recorded in the three Synoptic Gospels (but not in the Fourth Gospel) and also by Paul in his first letter to the Corinthians. What precisely happened on this occasion is impossible to determine, because of significant differences in the various accounts. We cannot even be sure whether it was a Passover meal, since the Fourth Gospel, possibly in order to describe Jesus' death as a passover sacrifice, places his death (not the Last Supper as in the Synoptics) on the same day as the celebration of the Passover. If the Fourth Evangelist is more historical than the Synoptic Gospels in this respect, the Last Supper, although it would have naturally had overtones of the Passover to be celebrated the following evening, would have been a communal meal of Jesus' *chaburah* (religious fellowship), such as was common in those days.[14]

There are also some difficulties, which Christians as a whole have not always appreciated, in attributing to Jesus the words which identify the wine with his blood. The Jews had a particular horror of drinking blood, derived from the strong prohibitions of the Old Testament. Even a symbolic reference would have been very difficult.[15] It is possible that Jesus, who elsewhere used the metaphor of a cup to refer to his death (Mark 10.38), did not actually use the image of blood in what he said over the cup, but that this was added very early on in a Hellenistic milieu in order to make explicit that the eucharist meant sharing sacramentally in Jesus' death. The longer version of the Last Supper in St Luke's Gospel, which includes a saying over the cup after supper as well as before the supper, suggests that this may have been the case, with the words: 'This is the new covenant sealed by my blood' (Luke 22.20).

Another problem concerns the command to continue to repeat the rite in remembrance of Jesus. Such a command is found only in Paul's account; but it is probable that elsewhere, where it is not found, it was simply assumed. All the accounts are likely to have been influenced by the liturgical rites of the churches from which the Evangelists and St Paul wrote.

It has sometimes been said that Paul and not Jesus instituted the eucharist, and that Paul moulded the accounts of the Last Supper so that it became a means of sharing in the covenant sacrifice of Christ, with the result that the commemoration became similar to one of the rites of the mystery religions by which believers were incorporated into the god. This is very improbable. Paul makes clear in writing to the Corinthians that he is standing within a tradition, and not inaugurating one. It is impossible to believe that all the Synoptic accounts are the result of Pauline innovation. But it is exceedingly improbable that Jesus intended the Church that came after him to go on celebrating this rite for long, because it is clear from remarks made at the Last Supper that he hoped the Messianic Banquet in the Kingdom of God would become a reality very soon. He was mistaken in that expectation, and the Church was right to continue to use his institution of the eucharist as a way of sacramental representation of what God had done through him for mankind.

We shall never know exactly what Jesus said to his disciples at the Last Supper. If there was a development by the Church in the direction indicated above, this is not of great moment. The rite itself stems from Jesus himself in which the past events of his death and resurrection are brought forward into the present – this is what is meant by the word *anamnesis* (do this in *remembrance* of me) – and in which Christians are brought into union with one another and with Christ himself. The rite also looks forward to the future consummation in the Kingdom of God, so that when we share in the eucharist we have a glimpse of heaven.

The eucharist has developed into the most important service among the mainstream Christian churches, and indeed it was the only rite (according to Paul) which Jesus himself specifically commanded. The commemoration first was made at common meals among the Christian congregations, and it only developed later into a separate rite divorced from eating and drinking, possibly on account of the kind of abuse to which this led and to which Paul referred in his letter to the Corinthians. The various names for the rite show the difference of emphasis on its meaning among different churches today; the Lord's Supper, the Liturgy, the Holy Mysteries, the Mass, the Holy Communion. There have been endless controversies over eucharistic doctrine. It was rightly regarded as a great achievement when the Anglican–Roman Catholic International Commission produced in 1971 a report on the eucharist unanimously agreed by its Anglican and Roman Catholic representatives. Here we shall concentrate on three areas only; the nature of the eucharistic action, the connection between the eucharistic elements and the presence of Christ, and authority to preside at the eucharistic celebration.

The eucharistic action

The eucharist is essentially an action. In form it now contains two services put together. The first part is the ministry of the Word, with prayers and Bible-reading, and the second part forms the ministry of the sacrament. The latter comprises a fourfold action; offering the elements, blessing them, breaking the bread and pouring out the wine, and giving back the consecrated elements to the people. This is a liturgical and sacramental representation of what Jesus himself did according to the Gospel accounts of the institution of the rite at the Last Supper. Much more doubtful however has been the recent attempt to portray this as a fourfold action representing the death and resurrection of Christ; his self-offering, his consecration by God's acceptance of his offering, his body broken on the Cross and his blood outpoured, and God's giving back to him his life renewed in resurrection. It is now realized that such an interpretation is both novel and far-fetched.

Where then does the action lie? It is a service of offering, usually conceived in terms of sacrifice. There is offering of bread and wine at the offertory to be used as the 'matter' of the sacrament. There is the commemoration of Christ's self-offering on the cross, the 'one perfect and sufficient sacrifice, oblation . . . for the sins of the whole world'. There is the grateful offering of the consecrated elements to God, 'we offer you through him this sacrifice of praise and thanksgiving'. There is the offering of the congregation, renewed through sacramental communion with Christ, at the end of the service, 'through him we offer our souls and bodies to be a living sacrifice . . .'. What is the relationship between all these different forms of offering?

It used to be generally believed (both within the Roman Catholic Church and by its critics outside it) that, according to Roman doctrine, the eucharist is a repetition of the self-offering of Christ on the cross. But if this view were ever held by theologians, it is so no longer. The ARCIC report makes clear that 'there can be no repetition of or addition to what was then accomplished once for all by Christ'.[16] Yet it is not merely a commemoration, comparable to the 'three hours devotion' on Good Friday. *Anamnesis*, as we have seen, means not just remembering the past but bringing it into the present. The self-offering of Christ is neither continued nor repeated in the eucharist. Its essence contains the representation of Christ's self-offering not in the way in which Christ accomplished it once for all, but in a *sacramental* mode. The offertory has significance only in the offering of bread and wine to enable this sacramental representation to take place, and the occasion when the worshippers make their offering of alms and prayers. The bread and the wine are offered to God in the prayer of thanksgiving and we pray to God to 'accept this sacrifice of praise and thanksgiving': and finally in the closing prayer the congregation join themselves in union with Christ's self-offering.

The presence of Christ in the eucharist

There has been great controversy over the mode of Christ's presence in the eucharist. There is no doubt about the reality of his presence, but differences appear about the mode of his presence, spiritual or sacramental, and about where he is present. Those who regard it as a mere commemoration believe there is nothing more than his universal spiritual presence. Others locate his sacramental presence in the elements themselves, while still others regard Christ as spiritually present only in the faithful reception of the elements by the worshippers (receptionism). Since presence was associated with being and existence, the mode of Christ's presence was usually discussed in terms of substance. This was supported by the 'words of institution': 'This *is* my body', 'This *is* my blood'. However in the original Aramaic (or Hebrew) in which Jesus originally spoke these words, there was no verb to join together 'this' and 'my body/blood'. Jesus would have simply said: 'This – my body'. This could have meant 'This is my body', but it could equally well have meant: 'This has the value of my body' or even 'This symbolizes my body'.

It has however been generally assumed that Jesus intended to identify the bread with his body. What happens then at consecration? Lutherans believe that the substance of Christ is added to the substance of the bread and the wine after consecration ('consubstantiation'), while Roman Catholics believe – or used to believe – that at the words of consecration the 'accidents' of bread and wine remain (that is to say, all its outward and phenomenological aspects) but the substance (inner reality) is miraculously changed into the substance of Christ (transubstantiation). However a footnote to the ARCIC report states that the word is used in contemporary Roman Catholic theology not to describe the mode of

Christ's presence, but 'the fact of Christ's presence and the mysterious and radical change that takes place'.[17]

Even this seems rather like magic. Although consecration takes the form of a prayer and relies on the faithfulness of God, it is necessary for a certain formula to be used by a duly authorized person empowered to officiate in order to guaranee the authenticity of the sacrament. This produces automatically a mysterious and radical change in bread and wine. But if the right formula has not been used, and the celebrant has not been duly authorized, there can be no certainty that he has been empowered, and that a change in the elements has taken place. If the right words and the right officiant are needed to produce a change in the elements of bread and wine, we have to ask whether this is compatible with our doctrine of God, who works through the natural laws of his creation. Is every celebration of the eucharist a miracle in which these natural laws are breached?

The words of consecration are 'performative' in the sense that they do accomplish something, just as the words in the wedding service, 'I thee wed', are performative in as much as thereafter the couple concerned are married. But just what do these words accomplish? Is it not possible that God puts a new value on the bread and the wine in response to these words of the eucharistic prayer, so that when consecrated they have the value of Christ ('transvaluation'), or alternatively that God places a new meaning on the elements ('transignification')? There then would be no change in the elements as such; but, once consecrated, they would have this new value or meaning placed upon them by God, which they would continue to have (as people remain married after the words 'I thee wed').

If the eucharistic elements are not all required for consumption during the liturgy, whether they have been changed in themselves, or whether they are bearers of a new value or meaning, it is appropriate that they should be consumed immediately the service is ended, or if they are reserved for future use that they should be treated with all respect. In private worship they are sometimes exposed for adoration, provided that the emphasis of such adoration is focused on the eucharistic action which formed the reason for their consecration, so that they are used for the worship of Christ who died and rose again for us, and do not become objects of worship in themselves. Similarly if in the eucharist the bread runs out in the distribution, it is not sufficient merely to take more bread, but once again it needs to be given the value and meaning of Christ in response to a suitable prayer.

Is Christ truly present in this way? When a new value and a new meaning is put on a piece of metal so that it becomes a coin, it has a permanent new value and meaning. It *is* a coin, not just a piece of base metal. If in the sight of God and in the conviction of worshippers a new value has been put on the bread and the wine, it has a permanent new meaning and status. It is not a mere symbol. The power of Christ works through it, because it has the value of Christ. When the eucharist is celebrated in a place which is plagued by hauntings of the past or by apparently poltergeistic activities, the trouble normally dies down, which is a corroboration of the conviction that the consecrated bread are wine are not just symbols, but are potent with the power of Christ.

The eucharist remains an unfathomable mystery, and no theory can plumb its depths, so that there is truth in the ditty attributed to Queen Elizabeth I:

His was the Word that spake it:
He took the bread and brake it:
And what that Word did make it,
I do believe and take it.

Transvaluation and transignification do however point the way to an interpretation which is both credible and faithful to the evidence and consonant with the tradition of the Church.

The president of the eucharist

The contemporary habit of concelebration may result in difficulty in knowing just who are celebrating, or even how the celebrants may be recognized. Concelebrants may stand at the Holy Table with the president, but so also may servers. Concelebrants do not always hold a hand aloft during the prayer of thanksgiving, they do not always stand apart from the congregation, they are not always specially robed, and sometimes they speak no words. In any case none of these – stance, hand-raising, robes or spoken words by themselves – constitutes the act of celebrating the eucharist. It seems strange to reduce this in essence to a matter of intention, but in the light of present practice, that seems to be the case so far as concelebrants are concerned.

However there is no doubt about who is presiding at a celebration. The eucharist is such a solemn service that it is thought inappropriate that any church member should preside at its celebration. Almost all mainstream churches require authorization before a person may celebrate Holy Communion. In a move towards lay celebration, some people press that lay people should be specially authorized to do this. But since ordination constitutes this authorization, this is tantamount to requiring more lay people to be ordained. Any other authorization than ordination would mean two separate rites for the same end, which would make for utter confusion.

It is sometimes said (and it is in fact authoritative Roman Catholic doctrine) that the person presiding at the eucharist acts *in persona Christi*. This phrase needs unpacking. It could mean that the celebrant impersonates Christ, and must therefore share his gender, and generally resemble him. This is absurd, if only because we have no idea what Jesus looked like, and impersonation always involves pretence. The more natural meaning is that a celebrant acts as the representative of Christ. But this needs further definition. In what way does such a person represent Christ? He cannot repeat the 'once only, once for all' self-offering of Christ. It was Christ and no one else who freely offered himself in obedience to God on the Cross. The celebrant at the eucharist presides over the sacramental representation of that self-offering by the use of bread and wine. He therefore does not *himself* represent Christ, but he presides over a rite in which *the bread and the wine* represent Christ, and these are used for a sacramental representation of Christ's self-offering of himself to the Father.[18] A priest is not given at ordination any magical powers which enable him to manufacture Christ's body and blood from bread and wine. On the contrary, he leads the prayers of the congregation to ask God to consecrate the elements. At ordination authorization is given to him to preside over this central rite of the Christian Church whereby people share in the self-offering of Christ and are identified with him afresh through their reception of the sacrament of his Body and Blood.

Other sacraments

The Council of Florence (1430) fixed the number of sacraments at seven, following Peter Lombard and Thomas Aquinas. (One medieval theologian had suggested thirty!) The two sacraments of baptism and the eucharist from early times were given a special place. Of the remaining five, we have already considered confirmation in connection with baptism. As for marriage, according to traditional theology the couple enact the sacrament themselves by pledging their troth to each other for life in the sight of God. It is however difficult to find any biblical authority for regarding this pledge as itself a sacrament. St Paul certainly called marriage 'a great mystery', but this does not in itself constitute the act of marriage as a sacrament. Marriage is best not itself described as a sacrament, but the married state should be regarded as sacramental, as the spouses through their outward and visible bodies express to each other the inner meaning of their love and commitment to each other.

Penance is also classed by some as a sacrament. Without doubt private confession with absolution has brought peace and relief to millions of people, but this in itself does not constitute it as a sacrament. Again, it is not possible to find scriptural authority for regarding it as such. Its sacramental 'form' would be the spoken voice of the priest, which is material in the sense that it emits vibrations which impinge on the auditory nerves, just as the words spoken by bride and bridegroom at the heart of the marriage service are believed to supply the 'form' of the sacrament of marriage. In the other sacraments the form is visible rather than audible (e.g. water, or bread and wine, or the laying on of hands).

Orders are sacramentally given with the laying on of hands; but it is not easy to find any biblical warrant for regarding sacramental ordination as laid down by Christ. Jewish elders were ordained with the laying on of hands, and it seems probable that the Church continued the custom. Nonetheless the sacrament of holy orders has form and matter similar to those of the other sacraments, and grace is certainly imparted at ordination, so that it is rightly regarded as a sacrament. According to traditional belief, baptism, confirmation and ordination leave an indelible character on the soul. They certainly cannot be repeated; but it is best to see them in terms of a person's vocation rather than as implanting a permanent character on the soul (see p. 213).

There remains to be considered unction. This used to be reserved for the deathbed, but it is now generally accepted to be best understood as the sacrament of healing, in accordance with Scripture (James 5.14). Unction and the laying on of hands are customarily used at healing services or at the eucharist. Many people have received much blessing from their use, and on occasion extraordinary relief has been reported. There has been in the Church as a whole a remarkable recovery of the healing ministry. Sometimes cures have seemed miraculous; but it must be remembered that the body contains within itself remarkable powers of self-recovery, and when instantaneous healings occur, we are witnessing a remarkable speeding up, under the influence of divine grace, of the natural processes of healing. In some species there are remarkable capabilities of regeneration even from serious bodily loss, and it seems that on occasion this can happen with the human species under the impulse of divine healing. Sacramental healing is only one mode of spiritual healing. Extraordinary recoveries have been reported through prayer or meditation.

The need for sacraments

Sacraments are badly needed today, when signs have largely taken the place of symbols, and when modern technology requires intelligence rather than imagination. 'How great is the need for symbol which reaches down to the depths of the racial unconscious, yet stretches up towards the height of the transcendent, which comes to terms with the past estrangement yet leaps towards the future reconciliation. Wherever symbols exist today, life is still open, progress is still possible. And because God has not left himself without witness, they do in fact exist in many forms and in many contexts.'[19] Sacraments are special symbols, given to us by God through the Church as means of grace, binding us to him and to one another.

Notes

1. See E. R. Bevan, *Symbolism and Belief* (London, 1958), pp. 11ff.

2. See A. Souter, *The Text and Canon of the New Testament* (London, 1913; 1954 edn), pp. 167–80.

3. See K. Aland, *The Problem of the New Testament Canon* (London, 1952).

4. H. Montefiore, *Can Man Survive? – The Question Mark and Other Essays* (London, 1970), p. 163.

5. See H. de Lubac, *The Splendour of the Church* (London, 1956), p. 147.

6. See W. Temple, 'The sacramental universe' in *Nature, Man and God* (London, 1934), pp. 473–95.

7. O. Cullmann, *Baptism in the New Testament* (London, 1950), pp. 19–20.

8. See W. Flemington, *The New Testament Doctrine of Baptism* (London, 1948), pp. 3–11.

9. See F. L. Cross, *1 Peter* (London, 1954).

10. See O. Cullmann, *op. cit.*, p. 23; J. Jeremias, *The Origins of Infant Baptism* (London, 1963).

11. See R. H. White, *The Biblical Doctrine of Initiation* (London, 1960), pp. 296–300.

12. See G. Dix, *The Theology of Baptism in Relation to Confirmation* (London, 1946)

13. See G. W. H. Lampe, *The Seal of the Spirit* (London, 1951).

14. See J. Jeremias, *The Eucharistic Words of Jesus* (Oxford, 1955), who argues that the Last Supper was a Passover meal.

15. See J. Fenton, 'Eating people', *Theology* XCIV. 762 (November/December 1991), pp. 414–23.

16. 'Eucharistic Doctrine', II.5 in ARCIC, *The Final Report* (London, 1982), p. 13.

17. *Ibid.*, p. 14.

18. See J. Baker, 'Eucharistic presidency and women's ordination', *Theology* (September 1985), pp. 359ff.

19. D. W. Dillistone, *Christianity and Symbolism* (London, 1953), p. 304.

chapter 10

Ministry in the Church

The beginnings of the ministry

When we think of 'holy orders' today we naturally think of the contemporary Church, with its organized life, its formal ordinations, its rules and regulations for the clergy. It is hard for us to imagine the situation of the primitive Church. That situation has been well described as follows:

It is difficult for us to appreciate the outlook of those who could describe themselves as people who 'were enlightened and tasted of the heavenly gift, and were made partakers of the Holy Ghost, and tasted the good word of God and the powers of the age to come'. They had passed through the tremendous mystery of initiation; they had, in an effective symbol, died and risen from the grave; they had passed through the deep to taste the milk and honey of the promised land, and, sealed as Christ's possession, had taken the spiritual food of the Messianic banquet . . . In such an *ecclesia* of the redeemed, constitutional questions of ministerial authority can hardly have possessed any ultimate importance. The Church on earth was an earnest of the coming Kingdom. Ministries it had in plenty and ministers by whom they were exercised, but all alike were gifts and endowments of the Spirit. The Spirit is the energizing principle of the whole body.[1]

Nonetheless, as Paul found out to his cost at Corinth, questions of ministerial authority did arise, when people began to doubt his authority as an Apostle. Two particular characteristics of New Testament ministry stand out; that of *apostellein* (and its related words including *apostolos* or apostle) meaning to 'send out', and *diakonein* (and its cognate forms including *diakonos* or deacon) meaning to 'serve'. The Son was sent into the world by the Father, and in turn the Son sent out his *apostoloi* with delegated power. (The word *apostolos* translates the Hebrew *shaliach*, which can mean an accredited envoy.)[2] The Twelve were Apostles, but apart from the special case of Paul, and the appointment of Matthias to take the place of Judas Iscariot, there is no real evidence that the ministry of the original Apostles was continued, particularly as it was a prerequisite for the office to have seen the Lord. Paul in Romans 16.7 does mention as apostles Andronicus and Junia: there is some textual confusion here, probably because Junia was a woman (see p. 176); but since they are not mentioned at the head of the list of people to whom Paul sent greetings, it is unlikely that they were of the same standing as the Apostles. People were 'sent' to preach the Gospel and probably these are the 'apostles' to whom Paul here refers. Envoys were set apart for particular work. The act of 'sending' out apostles was naturally connected with 'authority', for there was no point in sending them unless they had authority to carry out what they were sent to do. Being 'sent' was a form of 'service', both to God and to fellow Christians, after the pattern of Jesus who was sent by his Father and who described himself as a servant. The word 'servant' is used in the New Testament in connection with all sorts of Christian service, including the service of the Word, although later it became associated with the 'service of tables' and the administrative service of 'deacons'.

Leaders were required in local churches, and the Apostles no doubt appointed them on their travels when leaving the churches they had founded, but there is no evidence that the eldership was restricted to those whom the Apostles ordained. It is probable that from the beginning these 'elders' were appointed by the local churches with the laying on of hands, after the Jewish custom; but there is no evidence to suggest that, in the case of churches founded by others, the elders had to be later 'ordained' by an Apostle. When the task of pastoral oversight was to the forefront, these elders were probably called overseers or *episkopoi*. It is exceedingly improbable that all *episkopoi* were appointed by one of the Twelve. There are differing theories about how a chief overseer was appointed, whether from 'below' by the 'college' of elders or whether 'from above' by an Apostle or his deputy (e.g. Titus or Timothy), or by either: we just do not know.[3] Paul had not visited Colossae when he sent them the letter included in the New Testament canon, and since he was scrupulous not to trespass on another's territory, we may assume that no other Apostle had been there. Presumably they appointed their own elders. Yet Paul did not cast any doubt upon the authority of those who ministered there.

There is a tunnel period; and at the end of this period there emerged the threefold order of *episkopos* (bishop), *presbyteros* (presbyter or priest) and *diakonos*. As the ARCIC report on *Ministry and Ordination* puts it: 'Just as the formation of the canon of the New Testament was a process incomplete until the second half of the second century, so also the full emergence of the threefold ministry of bishop, presbyter and deacon required a longer period than the apostolic age. Thereafter this threefold structure became universal in the Church.'[4]

The apostolic ministry today

The actual form of the ministries of the New Testament are of little interest to us, because they were created by the Spirit to meet the needs of the time. What is important is that the essentials of New Testament ministry are reflected in the orders of the contemporary Church. What are the essentials of the apostolic ministry? This again is well expressed in the ARCIC report:

In the New Testament a variety of images is used to describe the functions of this minister. He is Servant both of Christ and of the Church. As herald and ambassador he is an authoritative representative of Christ and proclaims his message of reconciliation. As teacher he explains and applies the word of God to the community. As shepherd he exercises pastoral care and guides the flock. He is a steward who may only provide for the household of God what belongs to Christ. He is to be an example both in holiness and in compassion.[5]

All these functions belong to the apostolic ministry today.

It was only natural that ministers, who preached the word of reconciliation and were responsible for the unity of the local church, should preside at the celebration of the sacrament of the eucharist, and no one else could so act without their consent. They 'offered the gifts', to use the phrase employed in the apostolic Church. There is evidence for this as early as the time of Ignatius (martyred AD 107). In some cases no doubt they also exercised the ministry of prophecy in the church, but this was usually a separate gift of the Spirit. There is always a certain tension between exercising both the gift of prophecy and the pastoral ministry at the same time.

The Christian ministers, whether called *presbyteroi* or *episkopoi*, obviously exercised a vital role in the Church. They formed the focus of the local congregation. Authority was exercised through them, even though they were servants of the congregation. It could not be said that the local *ekklesia* depended on them, because it depended on the Holy Spirit who energized it and give it life, and through whom were received the gifts of faith, love and hope. But without the elders, the church would have been formless and without leadership. The whole church was priestly, in the sense that all its members formed, in the words of 1 Peter, 'a chosen race, a royal priesthood, a dedicated nation, and a people claimed by God for his own' (1 Pet 2.9). Those called to be *presbyteroi* or *episkopoi* of the local congregation needed special gifts to act as leaders, just as those called to other special ministries within the congregation need their special gifts of the Spirit to carry these out. As the ARCIC report puts it, 'their ministry is not an extension of the common Christian ministry, but belongs to another realm of the gifts of the Spirit'.

Originally there were in a local congregation these presbyters or *episkopoi*, that is, elders or overseers. Later one person was appointed to be the chief presbyter. He became the *episkopos* or local bishop, surrounded by his elders. The bishop then acted as the equivalent of the parish priest of today's local church. It was not until later that the *episkopos* had charge of more than one congregation (or parish as we would say today). Presbyters then took charge of the local congregation, and became the representatives of the bishop. Meanwhile the office of deacon emerged with special liturgical functions, and with great ecclesiastical but little spiritual authority. It was a permanent office.

Authority lay with the bishops, who emphasized the unity of the whole Church by joining together to ordain another person into the episcopal order. Similarly within a diocese, the bishop, who carried out the ordination of presbyters, emphasized the unity of the diocese by joining with his presbyters at the ordination of new presbyters. Originally he presided over baptisms on Easter Eve. The bishop was the outward link between dioceses and he was the focus of unity within a diocese. In this way bishops witnessed to the unity of the Church. This was part of their apostolic ministry in the primitive Church;[6] and it still is today, although the present disunity means that their witness is confined to the particular denomination to which they belong; Roman Catholic, Old Catholic, Eastern Orthodox or Anglican. (In some parts of the world there are Methodist, Lutheran and even Presbyterian bishops, although similar claims would not be made for them as a focus of unity within the apostolic succession.)

As the Church grew, various dioceses grouped themselves in what today might be called 'provinces' under a particular bishop, and later under an archbishop. These further arrangements helped in the maintenance of Church discipline and in the pastoral oversight of the senior ministers of the Church, but it did not produce a new 'order'; it was a matter of jurisdiction rather than theology.

The importance of the Bishop of Rome stemmed from two factors: he was the successor of Peter and he was bishop of the capital city of the Empire. This led to a primacy of ecclesiastical jurisdiction (and in time to a claim of universal jurisdiction), and later to a primacy of spiritual authority. We have already noted that the Petrine texts in the New Testament say nothing about the transference of Petrine authority to his successors (see p. 178). Many holders of the papal office have not shown themselves to be 'servants of the servants of God'. They have behaved rather like temporal rulers, acting as dictators in a secular state. Claims of authoritative utterance ill accord with the actual record, in which we find later Bishops of Rome contradicting authoritative statements of earlier ones. So-called infallible definitions of the faith are not promised in Scripture, nor can they always be shewn to stem from scriptural truth. A particular incumbent of the papal office may be very highly respected and even venerated by those outside the Roman Catholic Church, who may greatly value his spirituality and pastoral ministry, but at the same time such people cannot accept the ecclesiastical and spiritual claims of the Bishop of Rome.

At first sight it would seem helpful to have one person who could represent the universal Church. There were theological grounds as well as jurisdictional needs that led to the Bishop of Rome's being regarded not merely as *primus inter pares* (first among equals) among bishops, but as the ruler of the universal Church. As the Church grew, there was need for a focus of unity for the Western Church, just as the Patriarch of Constantinople fulfilled this role for the Eastern Church. The need was then felt for someone who could symbolize the Church as a whole, and gradually the Bishop of Rome, the holder of the Petrine see in the capital of the Western Empire, assumed the prerogatives of Peter as ruler of the universal Church, amassing more and more spiritual authority until finally Vatican I pronounced the dogma of his infallibility, which was somewhat modified at Vatican II by the requirement that he should act in concert with his fellow bishops.

The need for a single focus of unity for the whole Church has led some to favour a universal primate, a greatly reformed version of the present papacy. Certainly a college of bishops needs a chairperson; but since there is always conflict in the Church, and this has existed from the earliest times, it is difficult to imagine that a universal primate would be able to carry out a representative role for the whole Church. Nor can deeply-held theological differences be settled by the equivalent of an ukase from on high. We have already noted that the unity of the Church is not a mathematical unity (see p. 170), and so there is no need for one single person to act as its chief representative. The unity of a college of primates, when it can be achieved, is a more appropriate way of showing the true unity of the Church, which is more like the unity of a family. In any case, there seems no prospect, as we have already noted, of agreement on these matters between all the divided churches in the foreseeable future.

Apostolic succession

Can the apostolic ministry be expressed in other ways than the traditional threefold ministry? Presbyterians, for example, equating *episkopos* with *presbyteros*, look on the local minister as a kind of bishop. Except for some Lutheran national churches, Protestant churches have not retained the apostolic succession in their ordinations. Men (and women) in these churches who have experienced a call to the ministry are ordained after training, after having had this call validated by their church authorities, without this manual link with the past. These ministries have in most cases been manifestly blessed by the Holy Spirit. Their ministers carry out apostolic functions in preaching and teaching and shepherding the flock of Christ. Although there are differences of emphasis in both life-style, customs and teaching from those associated with the threefold ministry, there is agreement on the basic essentials of the work. Looking to the richness of God's grace to supply all their needs, they would strenuously deny that there is anything necessary that they lack.

We approach here an important theological principle, namely to be cautious of denying the opposite of what is affirmed. Those who affirm the apostolic ministry in its traditional form should not pass judgement on the orders of those who are outside the traditional threefold ministry. Instead they should content themselves with stating why they consider it necessary themselves to insist on the traditional threefold ministry.

So far as the apostolic succession is concerned, it must be acknowledged that during the history of the Church there has been a change of emphasis. In the early Church, it was the succession in a see that was important, although subsequent research has shewn that there was originally a confused situation, with no clear evidence of episcopal succession, particularly in Rome and Alexandria. In some cases the episcopate seems to have emerged out of the presbyterate. Despite differing patterns emerging in different churches, it came to be believed in the early Church that the body of apostolic truth had been handed to a church by its founding Apostle, and then handed down to each successor in the see. But as sees proliferated, the phrase 'apostolic succession' came to have a different meaning. It was used in connection not with succession in a see but with ordination by a bishop who claimed to trace his descent in ordination back to the Apostles.

It is easy to caricature the idea of apostolic succession as though there were some special kind of *mana* originating with the Apostles which was passed on magically by hand at ordination. This is a travesty of the doctrine. Certainly ordination is a sacrament, so that through the laying on of hands grace is bestowed to carry out the work of a priest as well as authority to undertake it, just as at the sacrament of confirmation the bishop lays his hands on lay people, strengthening them for service within the Church. The true significance of apostolic succession, however, is that it is the outward sign of a body of traditions the continuity of which can be traced back to the earliest days of the Church. This does not guarantee any kind of immunity from sin or from error, still less does it prove in itself purity of doctrine. But a church which retains the apostolic succession in ordination shows a proper respect for its origins. It is not starting out anew with a fresh Gospel, or initiating a new church, but continuing to preach the Gospel once 'handed down' within the Church of God which has continued down the centuries. Through the apostolic succession it is proclaiming in an outward way its identity with the catholic Church across the world and down the ages. It is showing that its ministry is not serving a sectarian congregation, but a local embodiment of the one Church of God.

In fact, churches which keep the apostolic succession almost without exception uphold the traditions of the catholic Church in liturgical action, in the liturgical year and in the threefold ministry as well as in other ways. This outward sign in itself is not enough. It needs to be accompanied by the inward spirit of catholic spirituality. Yet it remains a visible symbol without which the inner reality is likely to be missing. Those who have kept this sign usually would not wish to be without it.

It is sometimes claimed that a person duly ordained within the apostolic ministry has a 'valid' ministry, implying that those ordained without it have an invalid or defective ministry. It is said that for a sacrament to be valid it needs to have the right form (in this case the laying on of hands), the right matter (the words of ordination) and a right intention (to do as the Church does). In modern parlance 'validity' tends to be used in a semi-legal sense. Official Roman Catholic doctrine, because of doubts whether Anglicans have a 'right intention', still holds Anglican orders to be not only invalid, but 'absolutely null and utterly void', so that it is uncertain whether God will honour sacraments which Anglican priests have administered. Such a view seems to accord ill with a doctrine of a God whose nature is absolute love. But the same view until recently was held in Anglican circles about Free Church ministers ordained by rites without the apostolic succession. In fact the Latin word from which 'valid' is derived – *validus* – means 'strong'; and that is its proper meaning in this connection. A ministry outside the apostolic succession is not necessarily defective; but to be ordained within it strengthens ordained ministry for the reasons suggested above.

There are extreme conditions in which this view might be modified. If a church with the apostolic succession were so lacking in the essentials of Christianity, or even appeared to be denying them, it could be right to secede in schism from the main body without having the opportunity for retaining the apostolic succession. But in such a case it would be wise to restore it as soon as possible. In the reformed Church of England, happily, there was no such situation. The apostolic succession was retained, and extreme care was taken to see that the due essentials of catholic order were kept in the consecration of bishops.

The theology of episcopacy

To follow in the footsteps of the primitive undivided Church is not a sufficient justification in itself for episcopacy. Democracy hardly flourished in those far-off days, and there was a deficient doctrine of the laity. An episcopal ministry might at first sight seem to be the natural form of church order in an age when there was an autocratic form of government. But episcopacy is not to be equated with the practice of prelacy as it developed in the seventeenth century Church of England or among the prince bishops of the Lutheran churches, or with some developed styles of Roman Catholic episcopacy. Primitive episcopacy involved the bishop acting with his presbyters and with the consent of the people, more in the nature of the assembly of Acts 15. This is well expressed in ordination, where the bishop acts with his presbyters and with the good will and approval of the people. It is also expressed in the Church of England by 'the bishop-in-synod'.

There are three main theologies of episcopacy. One is a pragmatic one; that it is the form of church government which works best. It is said to be a matter of the *bene esse* (wellbeing) of the Church.[7] Pragmatic arguments, however, are seldom conclusive. Episcopacy has worked exceedingly well, but it has also functioned exceedingly badly, especially when it has been corrupted by the tendencies noted above. It has stamped on initiative; it has downgraded the order of presbyter and paid no respect to the laity who comprise, after all, more than 99 per cent of the Church. No doubt an equal number of examples could be given of episcopacy working well, so that in these cases it truly is of the *bene esse* of the Church; occasions when bishops have given signal examples of holiness to the whole flock of Christ which they have shepherded in a spirit of humble service; occasions when they have devoted themselves to the pastoral ministry and have upheld and supported and encouraged their priests, and occasions when the episcopate has been a protection to the laity against power-hungry clergy. But it is hardly a theological argument in favour of episcopacy to affirm that it can work well. That is to suggest that episcopacy is a mere matter of organization, rather than a key ingredient of a living organism.

Another view of episcopacy is that it is necessary in order that the Church may exist. Episcopacy is said to be of the *esse* (essential nature) of the Church.[8] This view is very difficult to establish. Although we have rejected the Roman theory (see p. 179), it is at least comprehensible that all authority in the Church should be invested in one bishop acting in conjunction with his college of bishops, and that this authority should spread downwards through the presbyters to the laity. On this view there is a pyramid of authority in which the bishops play their part as a vital ingredient. But to say that a church depends for its very existence on a bishop ordained within the apostolic succession offends against both experience and doctrine. It is almost as though, in order to find a safe haven between the two opposing positions of Rome and Protestantism, Anglicans have tried to establish a middle way by magnifying the bishop. What possible theory could successfully establish the bishop as the cornerstone without which the whole building collapses? There is no scriptural warrant for such a belief; nor in the early Church, beset by heresies and schisms, did the existence of a bishop *per se* constitute the church. It was rather the existence of a bishop as the successor in the see which could trace its origin back to the time of the apostles which validated the church and its teaching. After all, entry into the Church is effected by baptism, and baptism does not *require* a bishop (although in the early Church baptism was usually administered by or in the presence of the bishop on Easter Eve): indeed, in extreme circumstances baptism may be validly administered by a lay person. The bishop is the servant of the church, the agent of the Gospel and the preacher of the Kingdom;

and all three, the Church and Gospel and Kingdom, are theologically prior to the bishop.

A third possible line of explanation for episcopacy also presents itself. Episcopacy may be said to be a matter of the *plene esse* (fullness) of the Church.[9] Episcopacy represents the apostolic ministry and expresses the fullness of the Gospel. Episcopacy is a form of church order which enables the church to be itself. It presents a formal order of obedience by which people may express their obedience to Christ. It provides an outward focus of unity by which those within a diocese may express their unity, and the college of bishops, acting together, expresses the unity of the worldwide Church in so far as this is not broken by schisms. Episcopacy is a form of church government which proclaims continuity with the Church back to apostolic times. The apostolic succession embodied in episcopacy bears witness to the objectivity of the Gospel. This objective witness is needed as much as the subjective assurance that faith brings. The laying on of hands in episcopal ordination is 'the fullness of the sign of apostolic succession', to use a phrase used by the French Groupe de Dombes.[10] Episcopal ordination takes place within the eucharist, which symbolizes its dependence on the death and resurrection of Christ. Episcopacy therefore provides an expression of the fullness of the Gospel in terms of Church order. 'The growth of all Christians into the measure of the stature of the fullness of Christ means their growth with all Christians in the unity of the one Body, and of this unity the Episcopate is the expression.'[11] The distinguished author from whom this quotation is taken had earlier stated that episcopacy is of the *esse* of the universal Church, but as we have seen he is careful here to qualify his meaning. He does not write that episcopacy is the *only* expression of the fullness of the Gospel in terms of church order. The fact that episcopacy does express the fullness of the Gospel in this way does not imply that without it there can be no church, nor does it follow that other forms of church order may not have a similar function.

The theology of the priesthood and the diaconate

A bishop always remains a priest and a deacon. Peter in the first Epistle standing in his name speaks of himself as an Apostle, a 'fellow elder' and a servant. Jesus is the exemplar of all three orders. As the One sent from the Father he is the prototype of the apostolic ministry, as 'the great high priest' of Hebrews he is the archetypal priest, and when he said that he came not to be served but to serve he showed himself the exemplar of deacons.

A priest is ordained by a bishop assisted by other priests, just as a bishop is consecrated by (at least three) bishops, usually under the presidency of the metropolitan bishop or archbishop. Anglican orders have been criticized on changing grounds by the Roman Catholic Church. First, it was said that there was no proper apostolic succession (a charge now dropped). Then, it was alleged that the form of consecration and ordination is deficient on two grounds; first, there is in Anglican rites no *porrectio instrumentorum*, the handing over of the symbols of the office (but this was not done in the early liturgies), and secondly the same formula is used in making priests and bishops (but the different rites show clearly that a different office is being conferred). Finally in 1898 the encyclical *Apostolicae Curae* ruled that, since there was no explicit mention in the Anglican ordinal of a sacrificing priesthood, there was a defect of intention on the part of the church which rendered Anglican orders 'absolutely null and utterly void'. This was hotly contested in the *Responsio* of the then Archbishops of Canterbury and York. Although subsequent research has shown that ecclesiastical rather than doctrinal motives predominated in this negative verdict, the Encyclical has never been superseded, despite the plea by the Anglican–Roman Catholic International Commission for a degree of intercommunion between the two confessions.

The functions of a priest are well set out in the Ordinal of the Alternative Service Book of the Church of England. These may be summed up in the three images of 'messengers, watchmen and stewards'. A priest is minister of the Word (messenger) and sacraments (steward) and acts as pastor to the flock of Christ (watchman). Thus priests exist as ministers in their own right; but they also (according to the Church of England) promise obedience to the bishop 'in all things lawful and right'. Since 'right' is not further defined, this gives a broad discretion. At their ordination their intentions and commitments are plainly spelled out and affirmed. There is much confusion in the contemporary church about the role and function of a priest, perhaps because many of the worldly honours previously accorded to the priesthood have been swept away as society has become more secular. Priests have three priorities; first, the pastoral care of their flock, secondly the well-being of the community in which they live, and thirdly the preparation for the coming of God's Kingdom in the world as a whole.

If these roles are to be fulfilled, holiness of life is prerequisite for priests, and their hearts and minds need to be steeped in the Scriptures, and they need to live a life which is open to the Spirit, with attitudes modelled on those of Jesus. A priest's role does not consist primarily in 'welfare work': others are called to that vocation. The priest's primary role is to lead the worship of God and to inspire lay people to commit themselves fully to God in Christ and to make their proper Christian contribution in the secular world where they live and work, and so far as the local community is concerned, to inspire others to make their contribution. Priests are not called (except in exceptional circumstances) to immerse themselves in secular work, but to point out the spiritual dimension involved in all work in the world. There will however be non-stipendiary priests who earn their living in the secular world, and who assist at their parish church. Their priorities will be rather different; but they are adjuncts and not substitutes for the full-time ministry.

The role of a priest is somewhat paradoxical. On the one hand priests are needed for the building up of Church communities and for their adequate pastoral care, but on the other hand they must try to be expendable in the sense that the job of priests is to enable others to play their full share in carrying out these very activities. But they must not encourage members of their congregations to spend so much time on church activities that they do not have time or energy for their more important contribution as Christians in the world in which they live.

As we have already noted (see p. 199) it is better not to suppose that an 'indelible character' is imprinted on a priest at his ordination. A person is a priest by vocation. It is always possible to mistake a vocation, just as it is possible later to deny it; and in changing circumstances a person's vocation may conceivably change.

A priest is the representative of the Church because a priest's vocation has been tested by the Church, accepted by the bishop, and ordained by him and his presbyters with the agreement of the congregation. As president at the eucharist a priest acts as the representative of the Church. But a priest is ordained primarily in order to represent Christ. Of course all Christians ought to represent Christ, as their very name implies; but a priest, in so much as it is his duty to minister the Word and Sacraments in Christ's name, is Christ's representative in a special sense.

As for a deacon, his job is primarily to assist a priest, and to undertake administrative and pastoral work in the congregation. In the Church of England (apart from women deacons during the time before women could be priested) the order has been used in the past as an apprenticeship for the priesthood. Various churches have evolved their different traditions for the diaconate. According to the Church of England they may officiate at all services, except for the Prayer of Thanksgiving at the heart of the eucharist; and they are not permitted to pronounce God's blessing in a liturgical service (although by an anomaly they are allowed to conduct a wedding service in which the bride and bridegroom are blessed), nor are they permitted to absolve sins in God's name. These two functions are reserved traditionally for the greater authority accorded to the priesthood. However deacons are nowadays increasingly put in charge of parishes, even though help has to be imported for the eucharist (unless communion is given from the Reserved Sacrament).

The gender of a priest

It is only during the present century that controversy has arisen over the gender of a priest. In the past it has always been assumed that a priest would be male. With increasing consciousness of discrimination against the female half of the human race, and with an increasing number of women who have been conscious of a call to the priesthood which appears to be authentic when measured by the same criteria as those by which male vocations are judged, there has been a vigorous movement towards the acceptance of women's ordination to the priesthood. Women have for some time been ordained as ministers in Protestant churches (Lutheran, Methodist, Presbyterian, Congregationalist, United Reformed, Baptist). The Eastern Orthodox Churches have regarded the ordination of women as contrary to their unalterable tradition. The Roman Catholic Church has declared against their ordination.[12] The Anglican Communion is split, with a large number of its provinces (including the two provinces of the Church of England) deciding to ordain them but others not recognizing their ordination. The split in the Anglican Communion mirrors the split in the universal Church, with the two largest churches, Eastern Orthodoxy and Roman Catholicism, strongly opposed (at present) to their ordination. Because of this split, it is necessary to consider the arguments both in favour and against.

Attention has centred on the reasons given against their ordination (with counter-arguments in refutation) rather than on the positive reasons which support it. There are those (so far as Anglicans are concerned) who claim that neither the Anglican Communion nor any of its autonomous churches has authority to change the universal custom of the Western Catholic Church and the Eastern Orthodox churches without the authority of an ecumenical Council behind such a major change. But there is no chance of calling an ecumenical Council in the foreseeable future; and a church is surely not thereby inhibited from taking any new and creative step. In any case, members of a church which broke away from the Roman Catholic Church at the Reformation can hardly remain Anglican and then claim that no step of this kind can be taken without the agreement of that very church with which it is in schism.

Some who object to women's ordination to the priesthood allege that only those who belong to the male gender can act *in persona Christi*. There is a confusion here. Sexuality is certainly basic to human personality, but the same cannot be said of a particular gender. As the 'Nicene' Creed makes clear, it is important that we hold that Jesus was a human being (*anthropos*), not that he was a man (*aner*). In any case we have already examined and found wanting the Roman Catholic claim that the priest in the eucharist does act *in persona Christi* (see p. 198). He does not act the part of Christ; on the contrary he presides over the sacramental representation of Christ's death and resurrection under the forms of bread and wine.

It is also claimed that because Jesus did not choose any women among the Twelve Apostles, it follows that the Church must not ordain women. However in New Testament times, the attitude to women was very different from what it is today. A woman was the property of her husband. She was regarded as inferior to him (a man's blessing used to be 'Blessed art thou, O Lord, who hast not made me a woman'). She did the manual work in the household, and while she could not divorce her husband, he could divorce her, even, in the opinion of a famous Rabbi of the time, if she did not cook a good dinner. With such contemporary attitudes Jesus could not give authority to women, because that authority would not have been recognized. He did however go out of his way to honour them and to make friends with them. In any case, the Holy Spirit can guide the Church into a fuller apprehension of truth. At the assembly recorded in Acts 15, the Jerusalem Church decided that Gentiles could be admitted to the Church, a far greater change than that of ordaining women. After all, Jesus did not choose any Gentiles to be of the number of the Twelve, but no one today would confine ordination to Jewish Christians.

The Church which started as a Jewish sect naturally took over many of these prejudices against women. Thus women were to be obedient to their husbands in all things (Eph 5.24), the younger married women were to stay at home (Titus 2.5), women were not to adorn their hair, they should not wear gold or pearl ornaments (1 Tim 2.9), they must not pray in public without a headcovering (1 Cor 11.6), and they must keep silence in the assembly (1 Cor 14.34). In one passage Paul described man as head of a woman (1 Cor 11.3). However the Greek word *kephale* is never used in first-century Greek in the sense of chief or directing force. It either designates the head in contrast to other parts of the body, or it can mean origin, which is probably its meaning here, with a reference to Eve being formed from Adam's rib.

There are those who under the influence of these texts regard it as contrary to Scripture to accord to women the authority of the priesthood. However in another passage Paul rose above the presuppositions of the culture in which he lived and applied to the status of woman the criteria of the Gospel. He wrote to the Galatians that in Christ distinctions of race, class and sex were done away: all are 'one person' in Christ (Gal 3.28). He might have reflected that according to the first chapter of Genesis man and woman together comprise the image of God (see p. 50). These objections to women's ordination based on texts from Scripture constitute a dangerous mode of argument; for it is often possible to quote another text in Scripture in refutation.

Perhaps a more serious argument is based on Christian symbolism. In Scripture the Church is described in female terms, and Christ naturally in male terms. Indeed Paul wrote of Christ and his Church as indissolubly united as a man is married to his wife (Eph 5.32). Those who object to women's ordination on symbolic grounds see special significance in Jesus' own male gender. But, as we have noted above, the importance of the Incarnation lay not in the fact that Jesus belonged to the male sex, but in the assertion that in Christ God became a human being.

Those who object to women's ordination on symbolic grounds claim that there would be symbolic confusion if a woman priest were to represent Christ, because this would mean a woman representing a man. How could a woman speak in the name of God the Father, any more than she can speak in the name of God the Son? But all female Christians are made in the image of God as much as male Christians. They are called to represent Christ, and they do this without any confusion of symbolism. In the same way there is no confusion when a male priest represents the Church, despite the latter being symbolized in female terms. And we have already noted that in God there is no gender, and that there is a positive value in applying some female imagery to him as well as the customary male imagery (see pp. 130f.). These arguments from symbolism do not hold water any more than the more strictly theological arguments.

These are the main objections to women's ordination to the priesthood. It was necessary to look at them first because the proper question is not 'Should women be ordained?' but 'Are there any overriding arguments to prevent their ordination?' Scripture and tradition do not tell us all that we ought to do, but they can provide overriding reasons why we should not do certain things.

There are positive reasons for women's priesting which need to be affirmed as well as negative ones which may be refuted. The priesthood is not only representative of God to humanity, but also representative of humanity to God. There was a time when women felt able to be represented exclusively by men, but that time, at least in the West, has now passed. Therefore both men and women are needed for a fully representative ministry. There is a wholeness when they work together because they complement each other. The decision by a church to ordain women affirms all the women in that church (and the number of female members is usually larger than male members). Furthermore it even tends to affirm women who are not members of such a church, but who are members of the communities which it serves. Moreover, the admission of women to any role of authority in an institution tends to humanize it. Some characteristics which are more commonly found in women rather than men (e.g. an ability to effect reconciliation) are needed in the priesthood. Many women are feeling the call to a priestly vocation, and in the absence of decisive reasons against their ordination, it is wrong to frustrate that calling if it has been tested by the Church.[13]

These then are the main arguments against and in favour of the ordination of women to the priesthood. In all matters concerning sexuality it is wise to remember that arguments which are rationally argued on either side may be motivated by deeper assumptions which are psychosexual in nature. The decisions of celibate males about the female sex, however eminent their positions may be, need to be especially examined. Males, married or celibate, who exercise priestly power may be unwilling to share that power with females. Males who are not wholly emancipated from childhood attitudes may be frightened of returning to their mother's apron-strings. The image of woman may still be a potent symbol of male temptation, so that to ordain women to the priesthood would seem to symbolize a relaxation of male sexual restraint. Some women may fear it for the same reason. It is easier to ask questions on these themes than to answer them. But they need to be asked, because women should only be ordained if they can be accepted within the church as representatives of Christ and of the Church, and psychosexual neuroses outlined above may tend to prevent full-hearted acceptance. But the very fact of ordaining women to the priesthood could be a means of ameliorating these neuroses.

Notes

1. G. W. H. Lampe, *Aspects of the New Testament Ministry* (London, 1949), p. 2.

2. On the use and meaning of these words, see K. H. Rengstorf, *Apostleship* (London, 1952), pp. 1-31.

3. For two conflicting views, see Dissertation I in J. B. Lightfoot, *Commentary on Ephesians* (London, 1883), pp. 227f.

4. ARCIC, *The Final Report* (London, 1982), p. 32.

5. *Ibid.*, p. 33.

6. For a discussion of the origin of the bishop's office in the Church, see W. Telfer, *The Office of a Bishop* (London, 1962); and for a description of their ministry, see A. G. Hebert, *Apostle and Bishop* (London, 1963).

7. See F. J. Taylor, *The Church of God* (London, 1946).

8. See *The Apostolic Ministry*, ed. K. E. Kirk (London, 1946).

9. See H. Montefiore, 'The historic episcopate' in *The Historic Episcopate*, ed. K. M. Carey (London, 1954).

10. The Groupe de Dombes was a group of French Roman Catholic priests and Reformed ministers who met 1937–87 and produced *Pour la Communion des Églises* (Paris, 1988).

11 A. M. Ramsey, *The Gospel and the Catholic Church* (London, 1936; 1956 edn), pp. 84–5.

12. For detailed discussion of Roman Catholic arguments, see ch. 8, 'Women and the ministerial priesthood' in H. Montefiore, *So Far and Yet So Near* (London, 1986).

13. For a more detailed discussion, see H. Montefiore, 'The theology of the priesthood' in *Yes to Women Priests*, ed. H. Montefiore (London, 1979).

chapter 11

The Last Things

New Testament expectations of the Last Things

We are surrounded by mystery on every side. Scientists may talk about the 'Theory of Everything', but in fact there are mysteries in the material world which are as yet far beyond human understanding – for example, why there are uncertainties in the quantum world, or how elementary particles are mysteriously connected wherever they may be. There are deep mysteries of personal relationship too, to say nothing of those which pertain to the paranormal. The deepest mysteries of all relate to our relationship with God, and the most impenetrable of these is what happens to human beings when they die. For all the apparent certainties of revelation, we do not know. 'What we shall be has not yet been disclosed, but we know that when it is disclosed we shall be like him, because we shall see him as he is' (1 John 3.2). All that we can be fully assured about is that we shall be held in Christ within the love of God, and it is our hope to be with him in eternity for ever.

We have to bear this in mind when we look to the Scriptures for help. The spiritual truths which they express are of permanent value to us, but the eschatological framework in which these are expressed belong to the age in which they were formulated. In the New Testament period the end of the world was expected imminently. Jesus preached that the Kingdom of God was already dawning. The New Testament Church believed that with the resurrection of Jesus the Last Things had already begun, and that he was 'the firstfruits of them that sleep' (1 Cor 15.20), that is, the harbinger of the general resurrection of the dead at the close of this world order. This expectation coloured all their religious thinking.

As we have already noted, Jesus' own perspective altered somewhat. When sending out the Twelve on their preaching mission, Jesus told them that they would not have completed it before the Kingdom had come with power; but later he said that he did not know the day or the hour of the End. Again, Paul writing his second letter to the Thessalonians believed that the End would come in the lifetime of his hearers, and painted a somewhat bizarre picture of the dead rising from their graves together with the living to meet the returning Christ in the air (1 Thess 4.17). Later when writing to the Corinthians the perspective had changed a little – he wrote 'We shall not all die', meaning that some would have died before the end (1 Cor 15.51). By the time the Epistle to the Romans was written, he wrote simply that 'now is our salvation nearer than when we believed' (Rom 13.11), while by the time of the Epistle to the Ephesians no indication whatsoever was given for the time of the End (Eph 1.10).

Although the perspective may change, there breathes throughout New Testament eschatology (beliefs about the Last Things) the fervent expectation of being with Christ after death, and of being filled with love and joy. The Son will be surrounded by his sanctified ones. The Book of Revelation, which is full of vivid imagery derived mostly from the Old Testament, gives colourful expression to this truth, with the Lamb in the midst of the throne. However the Lamb is Christ, not God himself. The picture that is painted, derived from the imagery of the eucharist, is of God sitting on the throne, surrounded by elders and living creatures. The primacy is given to God. So also with Paul, who writes that at the End, Christ will make himself subordinate to God, and will hand back to him all authority, that God may be all in all (1 Cor 15.28).

It is necessary in thinking about eschatology to consider various aspects in turn.

The end of the world

The presuppositions of our contemporary world are very different from those of New Testament times. Most Christians today no longer believe in the imminence of the End. God's purposes for his world, so far as we can understand them, seem as yet very incomplete; so why should he specially intervene to bring this world to an end? Such intervention is not his normal mode of operation.

Whereas today we usually think of the end in terms of our personal future, the New Testament outlook concerns the future of the world.[1] The Scriptures sometimes speak of a cosmic disintegration resulting in a new heaven and a new earth; but from our contemporary knowledge of the cosmos there is no indication that there could be a catastrophic end to the

Milky Way (to which we belong) without special divine intervention. It is improbable that abuse of the environment would cause the sudden demise of humanity rather than a gradual extinction. It is always possible, however, that some catastrophic event could spell the end for humanity in this particular planet. Sixty-five million years ago a planetesimal collided with the earth, killing 90 per cent of all species, and causing a perturbation of climate which took a long time to return to normal. It has been estimated that Comet Swift–Tuttle might hit the earth on 14 August 2126. Even this (remote) possibility does not inspire in us fervent eschatological expectation reminiscent of that in New Testament times. If the comet is due to collide with Planet Earth (and no one can make calculations sufficiently accurate to be certain, especially as it would only take three and a half minutes to cross the Earth's orbit), there are likely to be strenuous efforts to deflect it by nuclear-tipped missiles, which might be successful. The Earth has withstood many shocks for over three and a half billion years, and doubtless it would withstand this comet's impact (although humanity would not). Eventually however in the far distant future the sun will swell into a red giant and Planet Earth will become too hot for life. There are those who hope that by that time humanity will have found the means to migrate to another part of the Milky Way, although that must remain a matter of doubt; and in any case our galaxy might be sucked into a black hole. Even if the universe is open (i.e. will expand for ever), there would eventually come a 'heat death' in which life would be extinct. But it seems unlikely that the End will come soon. There are however two abiding truths of New Testament eschatology which remain valid for us today. In the first place, the decision of faith always confronts us with an urgency similar to that when faced by the end of all things; and secondly, Christian hope does not spell optimism for the future of the planet or of the human race, but the hope of eternal life in Christ Jesus. Certainly we pray in the Lord's Prayer 'Thy Kingdom come', but this prayer was originally eschatological throughout, and the petition was for the transformation of the world at the end of time so that it becomes a 'second heaven'. We do not think in this apocalyptic way today, and so when we pray this today we ask for God's Kingdom to come more fully on earth, just as in heaven it will be fully realized.

Death

According to Genesis, death was the penalty of Adam's sin of disobedience; not the immediate prospect of death, but the removal of the chance of immortality through the Tree of Life in the Garden of Eden, so that death would at some time intervene. This belief in the connection between sin and death, derived from the Old Testament, was held by early Christians. Paul wrote: 'It was through one man that sin entered the world, and through sin death, and thus death pervaded the whole human race, inasmuch as all men have sinned' (Rom 5.12). The Christian hope of eternal life brought by Christ was understood as the putting right of Adam's sin which had resulted in mortality.

Sin certainly can result in death; but we can no longer believe that there is a necessary connection between the two. There is fossil evidence of animal sickness and of course animal death long before *homo sapiens* appeared on the scene; and the death of human beings is simply part of the mortality of all living species. We do not yet know exactly how the ageing process functions, but we do know that it is built into our bodies. It would be a terrible thing if scientists do discover how this process can be stopped (or even reversed) because human beings are so constituted psychologically that they need a time-span bounded by birth and death in the same way as they need a daily rhythm with its boundaries of consciousness and sleep. If human beings were to learn how to become immortal so far as the ageing process is concerned, the earth would become hopelessly overpopulated, leading to their death by starvation; so they would have gained little advantage. A rhythm of nature has evolved whereby dead bodies fertilize the earth out of which new life springs. Death certainly reminds us of the contingency and transitoriness of this life, and the prospect of death increases our longing for eternal life. In much of today's secular Western world, death has become the great unmentionable, taking the place of sex in the Victorian age. Few people today have even seen a dead body. This taboo has arisen because for so many people death is now believed to be the end. Paul thought of death as 'the last enemy' (1 Cor 15.26), because he thought of sin and death as demonic powers unleashed by Adam's sin. In the light of our knowledge of the ageing process we no longer think of death in those terms. For us it is the ending of the earthly chapter of our pilgrimage as we begin on what lies ahead, a kind of rite of passage. In the secular world the two key moments are birth and death. In the Christian world the key moments are new life in Christ, and the conclusion of God's purposes for his universe.

Resurrection

The general case for the existence of life after death does not rest primarily on New Testament evidence, but on more general considerations of God's purposes in creation, as well as on evidence for life after death. This evidence is found in such phenomena as near-death experiences, 'veridical hallucinations' shortly after the death of a loved one, the evidence of mediums and other paranormal phenomena. We cannot enter into a detailed discussion of these factors here, because it is part of the Christian faith that life does not end at death.[2]

It is impossible to account for the rise of Christianity without accepting that the earliest Christians were certain that, against all expectation, Jesus had risen from the dead. It is very difficult to refute the Gospel evidence of resurrection appearances, and there is good attestation for the Empty Tomb. For those who actually saw the risen Lord, his resurrection was proof of the general resurrection of all mankind after death. He was regarded, as we have noted, as the 'firstfruits of them that sleep'. Today there is less certainty about exactly what the disciples actually saw, but at the same time the evidence is convincing that they knew that he was alive, although he had died.[3] Since his body was reported missing from the tomb, it used to be thought that our bodies also would rise from the dead at the general resurrection in a new form of body. Despite Paul's assertion that flesh and blood can never inherit the Kingdom of God (1 Cor 15.50), the phrase 'resurrection of the flesh' crept into the Creed. (For this reason it was customary to bury a priest facing in the opposite direction from that of his flock, so that at the resurrection he would still be facing them.) Today such a belief about our resurrection is no longer credible. The body disintegrates at death or is burnt, and its components will not reassemble in bodily form.

Jesus' own resurrection body, according to the evidence of the New Testament, appeared to be solid, so that Mary Magdalene wanted to touch him; but at the same time he could appear and disappear at will, and could apparently pass through closed doors. The word body here does not signify a physical object, but the mode of existence beyond death. We have already suggested that these appearances were those of his spiritual or 'subtle body' (see p. 148). These resurrection appearances ceased after a period. There were particular reasons for their occurrence; to give commands to his disciples as well as to assure them of his existence. Since it is most unusual for ordinary human beings to appear in this way to their friends after their death, it is unlikely that our resurrection bodies will be similar to his. It is more likely that they will resemble his ascended and glorified body (1 John 3.2). But we know nothing about this; and we must remain silent about the nature of our future bodies, except to note that they will be immaterial. Unless our future existence is to be entirely passive, it is vital that we are given some kind of body with which to express ourselves and to communicate with others.

In the Hellenistic world of New Testament times, the immortal soul was generally believed to be imprisoned within the mortal body, and liberation consisted in freeing the soul so that it might regain its natural habitat. Jewish insistence on the goodness of the material world, echoed in New Testament writings, is directly opposed to this Hellenistic viewpoint. Not all Christians, however, have believed in personal resurrection. Some have held that future life means preservation within the divine mind;[4] others have held that resurrection stands for the divine view of a personal existence,[5] or the moral quality of a present life.[6] Such views, however, ignore both the evidence of Jesus' resurrection, and the evident incompleteness and imperfection of human lives. If God brought human beings into being for an existence which despite their gross imperfections comes to a final end at death, one wonders why he ever bothered to initiate a cosmic process which has resulted in the evolution of inevitably flawed human beings who have no chance to be perfected. We all need further opportunities to achieve the destiny for which God created us.

According to New Testament doctrine, the resurrection body springs out of our mortal body as shoots spring out of seed (1 Cor 15.35ff.). Illuminating as this analogy is, it hardly explains the continuity between the two processes, because shoots and seed are made of similar substances, whereas physical and resurrection bodies are not. Nowadays, the mind is commonly taken to be an aspect of the functioning of the brain, and the brain is known to disintegrate at death, so that it becomes difficult to understand how there can be any continuity.[7] Perhaps partly for this reason, some people understand resurrection as an entirely new miraculously created mode of existence of a person who has disintegrated at death, in which his personhood is completely recreated. It is however difficult to understand how God would use such a clumsy way in which to achieve this continuity. Surely there must be some means by which the resurrection bodies achieve direct continuity with their mortal bodies without billions of these miraculous reassemblies?

An analogy may perhaps be found in the hardware and software of a computer. The software has to be embodied in hardware for a computer to function. Some computers are 'compatible' so that embodiment may take place in a different kind of computer. In rather the same way (the analogy is naturally imperfect) it is possible that the soul is embodied after death as a person in a different kind of body, non-material instead of material. The soul may come into being and develop within the physical body in which it becomes naturally embodied, and at death it may be embodied in a new immaterial (resurrection) body. It is even possible that there are other bodies (such as the so-called 'astral body') besides the physical being, which together comprise a human being. The other bodies may decay after death like the physical body, so that only the soul remains which is then embodied afresh in the resurrection body. In this sphere we can only speak with diffidence about mysteries beyond our understanding. There are good reasons, however, to discard reductionist views about human personality. These are areas of human existence far beyond our knowledge and understanding.

Resurrection, not survival or immortality

Resurrection needs to be distinguished from both survival and immortality. Concepts of survival are current in particular among animist religions. They suggest a continuance of present life, but in a diminished form, since the spirit has been deprived of its body. It is a doctrine not of hope, but of despair. In its essentials, life simply goes on and on with attenuated force, with souls as shadows of the living, bloodless beings living in a grey and ghostlike underworld. A not dissimilar concept of survival is to be found in spiritualist religions, and many of the alleged messages received from the spirit world attest the triviality which is inherent in such a concept of survival. Its only point seems to be the concern about trifling matters which for many constitute all there is to present-day living. Christianity is intrinsically opposed to any concept of life after death which involves a diminishment or attenuation of living in this world. On the contrary, the teaching of the New Testament attests to an accentuation of life, fullness of life or 'eternal life'. This is already tasted in this life through union with Christ; for the world to come has already broken into this world through him. 'I came that they might have life, and have it in all its fullness' (John 10.10) characterizes the essential feature of eternal life.

Immortality involves the view that in each person there is something of the divine which is inherently immortal. It is therefore at root a pantheistic belief, since according to its tenets each person is part of the larger divine whole. We have already found reasons to reject pantheism (see pp. 124f.). The roots of this idea of the 'divine spark' are to be found in the belief in the ancient world that the world soul was split into small atomic pieces and buried in humanity, and that when liberated from the prison of the flesh these divine sparks will be reassembled again into the world soul. This belief found expression in Hellenistic mystery religions, and through the Orphic mysteries it influenced Socrates, and so it was spread abroad on a larger canvas. But there is nothing divine in humanity. We belong to a different order of existence. Human beings are made in the image of God, but they are created by God and dependent on his grace at every point. This is true of human beings in this world, and it is also true of our future existence in a resurrection body.

The concept of the resurrection body inevitably has its problems. We now know that *homo sapiens* did not suddenly appear on this planet: mankind was preceded by *homo habilis*, *homo erectus*, etc. What is the status of the earlier hominids? Do they have resurrection bodies? This is one of the many questions to which we can return no answer. What will be the status of infants who have died? It used to be thought that they existed in 'limbo', deprived of the state of beatitude which older people could enjoy, but happy in their state and ignorant of what might have been theirs. Will these infants have an opportunity to mature after death? We do not know the answer. And what will happen to people who die with their brains destroyed by Alzheimer's disease or other forms of senile dementia? What will happen to those whose life had been reduced to a permanent vegetative state? Will they be resurrected in full command of their faculties? If so, this suggests that the soul retains the potentiality of memory despite the fact that brain disease in this life may cause people completely to lose their memories. Aquinas believed that people would be resurrected as they had been at the age of 30. (What happens to those who died in their twenties?) This choice seems an arbitrary age, conceived no doubt when expectation of life was shorter than now. These are mysteries to which we cannot know the answers. They do not however seem in any way to cast doubt on the Christian doctrine of the resurrection of the body, but they raise questions about details which are unanswerable.

Purgatory

The concept of purgatory is not confined to Christianity. For example *Bardo Thodol*, the Tibetan Book of the Dead, describes the purgatorial sufferings of the soul in the intermediate state between death and rebirth.[8] Among the Christian churches, it is the Roman Catholic

Church which has developed the doctrine of purgatory. According to Article XXII of the Thirty-Nine Articles of the Church of England 'The Romish doctrine concerning Purgatory ... is a vain thing fondly invented, and grounded upon no warranty of Scripture, but rather repugnant to the Word of God'. Purgatory, according to traditional Roman doctrine, is 'the place or state of temporal punishment, where those who have died in the grace of God are expiating their venial faults and such pains as are still due to forgiven mortal sins, before being admitted to the Beatific Vision'.[9] The words of Jesus that there can be no forgiveness of sins against the Holy Spirit 'neither in this age nor in the age to come' (Matt 12.31) is thought to show that some sins may still remain to be forgiven in the age to come; and the Pauline passage about 'fire testing the worth of each man's works' (1 Cor 3.13) is believed by some to refer to purgatory.

Prayers for the dead should not be for forgiveness of another's sin but for their release from purgatorial punishment. There is however only a very slender scriptural base on which to found a doctrine of such importance. Yet the belief in purgatory is strongly embedded in the tradition of the early Eastern and Western Churches. Indulgences are still granted by the Roman Catholic Church, but only for the remission of penalties which still remain to be paid for sins which God has already forgiven. These penalties are due to be paid in purgatory. The concept of indulgences rests on various presuppositions. There is a 'treasury of merit' whereby the merits achieved by the saints may be set against penalties which are still owed forgiven sinners; and the Church, it is supposed, has the power to distribute these benefits to sinners in respect of our prayers or good works. Belief in purgatory is also to be found in other faiths.

It is congruous that the saints should aid us by their prayers (see p. 231), but it is incongruous that they should have been given benefits which may later be redistributed to others in need of them. It is incongruous because all God's gifts to mankind are of grace. Even if such distribution of benefits were to be possible, we have not seen, in our consideration of the Church, any authority given to it to exercise such powers. In any case, the idea that forgiven sins should still require the expiation of God-given penalties for sin even when God has forgiven the sins themselves, seems quite incompatible with the God of love; nor is it reflected in our experience of forgiveness by one person to another. For these reasons the conventional view of purgatory must be rejected.

There is however an aspect of purgatory which is of very great importance. If heaven may be compared to a party (and the image of the Messianic feast is commonly used in the Gospels), then we may reflect that people usually get ready to go to a party. They wash themselves so that they are clean when they arive, and it is customary to put on party clothes. It is commonly agreed that all sinful human beings, although called to be saints, are not yet ready for the very presence of God himself. They need further preparation. This is partly negative (washing), involving the stripping away of bad habits and wrong attitudes, and the 'dark night of the soul' in mystical experience may give us an anticipation of what lies ahead for all. Self-knowledge is always painful to acquire. But preparation for a party is also partly positive (dressing in party clothes) which involves being 'clothed upon' with a new body, and an opportunity for greater maturation and for the attainment of potentialities so that we not only display the image of God but become more like him. It is unfortunate that the traditional doctrine of purgatory has overstressed the negative aspects of what is called 'the intermediate state', because positive progress towards maturation is more important.

Some would hold that at the moment of death those who opt for God are miraculously changed so that they attain this fulfilment; but such a change to spiritual maturity is not warranted by the Scriptures, nor would it seem congruous with divine grace. In this life God does not miraculously change us, but he gives us grace to enable us to become more what we are. Purgatory should therefore be interpreted as representing the process by which a person after death makes further progress towards the ultimate goal of his existence.

Reincarnation?

Reincarnation is usually regarded with horror by Christians, as belonging to Eastern faiths and contrary to the Word of God as understood by Christianity. It is true that reincarnation has never been affirmed by the Christian Church, but in the light of what has been said about purgatory it deserves some consideration. The scriptural evidence for it is very slight. Jesus said that John the Baptist was to be identified with Elijah, if his hearers could bear it. Elijah was believed to have ascended into heaven in a chariot of fire and so he had not died; and his return was expected to herald the Last Days. However the words of Jesus could be interpreted to mean not reincarnation but that John was the person who should be regarded as the fulfilment of this belief about Elijah's return which is found in the closing verse of the Old Testament.

This one saying of Jesus is an extremely slender basis on which to hang such an important belief as reincarnation. Nor can it readily be construed from James 3.6 where the Greek text may be rendered in English 'the wheel of birth'. Nor can support be found in the Fathers. Origen, who is often thought to have believed in reincarnation, in fact held that the human soul had been created immortal, and was later incarnated in a human body.

The doctrine of reincarnation is often connected with the concept of *karma*, whereby each soul gets its reward or penalty for this life in the next. It is true that St Paul writes: 'a man reaps what he sows' (Gal 6.7), and the first two chapters of the Epistle to the Romans appear to support this view. But Paul is equally clear that whoever reaches out to God in faith is 'justified' (see p. 106) and forgiven. The doctrine of *karma* is that we all get our deserts in a future life; but Christian doctrine teaches that all are under the grace and judgement of God, and a 'clean sheet' is given in response to faith. However, the doctrine of reincarnation is not necessarily tied to *karma*. We have noted the immaturity of humanity during this life, and the need for further development after this life. It is possible that such development could take place not by embodiment in some future state but by reincarnation in another life on earth. Alternatively, it is possible that those who have died in infancy might be reincarnated so that they could begin the process of maturation on earth. Difficulties about the allocation of a soul to a body with a suitable genetical inheritance do not seem insurmountable. The doctrine of reincarnation receives considerable support from alleged instances of its having taken place. Experiences of *déjà vu* (the sense of repeating something that has happened before) can be dismissed as quirks of the human brain. However, it is not so easy to dismiss some of the evidence of mediums, and still more difficult the evidence of young children who have memories of the circumstances of an earlier life (including knowledge of places and relations) which correspond to what, after research, is found to have been the case. While some instances may be due to fraud, and others to telepathy, the general body of evidence is impressive.[10]

Prayer for the dead and the invocation of saints

Those who believe that our future fate is settled by God at the moment of our death naturally see no point in praying for the dead. Such a prayer could even be regarded as questioning God's judgement, or at best asking God to change his mind. We have already seen reason to question the scriptural basis of believing that the moment of death is of crucial importance (John 8.21ff: 'dying in your sins' does not necessarily imply an irrevocable status, nor does Hebrews 9.27: 'It is the lot of men to die once, and after death comes judgement'). In 1 Peter 4.6 the author asks 'Why was the Gospel preached to those who are dead?', which at first sight seems to suggest that the moment of death is not of such vital significance in deciding a person's eternal destiny. But the text may refer to the Gospel having been preached during their lifetime to people who are now dead.[11] However a reference a few verses earlier to Christ preaching to 'the spirits in prison' (another obscure reference which may refer to the fallen angels) shows at least that the preaching of the Gospel is not confined to this world. If it is held, as we have suggested, that everyone needs further progress after death towards spiritual maturity, it seems congruous for those still alive to offer prayers for progress on the part of those who are dead. If we can rightly offer prayers for them when they are alive, why cannot we rightly do so after they are dead?

The scriptural evidence for prayers for the dead is ambiguous. Prayers were offered for Onesiphorus and his household according to 2 Tim 1.16ff., but it is not entirely clear whether at the time he was still alive. It might be said that if baptism for the dead was permitted (1 Cor 15.29), then prayer for the dead should also be permitted. But the practice of baptizing for the dead is so obscure that little can be built upon it. There is certainly no clear instance in the New Testament where prayers are offered for the dead. But this again may be interpreted differently by different people. In any case the practice would have been affected by the expectation of an imminent Parousia.

Although instances can be found in second-century Christian literature, it was not until the third century AD that the practice of praying for the dead became common, and it is associated in particular with the eucharist and with inscriptions on tombstones. It is a natural instinct to commend a loved one to the mercy of God. The Church includes both the living and the dead, and we are all one in Christ, so that there is a spiritual interchange between people in Christ whether they are alive or dead. It is unfortunate that the question of praying for the dead has become connected with the Roman Catholic doctrine of purgatory, for those who reject the one can easily reject the other. There can be no objection to praying for the dead, although care should be taken over what exactly we lay before God in our intercessions. Since we do not know the state of the departed, our prayers can only be in the most general terms for their welfare and spiritual progress. They are in God's hands.

In the creeds of Christendom worshippers affirm their belief in 'the communion of saints'. This is an acknowledgement that the living and the dead are joined together by their union with Christ. It is a comfort and strength for Christians on earth to feel that they are one with the millions of Christians who have gone before them, some of whom have left them such signal examples of the Christian way. They are strengthened by the fellowship as well as by the example of the dead. They are comforted by the knowledge that they are still united to their loved ones who are now dead. The Church of God spans heaven and earth.

There used to be a clear distinction between the Church militant (here on earth), the Church expectant (in purgatory) and the Church triumphant (in heaven). The saints were regarded as being in heaven and therefore able to respond to our invocation to pray to God on our behalf, while the rest of the dead, still in purgatory and still paying the penalty of their forgiven sins, were in no state to do this. Such distinctions however should not be made. We simply do not know the condition of those who have departed in the Lord, other than they are in the nearer presence of God. Why should we not ask for their prayers, and invoke their intercessions on our behalf? If we pray for them why should we not ask them to pray for us? Again, we do not know what are the preoccupations of the departed, but it is hard to believe that they are not as concerned for those whom they loved and cared about on earth as we are for them. In such a case it seems appropriate to ask for their prayers.

It is the custom of the Orthodox and Roman Catholic churches, and of some congregations in the Anglican communion, to invoke in particular the prayers of Mary, the mother of Jesus. We have considered her position earlier (see pp. 94f.). Whatever we believe about her, there can be no doubt that she must have been a very remarkable person in her own right. Jesus in his human nature was dependent upon her for his upbringing, especially in those very early days when an infant's relationship with its mother powerfully affects the later development of character and behaviour. Jesus' character made such an impression on those who knew him that the combined witness of the New Testament is that he was without sin. This suggests a pre-eminent upbringing, which justifies us in regarding Mary as one of the major saints. It is right and proper to invoke her prayers along with others for the needs of the living, although whether she should be given the primacy of place among the saints is another matter.

In speaking of prayers for the departed, we have only considered the case of those who have died in Christ. May we pray for those who did not belong to the Church? To consider this question, we must consider whether they too have the prospect of salvation.

Salvation outside the Church

It was at one time the belief of Christendom that there is no salvation outside the Church. In an age when most people were reckoned to be Christians, and before the great schisms of the Church had taken place, the doctrine that it was necessary to belong to the Great Church in order to be saved was generally acceptable to Christians. Later, after the Reformation when there had been large-scale schism in the Church, the Roman Catholic Church introduced a distinction between membership *in re* (actual membership of the Church) and *in voto* (in spirit). Pope Pius IX wrote: 'We must hold it as no less certain that, those who, through no real fault of their own, are ignorant of the true religion, incur no guilt for this in the sight of God.' Invincible ignorance among Christians is not a sin.

More recently there has been a greater mingling of peoples belonging to different faiths, and this has led to greater understanding, and even to greater sympathy for them. Thus in Vatican II we read about the Jewish people that 'they remain most dear to God', and that Muslims 'along with us adore the one and merciful God'; nor 'is God himself far distant from those who in shadows and images seek the unknown God'. As for those who have no belief in God, 'divine providence does not deny the help necessary for salvation'.[12] The doctrine *Extra ecclesia nulla salus* (no salvation outside the Church) has been totally transformed. It is an interesting instance of the way in which doctrine can develop under the influence of a changing situation. It also forms an example of the theological danger of denying the opposite of what is affirmed. It remains true of course that salvation is found within the Church – that is the abiding truth in the doctrine – but it is not true that outside the Church there is no salvation. If it were true, we could hardly continue to believe in a God of love.

In the Church of England Article XVIII is headed 'Of obtaining eternal salvation only by the name of Christ', and Article XIII ('Of works before justification') describes works which do not spring out of faith in Jesus Christ as 'not pleasing to God and having the nature of sin'. These articles however, which date from 1562, depict earlier beliefs about salvation rather than contemporary views which have been influenced by a greater understanding of other faiths in the modern world. We have already considered in an earlier chapter the relationship of Christianity to other religions (see pp. 151–8).

Hell

Hell is very different from purgatory. Purgatory is a state of being when painful lessons have to be learnt, when people have to come to terms with their past attitudes and actions, and to become aware of and accept in its entirety the reality of their inner being. Hell is eternal separation from God, or rather – since God is everywhere – eternal inability to respond to God's love.

Hell, it is believed, is the sentence of condemnation passed by Christ at the Last Judgement on those who by their life, attitudes and lack of faith have deserved such a verdict. This Judgement is described in graphic imagery in the Book of Revelation; and Paul refers to it when he writes that 'we all have to pass before the judgement seat of God' (Rom 14.10), or 'of Christ' (2 Cor 5.10). The image of the Last Judgement was firmly planted in people's imagination during the Middle Ages by its depiction on the walls at the west end of many churches. In the Fourth Gospel the idea of the Last Judgement is still found, but it is somewhat modified. Christ, we are told, came not to judge the world but to save it (John 12.47). At the same time contemporary judgement is inevitable. 'As I hear I judge' (John 5.30). In fact we bring God's judgement on ourselves. The imagery of the last assize is a graphic way of expressing this truth. If anyone is condemned to hell, it is because it is no longer possible for that person to respond to the divine love.

Hell has often been connected with pain and suffering, as though it were the sphere where the eternal torments of an angry God are inflicted. But God is not an angry God: his nature is love, and his righteousness is manifested in forgiveness. (When we read in Scripture of the 'wrath of God' this refers not to divine anger but to the inevitable results of transgressing the divine law.[13]) So this concept of hell, which connects it with retribution, although it has been popular in many ages of Christendom, and can even be found in the New Testament itself, contains a fundamental misapprehension. To be eternally unable to respond to God's love must involve eternal frustration and eternal pain, because it involves a denial of a person's nature as created in the image of God; but this frustration and pain are inherent in the act of rejection rather than imposed from outside in anger and retribution. Perhaps if there are any such people, God in his mercy annihilates or 'decreates' them rather than allows them to suffer eternal frustration.

Every human being has to make choices in life for or against God, whether these choices are made explicitly about God, or whether they are moral choices which affect their deepest integrity as human beings.

(Many choices which appear to be choices against God are really only choices against the false ideas of God with which people may have been brought up, or which have been presented to them at school or from the pulpit or in other ways.) It is impossible to overestimate the reality or the seriousness of these spiritual and moral choices. They are brilliantly illustrated in the Gospel parable of the sheep and the goats. The choice is free and unconstrained, and made without hope of reward or fear of reprisal; but once made, its implications are infinite. 'The curse is upon you; go from my sight to the eternal fire that is ready for the devil and his angels. For when I was hungry you gave me nothing to eat, when thirsty nothing to drink . . .' (Matt 25.41ff.). The option of hell remains open for all of us as long as we are alive, for throughout life we are confronted by such choices. In one sense therefore, the question 'Is there anyone in hell?' cannot be answered until the end of the world, because so long as there are human beings on earth, they are free to choose the option of hell. 'It is *wilful* sin, the will turning away from God to the very end, that makes Hell. That soul is *in* Hell that finally rejects and turns away from God. It must be so. God himself can't alter that, it is the soul's own choice and abiding place – the abiding consequences.'[14]

Human beings are free to make these choices. Our choices are constrained to some extent by our environment and by our genes (see p. 64); but we still have real freedom to choose, especially in these fundamental matters. This freedom is not only inherent in our human experience, but it is also implicit in our doctrine of God. For grace is not irresistible, otherwise God would have created a species of robots, not human beings. God's great experiment in creation would not be justified by the emergence of rational creatures who love to order, and whose being is such that they have to obey his will, but by free rational beings who can freely respond to his love and who choose to obey his will.

But there is another side to this question. God's love is infinite. Is it possible for a human being to hold out against that love for all eternity? Would not that be a denial of divine omnipotence, an acknowledgement of the failure of the divine experiment in creation? Is it not in contradiction with the claim that Jesus died for the sins of all? We cannot set limits to the efficaciousness of divine love. Christian faith is faith in the omnipotence of love. 'I am convinced', wrote Paul, 'that there is nothing in death or life, in the realm of spirits or supernatural powers, in the world as it is or in the world as it shall be, in the forces of the universe, in heights or depths – nothing in all creation that can separate us from the love of God in Christ Jesus our Lord' (Rom 8.38–39). But Paul did not regard this conviction as an invitation to sit still and let events take their course, secure in the conviction that all would be saved. On the contrary, he claimed that he laboured harder than anyone in the cause of the Gospel. His conviction about the ultimate triumph of divine love, far from inducing in him an attitude of *laissez faire*, stimulated him to even greater efforts to spread the Good News throughout the whole world as it was known in his time.

Is it possible to hold together these two convictions – the eternal option of hell, and the conviction that human beings will in the end respond freely to divine love? Both convictions can be found in the New Testament, and that is why both universalists and their opponents can ground their case in New Testament texts. In terms of logic the two convictions cannot be integrated; but they are held together in Christian experience. We are aware of the power of human love which we cannot resist, even though we are also aware that there is no external compulsion on us to respond with our love; and if this is so with human love, how much more is it true with divine love? Again, we are aware in our human experience that we have choices which confront us with the seriousness of hell, and even though we have faith in the invincibility of divine love, that in no way detracts from the gravity of our choices and our knowledge that we may easily take the broad way, with many others, on the way to hell. We know in our hearts that we cannot trust ourselves to make the right choices. It is only because of our conviction that God never gives us up and loves us even when we are sinners that gives us courage to persevere. And so these two positions, seemingly opposed when set out in cold objective logic, cohere when seen in the perspective of subjective human experience.[15]

Heaven

It might seem at first sight that if heaven is the goal of human existence, a lot could be said about it. But even Richard Baxter, publishing in 1649 his 856-page work on *The Saints' Everlasting Rest*, devoted only a couple of pages to a description of heaven, and that entirely taken from biblical imagery. There are two possible ways of describing things heavenly. One is the *via negativa*, which points out dissimilarities between heaven and the things of this world. Thus heaven is not spatial, not temporal, not material. (It cannot be temporal, because time is as much a dimension as length and breadth and depth.) The other way of description, the *via analogica*, concentrates on points of resemblance. Thus the description of heaven as 'eating caviare to the sound of trumpets' focuses on the attractiveness of heaven and its glory. The way of analogy is particularly apposite for describing heaven, since in this life we already have a genuine foretaste of eternity. 'Realized eschatology' expresses the truth that the Last Things have already come, although it needs to be added that they have not fully come – daily life continues. Yet here and now we already have 'eternal life', and from this glimpse of the glory that is to be we can dare to extrapolate to the reality of what still lies ahead.

So far this discussion of the Last Things – death, the resurrection body, hell – has focused on the individual. Death is the loneliest event in human life, because it involves a journey which every individual has to make alone. Although our bodies are the means by which we communicate with others, yet they belong to each one of us individually and not to another. Hell is the result of the individual's choice: others may greatly influence us, but no one else but ourselves is responsible for our choices.

But the Christian life is not primarily about individuals: it is about human beings who are members one of another. They belong together in communities: they exist in solidarity with others. 'There can be no complete consummation for the individual until there is consummation also for society.'[16] Heaven is described in the Book of Revelation as a city where countless people reside, the new Jerusalem: it is significant that the Bible opens with a garden where two people commune with nature but ends with a city where many people live together. Heaven is not the flight of the alone to the Alone: it is the Kingdom of God where the sovereignty of God is recognized and affirmed by the whole company of those who live in him eternally. Hence the biblical imagery of feasting, whether a marriage feast which a king made for his son, or the Messianic banquet in the Kingdom of God.

The most striking imagery of heaven is to be found in the Book of Revelation. In it, we are told there is no Temple, for the Lord God Almighty and the Lamb are its temple. Here on earth a church building is set apart to mark the consecration of all creation: in heaven all is consecrated, and so there is no need of anywhere to be set apart. The city is described in terms of gold and precious stones, emphasizing its beauty and glory. There is no sun, because it is filled with the light of God himself. (Light is a natural metaphor to express the glory of God.) There is a countless multitude there, and our earthly worship in the eucharist is only a pale reflection of the worship of heaven. (We can only surmise, but perhaps corporate contemplation of God is likely to constitute the core of heavenly worship.) These images help to paint a picture, but it is only a picture, since there is neither time nor space in heaven. It is the sphere of the spiritual, not the material.

This leads to the question of what actually happens in heaven. This must remain a mystery for those who live on earth. But some things can be said. Whereas on earth we live by faith, in heaven we know God as he is. 'To know God is to know all things as He knows them and as they are in him. To see God is to see all things with His eyes.'[17] As Augustine wrote: 'Maybe when "we shall be like him" our thoughts . . . will no longer go from one thing to another but in a single perception we shall see all we know at one and the same time.'[18] Moral progress is always possible for created beings, even in heaven, for there is an endless possibility of progression into the divine likeness. Here on earth we strive after the good and the beautiful and the true: in heaven we have their fruition to contemplate and enjoy.

Quality of life is more important than quantity. 'No one ever wanted an endless quantity of life until discovery had been made of a new and quite particular and exceptional quality of life.'[19] Yet a major problem in trying to imagine heaven is that we live in time and heaven is eternal. Boethius' classical definition of eternity was 'the unending, complete and perfect possession of life all at once'. It is perhaps possible to get a glimpse of what this could mean by reflecting that when people speak, they may take some time to complete a sentence, and yet we can hold the whole meaning of what they are saying in our mind together; or again when we think of a tune, more than one note is in our mind at the same time. A distinction has been made between time as *chronos* (duration) and time as *kairos* (personal experience and action).[20] Heaven's time will be *kairos* time, not *chronos*.

There is a further aspect of heaven that must not be omitted, the close personal relationships both among people and between them and God. Paul came closest to this when he wrote that 'God would be all in all'. Although it is difficult to give this phrase a precise meaning, he must have intended it to signify that God so interpenetrates his creation that they become virtually indistinguishable from him. Men and women can have the experience of being most themselves when they are in such a deep relationship with one another that they are unconscious of their own individual being. This may be a pointer of that to which Paul was alluding.

'We see through a glass darkly, but then face to face.' In writing about heaven it is hard to improve on the words of Peter Abelard's hymn: '*O quanta qualia sunt illa sabbata* . . .':

O what their joy and their glory must be,
Those endless Sabbaths the blessed ones see!

Notes

1. See J. A. T. Robinson, *In the End God* (London, 1950), p. 10.

2. See H. Montefiore, *Reclaiming the High Ground* (London, 1990), pp. 126–33; J. Hick, *Death and Eternal Life* (London, 1976), pp. 129–30.

3. See H. Montefiore, *The Womb and the Tomb* (London, 1992), pp. 150–60.

4. See C. Hartshorne, *Logic of Perfection* (La Salle, Illinois, 1962), p. 253.

5. W. Pannenberg, *What is Man?*, quoted by J. Hick in *The Oxford Dictionary of the Mind*, ed. R. Gregory (Oxford, 1988), p. 772.

6. D. Z. Phillips, *Death and Immortality* (London, 1970).

7. See H. Montefiore, *Reclaiming the High Ground, op. cit.*, pp. 122–3.

8. See *The Tibetan Book of the Dead*, ed. W. Y. Evans-Wentz (Oxford, 1969).

9. *The Oxford Dictionary of the Christian Church*, ed. F. L. Cross (Oxford, 1958), pp. 1125–6. See also 'Reincarnation – Christian option?' in M. Perry, *Psychic Studies* (Wellingborough, 1986), pp. 175-90.

10. See I. Stevenson, *Children Who Remember Lost Lives* (Charlottesville, Virginia, 1987).

11. Essay 1 on '1 Peter 3.18—4.6' in E. G. Selwyn, *The First Epistle of St Peter* (London, 1946), pp. 313ff.

12. *Lumen Gentium*, para. 16.

13. C. H. Dodd, *The Epistle to the Romans* (London, 1932), p. 23.

14. *Letters from Baron Friedrich von Hügel to a Niece*, ed. G. Greene (London, 1928), p. XXXV.

15. See J. A. T. Robinson, *op. cit.*, pp. 108–23.

16. J. Baillie, *And the Life Everlasting* (Oxford, 1934), p. 249.

17. *Ibid.*, p. 222.

18. Augustine, *De Trinitate*, quoted by J. Baillie, *op. cit.*, p. 224.

19. J. Baillie, *op. cit.*, p. 205.

20. See J. A. T. Robinson, *op. cit.*, pp. 44–55.

chapter 12

Practical Christianity

Ethics and the Gospel

The foundation of the Gospel is the story of Jesus which constitutes the Good News, because it shows God coming to the aid of mankind. The Gospels show Jesus to be someone called by God and so totally filled with the Holy Spirit that he is transparent to God. He is God's image in human form, God incarnate. In his crucifixion he manifests the self-sacrificial suffering of God. This liberates us from ourselves, expressing to us our acceptance by God despite our unacceptability and setting us free from our past to become the people he wants us to become. The Good News of the Gospel is about this divine initiative, not about human morality.

But in a disintegrating society, where moral values instead of being public truth have become merely a private option for people to choose if they so wish, people (and especially people in positions of power who are responsible for law and order) look for a form of morality that will help to provide sanctions for society. Why not religion? Many people loosely attached to the Christian faith and most of those outside it think of Christianity not so much in terms of Gospel as of morality. Religious people, they suppose, are (or make themselves out to be) good people. But the truth is very different: the Christian Gospel is good news to those who know they are bad. Nonetheless there is a connection between Gospel and morality. Although the Gospel is primarily about forgiveness, it also has (or should have) as its fruit a changed personality resulting in altered attitudes and behaviour. People are not justified by good works: we have seen (pp. 106f.) that they can only be justified by grace received through faith. Yet unless that faith does make a difference to personal attitudes and behaviour, it is only skin-deep. 'So it is with faith: if it does not lead to action, it is itself a lifeless thing' (James 2.17).

The first duty of mankind is to love God with heart and soul and mind.

239

'This is the first and great commandment.' Why should we love God? Because in his love he is responsible for our creation, and because we owe all that we are and have to him. 'We love because he loved us first' (1 John 4.19). Since we are made in God's image, it is necessary for human beings to love if they are to be truly themselves. If they do not love God, they will love an idol in his stead. God is to be loved because there is no one and nothing in heaven and earth more worth loving.

The second great commandment is that we love our neighbour as ourselves. Jesus said that on these two commandments hang all the law and the prophets, that is, they lie at the root of all revealed truth about human behaviour. This second commandment is often misunderstood. It is not a command to love our neighbours more than ourselves, although it does not rule out the possibility of self-sacrifice on their behalf. We are commanded to love our neighbours equally as ourselves. We have already seen that self-love (which is quite different from selfishness) is necessary for our wellbeing (see p. 64). Yet loving our neighbour does not in itself define our neighbour. Jesus in telling the parable of the Good Samaritan extended the concept of neighbour. Samaritans were hated by Jews on principle; yet the Good Samaritan came to the aid of a Jew in trouble. The concept of helping one's neighbours was extended to helping one's enemies.

We have already noted that people are not mere individuals, but individuals-in-community. We belong to one another, and together we constitute a community. Communities exist at different levels; the close family, friends and the wider family, the local community, the community of work, even the country as a whole (see pp. 59f.). With the advent of instant communications, the world itself is becoming a community. Human beings live in solidarity, not like hermits and anchorites. It follows that loving our neighbour means more than loving other individuals: it includes loving people-in-community.

Personal behaviour

Human beings tend to be frustrated because their attitudes are often such as to deny their true nature. The Beatitudes in St Matthew's Gospel are frequently understood as ethical imperatives. It has often been said that the ethics of the Gospel are summed up by the Beatitudes. But this is not how they are presented by Jesus. He explains them as matters of fact, not as ethical imperatives. He tells them as illustrations of where true happiness actually lies. Those who know their need of God, the sorrowful, those of a gentle spirit, those who hunger and thirst after righteousness, those who show mercy, the pure, the peace-makers, those who suffer persecution for the cause of right – these people may not conform to the world's expectation of happiness; but in fact their attitudes lead, despite outward circumstances, to interior blessedness and joy. This is because to be truly human is to be aware of our creatureliness and to share the sorrows of others. Our human nature, to find real fulfilment, requires us to show compassion and to love justice. Those with an integrated personality display singlemindedness, and so they exhibit purity of intention. They are prepared to stand up for what they believe, come what may; and they desire to share with others the peace which they themselves experience. It is only when interior attitudes are consonant with their true nature that human beings can find real happiness.

It is these interior attitudes that determine our actions. Just because the Gospel is a message of God's love and acceptance of humanity, it affirms us as human beings, and starts the process of setting us free to be our true selves and to find the happiness of which the Beatitudes speak. But this process needs effort on our part, helped and strengthened at every point by the grace of God. It does not depend on our efforts, but without such efforts we lack the grace of God that helps us to progress. However there are many setbacks and backslidings for everyone on their journey through life, needing fresh starts and the knowledge of forgiveness again and again and again. It follows that, since we ourselves are in need of forgiveness, none of us is in any position to pass final judgement of condemnation on others. This is not to say that we have to shut our eyes to wrongdoing, or pretend that it does not exist.

It is important that we are aware of the difference between right and wrong actions, and distinguish these from good and bad. (Few actions are wholly good. Usually we have to choose between differing shades of grey. The right action is that which has a preponderance of good.) But we must not pass judgement on the people whose actions we believe to be wrong. In the first place, we may have made a wrong judgement ourselves in a case where choice has been difficult. Secondly we do not know other people's full motivation: that is known only to God. In the third place, while we are all responsible for our actions, some people have less responsibility for them than others, because of their environment and heredity; and we are not in a position to determine this: only God can do that. Lastly, we are so badly in need of forgiveness ourselves that we dare not withold it from others in need of it. Jesus' parable of the Unmerciful Servant is a graphic illustration of this truth. The servant, whose master had just forgiven him an enormous debt, insists on taking action against someone who owes him a trivial amount. Hence the teaching of Jesus: 'Judge not, that you be not judged.'

Personal morality

If we are to become the people that we are intended to be, we need the highest aspirations. 'Be perfect', Jesus said, 'as your Father in heaven is perfect' (Matt 5.48). What does perfection mean? It must be different for each individual, dependent in part on his or her particular gifts and potentialities. But a more objective standard than that is required. Jesus demanded our perfection as God in heaven is perfect. But we do not know God in heaven, and therefore we are in no position to model ourselves on his perfection. Yet we do have the story of Jesus, and in that story his character stands out clearly. Since Jesus is for us God in human terms, perfection for us must involve *imitatio Christi*, the imitation of Christ.

Perfection requires not only knowing the difference between right actions and wrong actions, but also how to distinguish between them. To rely simply on our own personal moral sense and intuitions is dangerous. Although we have a natural sense of right and wrong, and although we are promised help from the Holy Spirit of God, yet we are far from perfect and only too apt to give ourselves the benefit of the doubt in such matters. For all the God-givenness of human reason, it is as subject to corruption as any other aspect of our personality. In any case, when faced with a decision, we do not have the time in a particular situation to think through all the circumstances of the case. But we are not alone. We are members of the Church. We share in its common life, and we need to know, and we should hope to share, its common mind on matters of human behaviour. This does not mean that we always have to subject our views to those of the Church. Conscience is the moral reasoning of the individual in action, and everyone has a duty to obey their conscience, even if it is in conflict with the Church's teaching. But we also have a duty to inform our conscience about the moral teaching of the Church to which we belong.

The criteria of Christian morality

The teaching of the Church on moral issues is based on a combination of sources; the natural law, scriptural teaching, the tradition of the Church and moral reasoning.[1]

The natural law may be considered in three ways. By some it is thought to consist of general principles of conduct. But these are too broad to be of immediate practical use. We may agree that 'a greater good is to be preferred to a lesser evil'; but the principle itself hardly helps us to resolve a moral problem. Others regard those institutions which society has evolved, and which are universally or nearly universally supported by all human societies, as part of the natural law. Marriage could be cited as an example. But however much weight may be given to such institutions, it can hardly be proved that they are in themselves laws of nature. Society could have evolved other forms of association; and in the pluralism of our disintegrating Western cultures, it is difficult to discern institutions which are universally accepted or approved. There is a third way of regarding the natural law which has a better claim to acceptance. The world of nature has evolved in accordance with the 'laws' of nature and the constants of nature. There are also norms in the sphere of human activities, whereby it is possible to derive what ought to be the case from what is the case. To use organs or limbs of the human body for purposes other than those for which they evolved could rightly be called action which contradicts the natural law of their being.

The Scriptures give us a major source of authority for determining what constitutes right and wrong behaviour. It is likely however that all teaching, including biblical teaching, will be to some extent culturally determined, and that it will belong to the age in which it originated. Thus ideas about capital punishment have changed very considerably from the days when death by stoning for adultery as prescribed in the Old Testament was thought to be appropriate. Teaching in the New Testament will have a special authority for Christians. But this authority is not absolute. The decisions of the Church recorded in Acts 15 show how broad was the discretion given for the admission of Gentiles to baptism, a discretion which tended to be diminished in some Scriptural passages which reflect a later period. The moral codes found in the Epistles of the New Testament are to a considerable extent adapted from the Stoic morality of the day, so that they do not reflect specifically Christian laws of behaviour. In the Gospels we cannot always be sure when we are confronted with the authentic teaching of Jesus which has not been modified in transmission by the teaching of the Church. Furthermore it is easy to misunderstand some of Jesus' teaching by a lack of appreciation of the conventions of his day. 'It is easier for a camel to go through the eye of a needle than for a rich man to enter the Kingdom of Heaven' – this was not intended to be taken literally. As we have already noted, in Jesus' day exaggerated statements were regarded as vivid ways of inculcating moral truths.

The tradition of the Church is of great importance, because it shows the consensus of Christians of earlier times, and because they were open to the promptings of the Holy Spirit. This tradition therefore should not lightly be overthrown. But, once again, church traditions are partly shaped by cultural factors belonging to the age when they were formed; and so they are not unchangeable. The Church's teaching on usury (profit made from loans) is a case in point. Once it was forbidden. Nowadays it is encouraged, subject to certain safeguards.

When Scripture, tradition and the moral law agree, then the Church's authority on a moral matter is very strong. For example, Jesus clearly taught that marriage is meant to be permanent, and this teaching is confirmed by tradition, and also (when the psychological needs of men and women are taken into account) this is also confirmed by the natural law. Difficulties arise when the various sources of moral authority in the Church disagree, or where there have been new insights into moral issues. There are also difficult moral issues that have arisen which are entirely new, brought about by advances in technologies, especially medical technologies. Among these are *in vitro* fertilization and euthanasia.

Moral philosophy

A fourth source of authority for the making of moral decisions is the use of moral reasoning. Indeed, everyone must engage in some element of moral reasoning if they are to act in accordance with their conscience. There have been developed very sophisticated ways of reasoning about moral issues. Behind moral theology lies the discipline of moral philosophy. In any action there are three factors involved in making an ethical judgement: the intention of the agent, the nature of the act, and its probable consequences. Jesus himself in his teaching concentrated on the intention of the agent, because if a right action is done with a wrong intention, it is worthless in God's eyes, even if good use can be made of it.

At the same time, there is some point in the well-known adage: 'The road to hell is paved with good intentions.' Without an assessment of the nature of an act, and without regard to its probable consequences, a well-intentioned action can be disastrous in its effects. We have already looked at the nature of an act in considering the natural law. As for the consequences of an action, they are often unpredictable; but we may assess its probable consequences. However, it is quite wrong to judge the morality of an act simply by its consequences. This is very commonly done in our contemporary secular society, on the principle of utilitarianism. An action which benefits the greatest number of people is regarded as justified. Thus abortion is justified on the grounds that it benefits the mother-to-be who may request it. But this disregards the nature of the act, the deliberate killing of a potential human being (or, as some would say, an actual human being). Human personality is sacred, in as much as it is made in the image of God. This is not necessarily to say that there should never be any taking of human life, e.g. in warfare. There may be some circumstances in which warfare can be justified (and these have been developed in the doctrine of 'the just war'); but the situation must be extreme for this to happen. But (quite apart from the danger of a wrong conviction) it is unjustified for the state to kill someone simply on the grounds that that person has killed others. Similarly there need to be extreme circumstances (such as a grave threat to the life or health of the mother) in order to justify the deliberate killing of an embryo or foetus in the womb. In the case of a deformed baby, it is often alleged that this is to the benefit of the unborn child, but the instinct to live is very strong, and the huge majority of the human race, whatever their circumstances, would rather be alive than dead.

Moral theology

These considerations belong to moral philosophy. Their bearing on moral theology is obvious. Moral theology itself is usually considered as a separate subject of its own. However it ought to be intimately connected with other aspects of theology. Because the relationship between moral decisions and feelings of guilt is close, and difficult moral decisions ought to be taken in a spirit of prayer and intercession, there are connections here with spirituality. Since it involves matters of salvation and redemption, it has connections too with Christian doctrine. But moral theology is not a merely academic science: it has implications for practical Christianity. We have already noted that faith without works is dead. Works which deny faith make people miss the mark in aiming at salvation (as we saw, the Greek word *hamartanein*, to sin, means literally to miss the mark). 'My brothers, what use is it for a man to say that he has faith when he has nothing to show for it? Can that faith save him? Suppose a brother or a sister is in rags with not enough food for the day, and one of you says, "Good luck to you, keep yourself warm, and have plenty to eat", but does nothing to supply their bodily needs, what is the good of that?' (James 2.14–16). The same thought is echoed in the Johannine Epistles translated into the different idiom of divine love: 'If a man has enough to live on, and yet when he sees his brother in need shuts up his heart against him, how can it be said that the divine love dwells in him? My brothers, love must not be a matter of words or talk: it must be genuine and show itself in action' (1 John 3.17–18).

If there are so many sources to be considered in assessing whether an action is right or wrong, what principles should be used in this assessment? Here views have differed. This is to enter the field of casuistry, understood as the application of moral principles to actual cases. Casuistry has its origins in the practice of penance which began in the third century AD. Public penance was regarded almost as a second baptism. The idea behind penance was that in addition to forgiveness, punishment was required by God for sins; and it was better to endure this punishment in this world than in purgatory. A sinner who asked the bishop for penance was enrolled in the order of penitents, was excluded from communion, and before being readmitted to communion was committed to a course of prayer, fasting and almsgiving, the length of which depended on the seriousness of the sin committed. Even after readmission lifelong continence was imposed, and marriage was not permitted.

Naturally so harsh a system broke down. When in the Roman Catholic Church private confession became compulsory after the Council of Trent, it was necessary for priests to have some guidance for use in the confessional. 'Penitentials' were introduced, with lists of suitable penances for various sins. (Sexual sins inevitably feature prominently in these penitentials because natural selection has caused the instinct to reproduce to be one of the strongest drives of every species.[2])

At first sight penance seems far removed from the Gospel with its declaration of forgiveness, conditional only on our forgiveness of others (see p. 99). Overemphasis on mortal sins (that is, sins which if not forgiven would lead to hell) seems to deny the overriding importance of 'the fundamental option' (i.e. the fundamental choice of individuals for God, in the light of which those details of people's lives where they have 'missed the mark' seem of far lesser importance). But these penitentials, for all their shortcomings, served a useful purpose. They were a 'realistic acknowledgement of types of all too common human predicaments, and an awareness of the fact that law, even God's, does not automatically answer every query, but that for many much of life is a series of worried "But, what ifs"?'[3]

Out of this penitential tradition casuistry emerged. Various systems were adopted for deciding what was moral behaviour in particular cases. Probabilism does not mean what it seems. It is not the principle that the option which is more likely to be right should be chosen. Derived from the Latin *probabilis* (provable) any option that can be proved, that is to say, which may be rationally justified, is morally acceptable. This opened the door to plainly immoral behaviour and brought upon casuistry its bad name.

Probabiliorism is the principle that the option which is more likely to be rationally justified should be taken, while aequiprobabilism is the principle that one is justified in taking any one of two options which seem equally balanced. The principle most popular in the Church has been tutiorism, that the safer option should always be chosen. As an example of this option, in the Roman Catholic Church it is admitted that it is uncertain exactly when a fertilized ovum becomes a human person, but because it might be from the moment of fertilization, the safer option requires that abortion should never take place.

Objective and subjective criteria

One of the unfortunate results of casuistry is that it looks upon moral decisions as purely objective choices which a person must take. Christian morality becomes a moral law. The law determines what is objectively right and objectively wrong, and distinguishes between what is permitted and what is forbidden. This tends to overshadow the Gospel, which is about love and not about law. The Gospel requires the voluntary response of the human heart: the law requires the duty of obedience and submission. The love of God revealed in Christ invites us to take 'the fundamental option' of responding to this love by deciding for God, whereas the law tends to distance us from God by concentrating on our failures. The law is concerned with the minutiae of behaviour; but the Gospel addresses the whole person in terms of renewal and in a call for faith.

To criticize moral theology in this way should not be understood so as to depreciate its many achievements. Mankind does need moral principles of action on which to base behaviour. We do need to be able to state categorically whether a particular course of action is morally right or wrong, objectively speaking. We must not pull our punches, because this destroys the moral imperative of the Gospel, and the requirement to seek for perfection. Church people must have goals and ideals, and those outside the Church ought to be able to know what its standards and values are.

At the same time individual people struggling to conform themselves to behaviour which they believe to be right, must start from where they actually are. It is no good looking at matters purely in the abstract. It is necessary also to consider the personal dilemmas with which people are actually confronted at particular times in their life, living within a particular culture. Some actions may have been condemned by the Church on the grounds of some perfectly valid principle; but this principle may be opposed by some other principle which seems equally, or perhaps even more, important to the person actually concerned. It is necessary therefore to ask not only whether a particular option is in principle right or wrong, but also whether this option is more right for the individual person concerned than another option which involves another principle which may seem to override it.

For example, marriage is meant to be in principle lifelong. Remarriage must therefore seem to be always wrong in principle. Just as people's marriages fail for various reasons, so also those who remarry do so for differing reasons. Some whose marriages have ended may find it necessary to give and receive the intimacies of love and affection from another person in order to be their true selves. Or they may find that sexual continence is beyond their power to achieve. To forbid remarriage is to open up worse alternatives of inauthentic living, sexual promiscuity or inverted sexuality. Without this option they may find themselves becoming lonely and bitter. Although remarriage is wrong in principle, it may become the better option for some people whose marriages have totally broken down.

This position is very different from that known as 'situation ethics' which does away with objective morality altogether and according to which each person will make her or his own loving response in each situation without applying any objective principle. At first sight this appears to be a very Christian response. But who is to decide what is the most loving reaction to a situation? 'Situation ethics' does not take seriously enough the potential corruption of the reason. God does not illuminate all individuals so that they can instinctively make the most loving response to every situation which confronts them. We need objective norms of human behaviour as well as the realization that these cannot always be applied to complex individual situations in which individuals may find themselves.

This position also must be distanced from so-called 'pastoral theology' which so often appears to be a loophole for the weak, a softening of the demands of moral theology, in which pastors are exhorted to deal sensitively with penitents, to use 'prudent judgement' and not to hold people culpable where this is not appropriate. What is required is a moral theology which does not neglect objective moral principles and the imperative demand of the Gospel to seek perfection, but which also takes into account the actual situation of a person *not by way of concession* but as a vital and necessary ingredient in coming to a right moral decision. Moral theology ought to give weight to subjective realities as well as to objective principles. This is not to water down the demands of the Gospel, which are infinite. They call for heroism, determination and self-sacrifice. There are certainly individuals called upon to fulfil them literally. But there are others who are not. It is incumbent on all to respond to the limit of their abilities. As Niebuhr wrote in a telling phrase, the demands of the Gospel are 'impossible possibilities'. We must not give ourselves the benefit of the doubt by not taking them literally. At the same time they are not universally applicable to everyone. Since no one else can ever know the full story of a person's subjective situation, we have to leave it to people's informed conscience to judge for themselves what is right action for them in a particular case. Jesus himself seems to have recognized this when he replied to an enquiry about the impossibility of the rich entering the Kingdom: 'For men it is impossible, but not for God: everything is possible for God' (Mark 10.27); and again, when questioned about his stand against divorce he responded: 'This is something which not everyone can accept, but only those for whom God has appointed it' (Matt 19.11).

Behaviour of corporate groups and states

Morality is not confined to individuals. Groups and societies, corporations and companies are composed of human beings, and so they cannot escape moral issues: they act in a moral or an immoral manner. Corporate groups not only have moral obligations towards employees and (in the case of public companies) towards their shareholders, but they also have obligations to the wider community. Their operations may pollute the environment, or they may deprive people of an increasingly rare resource, or they may have adverse effects on employment or may result in holding the market to ransom. The Christian Gospel has inescapable implications for corporate bodies as well as for the individuals of whom they are composed. Christians who wield power in these bodies, in virtue of their Christian discipleship and as part of their Christian witness, should try to ensure that these bodies do act in a just and moral manner. This requirement of justice is not just for Christians;

it is laid upon everyone. But if Christians are in a minority in a corporate body, they may not be able to persuade their colleagues to this point of view. In extreme situations, where they feel that the injustice being perpetrated is incompatible with their Christian convictions, they may feel obliged to resign. However, if they do so, they will lose all future influence, and this will make it more unlikely that their colleagues will change their minds. This applies to governments as much as other corporate bodies.

The duty of government

Governments have a duty to see that primary needs of food and drink and shelter are available for all citizens, and also that justice is done to all. Christians can make personal contributions to meeting primary needs. This is particularly evident in overseas aid. But private generosity is not enough to meet public need. In the parable of the sheep and the goats, Jesus insisted that we shall be judged on practical works of mercy; giving bread to the hungry, water to the thirsty, housing for the homeless, clothes for the needy, and visiting those in prison. But personal charity is unable to cope with the extent and variety of these needs. Water and food supplies, housing, relief for the needy and arrangements for visiting in prisons need to be regulated on a national basis. They are the re-sponsibility of government: they are matters of politics. Christians, in order to fulfil the commands of Jesus in these and other matters, must be involved in political issues.

The Gospel is, as we have seen, about the Kingdom of God. The fullness of the Kingdom lies in the future, and so Christians pray, in the words of Jesus' prayer: 'Thy Kingdom come'. The Kingdom requires the acknowledgement of God's sovereignty over the hearts and minds of men and women. We already enjoy a foretaste of the Kingdom here and now, which was brought to us through the death and resurrection of Jesus. The Kingdom has a personal aspect, because it requires a personal response by individuals. But the idea that religion is a private affair, although very common today, is a recent distortion of the truth. The Kingdom of God also has a corporate aspect. It is about community, community united in its acknowledgement of the Fatherhood of God, and because of this, in its acceptance of the brotherhood of mankind. If the Kingdom is to come more fully on earth, there will have to be not only conversion on the part of individual men and women, but also changes approved by government in the structures of the society in which people live.

Liberation theology

There are those who are convinced that our first priority is to change the structures of society. These structures may so impede the coming of the Kingdom, in their view, that it is hopeless to preach the Good News of the Kingdom until they are changed. It is true, as we have seen, that structures do need to be changed, but mere change of structures does not in itself bring nearer the Kingdom. There were sincere Christians in the West who believed that when Russia changed its structures of society under Marxism–Leninism, this would hasten the coming of the Kingdom; but in fact it turned out to be not progress but retrogression.

Nonetheless we who do not live under extreme oppression are in no position to make judgements on those who do. The very fact that we have the opportunity to reflect on these matters at leisure contrasts with the tensions of those who live under terror or persecution. The oppressed millions of the subcontinents of South and Central America often lack all sense of self-esteem, living powerlessly in abject poverty under political oppression, while the wealth of the country is in the hands of a small minority of people who exploit their positions of power and are not accountable to government, or whose actions are winked at by government. People are subjected to violence, torture and even death at the hands of the authorities. Under such conditions there has arisen what has become known as 'Liberation theology'.

The biblical paradigm for such theology is the Exodus, with the deliverance of the chosen people from the bondage of Egypt into the promised land, involving their active revolt which was assisted by God in helping them to escape. (This paradigm was also used not only by Black theology in South Africa against Whites, but even earlier by Boers against the British.) Certainly in New Testament times the Jewish people lived under the Roman yoke, and there were those who plotted against Rome, and raised the standard of revolt, culminating in the disastrous war ending in the capture of Jerusalem in AD 70, and again later under Bar Cochba. No doubt the paradigm of the Exodus was not far from the minds of these revolutionaries. Jesus himself has been depicted as one of such; and he was indeed crucified by the Romans alongside two revolutionaries because the authorities believed he was potentially dangerous to them. But the evidence does not bear out the suggestion that he was sympathetic to revolution. He may have included Zealots among his twelve Apostles, but he distanced himself from political goals. He concentrated on doing his Father's will. It could be argued however that in those days, as well as in the early Church when it was faced with persecutions and martyrdom, the hope of the End was so vivid, and the Last Things were thought to be so imminent, that the political option never occurred to people. The evidence however suggests that the early Christians (quite apart from their inability to offer effective resistance), while resolutely refusing to compromise their commitment to Christ by paying tribute to Caesar, tried to distance themselves as far as possible from the state, and concentrated on giving no excuse for accusations of wrongdoing.

Liberation theologians do not think in terms of the imminent coming of the Last Things, but they concentrate on the actual situation in which Christians find themselves today. They put great emphasis on *praxis*. According to their way of thinking, action and involvement must take precedence over detached intellectual reflection. Christians, if they are to be true to the Gospel, must take 'the preferential option for the poor' and stand in solidarity with the oppressed against evil. One priest even went so far as to believe that the church to which he belonged was so implicated in oppression and injustice that he could best exercise his priesthood by helping revolution; but this was exceptional.[4] An early proponent of 'Liberation theology' wrote: 'All the political theologies, the theologies of hope, of revolution and of liberation, are not worth one act of genuine solidarity with the exploited social classes. They are not worth one act of hope, faith and love committed – in one way or another – in active participation to liberate man from everything that dehumanizes him and prevents him from living according to the will of the Father.'[5]

Such dehumanization, however, seems not to be permanent. The peoples of the USSR and Eastern Europe appear for the most part to have emerged from 75 years of dehumanizing dictatorship without much permanent damage to their human spirit. The Roman Catholic authorities, secure in Vatican City, found little difficulty in faulting the priority given by Liberation theologians to acts of solidarity with exploited social classes: 'The first liberation, to which all others must make reference, is that from sin . . . Structures, whether they are good or bad, are the results of men's actions and so are consequences more than causes. The root of evil, then, lies in free and responsible persons who have to be converted by the grace of Jesus Christ to live and act as new creatures in the love of neighbour.'[6]

Liberation theologians have been quick to point out that such a judgement ignores the distinction between private and social sin.[7] Into this internal disagreement within the Roman Catholic Church we cannot enter further. In Britain we live in a society which certainly includes a permanent underclass, and in which an increasing number of people are so imprisoned by its structures that they are marginalized and left without much hope. But in Western Europe there are few groups of people (apart from the Mafia) which amass great power and wealth in defiance of the law; and in this country the law itself can in principle be altered in Parliament through democratic procedures. The extreme conditions under which Liberation theology arose are not present, and probably for this reason it has had few proponents in the West. In our situation Christians rightly play their part in helping peaceful attempts to change society's structures where these tend to disadvantage the powerless, while at the same time acknowledging that the Kingdom can never come without a personal change of heart on the part of individuals. This change in turn will be followed by changes in the structure of society, but the change of heart is primary; and, as we have seen, change of heart is the result of the preaching of the Good News of the Kingdom. So political involvement by Christians is the effect, at one remove, of preaching the Good News; but in no sense can change of political structures be equated with the Kingdom.

Reasons for Christian political involvement

The reasons for political involvement by Christians are threefold:[8]

(1) We all have an obligation to speed the Kingdom of God. We have already noted that this obligation should be an effect of the preaching of the Gospel. The Kingdom itself can only come by the grace of God rather than by the efforts of mankind. Yet people can prepare for its coming. The Kingdom is not simply a spiritual concept involving the acknowledgement of the Fatherhood of God and the acceptance of the brotherhood of mankind. There are those who say that the Good News of the Gospel is concerned only with spiritual matters, such as salvation. But salvation is a word which includes wholeness in its meaning. Human beings have bodily needs which must be met, and material goods are needed if these are to be met. 'Earthly progress must be carefully distinguished from the growth of God's Kingdom. Nevertheless, to the extent that the former can contribute to the better ordering of human society, it is of vital concern for the Kingdom of God.'[9] The better ordering of human society is a political matter in which Christians must be involved.

(2) Christians were ordered by Jesus to love their neighbours as themselves. In corporate activities love expresses itself primarily as justice. Love involves preference; but to show individuals of a community preference is to disadvantage other members of the community. Loving

individuals means giving them preferential treatment. To give preferential treatment to certain people in a corporate body is to favour them unduly and so promotes injustice to the others. (It may be necessary to give preferential treatment to the powerless in society, but the object of this, far from giving special favours, is to promote justice so that they obtain their due which they otherwise would not get.) Justice for the citizens of a nation can only be obtained by political means. It follows that if we are to carry out the biblical command to love our neighbours as ourselves, we have to be involved politically.

(3) Christians must also give priority to the needs of the poor. In the Old Testament there are special injunctions to ensure that the poor are not neglected. In the New Testament Jesus pays special attention to the poor. Admittedly he said 'the poor will be always with you'. But Jesus gave them special honour, telling his disciples that the poor are blessed because theirs is the Kingdom of God. He went out of his way to make friends with those who were the outcasts of his society. Francis of Assisi spoke of 'my sister Poverty', and Bunyan noted that 'God's own are commonly of the poorer sort'.[10] But the honour given to the poor should not blind us to the need to relieve their condition. Every human being has inherent dignity, as created in the image of God; and so every human being ought to be treated with dignity regardless of his or her status in society and without regard to their poverty or wealth. Without this, people lack that self-esteem which is essential for their spiritual health. Jesus suggested that in helping the needy, people are coming into contact with himself. 'In as much as you did it to the least of my brothers, you did it to me.' As we have seen, charity is not enough: the poor need justice.

If individual Christians should involve themselves in politics, so also should the Church. One of the tasks of the Church is to challenge political decisions and political systems in the name of the Gospel. But the Church should never identify itself with any political party, for this would overlook its imperfections and would tend to downgrade other parties. The Church should make its views known on matters of principle when these affect political decisions. Every government is bound to take into account matters of expediency as well as those of principle. But the Church would be failing in its duty if it did not publicly as well as privately make its views known on the moral aspects of important political issues.

People have often had rather naive expectations of politics, expecting that through them the Kingdom of God on earth can be achieved. But Paul reminded us that 'flesh and blood cannot inherit the Kingdom of God'. There is no prospect that a perfect society can ever be achieved in this world: indeed the very attempt to produce it is likely to contribute to its imperfections. Politics are concerned with power, and so they tend to attract those who wish to exert power rather than to serve their fellow men and women. So sin inevitably enters into the very process of reform which is intended to remove it. It is easy to underestimate the sinfulness and self-regardingness of mankind. Corporate bodies tend to be more self regarding than individuals, because the sense of personal responsibility so easily becomes attenuated.

Selfishness must be distinguished from self interest. It is perfectly proper that every government should be concerned with self-interest. Indeed it would be seriously wrong if it did not, nor would it be likely to last long. We are commanded to love our neighbours as ourselves and not more than ourselves. As Archbishop Temple put it so well: 'The art of government is in fact the art of so ordering life that self-interest prompts what justice demands.'[11] That aphorism, however, could be improved: the art of government really consists in so ordering life that self-interest *is seen* to prompt what justice demands. It is often difficult to persuade people that justice really is in their self-interest. Justice demands more help for the underdeveloped world; but this is not often seen to promote the self-interest of a developed country. Yet this is not really the case, for without help underdeveloped countries will be forced to continue to degrade the environment worldwide, and it is in the self-interest of developed countries to prevent this from happening. And Third World markets could create jobs for the First World.

It is not the task of the Church to attempt to formulate a 'Christian economics'. Unrestrained capitalism certainly tends to marginalize the poor and to treat the people as 'the workforce', things rather than persons. But socialism, as evidenced in Eastern Europe and China, tends in the same direction, and a mixed economy may result in the depersonalization of large numbers of the population through unemployment. As we have noted, the Church should not recommend any particular political system. Indeed, it is not possible for the Church to lay down the kind of society most conducive to Christian living. This depends to a large extent on local circumstances, ethnic traditions, and the stage of development that has been reached. Western culture naturally assumes that the right form of society is democratic. But the imposition of parliamentary-style democracy on newly independent African states has proved disastrous, paving the way to demagogic centralism and national impoverishment; nor can a country like Russia, accustomed to totalitarian rule and a managed economy for 75 years, quickly adjust to attempts to introduce democratic government and a free market.

What matters most is not the political system under which people live but their basic attitudes and values. Jesus and the New Testament Church lived under the totalitarian system of Roman rule; yet the early Christians lived lives to the full in love and charity with their neighbours. Similarly, even under the tyranny of Soviet rule, the Russian people, with their underlying Christian values and attitudes, managed to find inner satisfactions despite outward oppression. What the Church can do is to offer basic principles translated into 'middle axioms'[12] to suit the circumstances of a particular society. Both capitalist and socialist societies tend to be dominated by economic considerations. The encyclical *Centesimus Annus* puts the point well:

The economy in fact is only one aspect and one dimension of the whole of human activity. If economic life is absolutized, if the production and consumption of goods become the centre of social life and society's only value, not subject to any other value, the reason is to be found not so much in the economic system itself as in the fact that the entire sociocultural system, by ignoring the ethical and religious dimension, has been weakened and ends by limiting itself to the production of goods and services alone.[13]

The same basic point was made by Archbishop William Temple in a different way:

As children of God, men and women are members one of another, and their true development is that of an ever richer personal experience in an ever wider and deeper fellowship. If then an economic system is abundantly successful in producing and distributing wealth, but creates and intensifies divisions and hostilities between men, that system is condemned, not on economic but on moral grounds; not because it fails to deliver the goods, but because it is a source of wrong relationships.[14]

All political systems and all economic systems, if they are to be adequate to the Christian Gospel, must embody five basic theological principles. The inherent dignity of all individual men and women must be upheld, and the furtherance of fellowship and co-operation among mankind must be promoted. Provision must be made for the basic material needs of people, and law and order must be maintained. We must respect the natural world, so that environmental degradation and consumption of non-renewable resources do not endanger life's eco-systems; nor must we steal the inheritance of future generations.[15]

Ethical criteria of the Kingdom of God

In this chapter we have discussed the moral choices which must be made in practical Christianity, both in personal living and in corporate life, including the responsibilities of government for which, in a democratic form of government, each individual must bear some responsibility. We cannot make the right moral choices without God's help. It is only by his grace working through human effort that the Kingdom can more fully come. That grace is not confined to Christians, for God wills all to be saved. St Paul puts the point with clarity: 'When Gentiles who do not possess the law carry out its precepts by the light of nature, then, although they have no law, they have their own law, for they display the effect of the law inscribed on their hearts. Their conscience is called as witness, and their own thoughts argue the case on either side, against them or even for them . . .' (Rom 2.14–15). God's Kingdom is not only where God is recognized as the Father of all, but also where individuals treat others as their brothers and sisters, and where corporate decisions are made for the good of all. Thus ethical choices have an integral connection with the Kingdom of God.

Notes

1. This and the following sections on personal morality draw heavily on my 'Introduction to sexual ethics' in J. Dominian and H. Montefiore, *God, Sex, and Love* (London, 1989), pp. 6–21.

2. See E. Morgan, *The Scars of Evolution* (London, 1990), p. 28.

3. J. Mahoney, *The Making of Moral Theology* (Oxford, 1987), p. 28.

4. Fr Camilo Torres was killed in Colombia as a guerrilla in 1966.

5. G. Gutiérrez, *A Theology of Liberation* (London, 1974), p. 308.

6. *Instructions on Certain Aspects of the Theology of Liberation*, IV, pp. 12–13.

7. J. L. Segundo, *The Theology of the Church* (London, 1985), p. 62.

8. I have followed closely here what I wrote in ch. 2 of my *Christianity and Politics* (London, 1990), pp. 17–25.

9. *Gaudium et Spes*, para. 39.

10. Cited by C. Hill, *A Turbulent, Seditious and Factious People* (Oxford, 1989), p. 87.

11. W. Temple, *Christianity and the Social Order* (London, 1942), p. 59.

12. See H. Montefiore, *Christianity and Politics, op. cit.*, p. 29.

13. John Paul II, *Centesimus Annus*, section 43.

14. W. Temple, *op. cit.*, p. 80.

15. H. Montefiore, *Preaching for Our Planet* (London, 1992).

chapter 13

Spirituality and Theology

Faith and belief

This book has attempted to give a reasoned statement of the Christian faith, showing it as an interconnected whole, and drawing on Scripture, tradition and reason in such a way that much of Christian belief can be expressed within the categories of modern knowledge, whether in terms of the natural or social sciences. Such reasoning is necessarily cerebral; and so the impression is given that the Christian faith belongs solely to the sphere of the intellect. In fact Christianity engages the whole person; the body, the mind, the will, the feelings, the unconscious, the soul. It is expressed in visual as much as by verbal symbols. It uses the 'right brain' as much as the 'left brain'. This chapter on spirituality comes last, partly because good spirituality must be founded on good theology, and partly because theology finds its consummation in spirituality, that is to say, in the actual practice of the Christian faith of which theology is the intellectual expression. Spirituality, as the word implies, is primarily concerned with the Spirit of God, that is to say, with the effect of God acting within and upon the human person, and then and only then with that person's response to God in his or her inner being and in the practice of a Christian life.

First comes faith, without which the whole Christian enterprise is an empty shell. Faith itself is the gift of God: it cannot be manufactured by human beings. Why God gives faith to one and withholds it from another is a divine mystery which we cannot hope to probe and about which it would be profitless to speculate. A person may shut his or her heart against faith; but no one can be blamed for the lack of faith itself, for that comes from God.

Arguments cannot prove the existence of God: many of them are crypto-theist in their assumptions, and the most they can achieve is to demonstrate that it is more probable that God exists than not. Belief is not the same as faith: it means belief in objective propositions. Assurance is not the same as faith: it means subjective feelings of certitude. Faith is a subjective–objective reality, that is to say, it is both about our convictions and also about Reality. But God is not an object. Since in a personal relationship with another person, we do not regard that other person as an object, so faith is best described in personal terms. In human relationships faith involves trust between two persons. In relation to God, Christians live in a relationship of trust towards him which permeates their whole being, consciously and unconsciously. Faith shows itself not only in unconscious attitudes, but also in conscious acts; in prayer, for example, and in action taken to carry out God's will. Faith may be of different kinds. At one end is *fides informis*, an unformed, vague faith, but nonetheless genuine: at the other extreme is *fides caritate formata*, faith fashioned by Christian love, involving not merely trust but a loving response to the love of God showered upon us.

Worship

If faith is a relationship, that relationship needs to be fostered not merely in a general way, but also by specific activities. It is not possible for two persons or more to have a significant relationship unless there is some meeting between them. Worship is the response of faith to God shown by the People of God. The word 'worship' means giving to God the worth that is his: that involves adoration and praise. Human beings are not mere individuals: they belong together, and when they meet together for worship, there is a strengthening of bonds between the community and God and also within the community itself. Worship as a communal activity is to be distinguished from prayer, which is an individual's activity. In worship a person contributes to an already existing stream of devotion, which extends from the local congregation into the universal Church, while in prayer a person is involved in a personal relationship which is supported by others but which remains essentially individual. Spirituality requires a corporate expression. Even the desert Fathers who lived an eremitical existence met together on the Lord's Day for communal worship.

God is worshipped with the head and with the heart. The whole person is involved, including the five senses; smell (when incense is used), sight, hearing, touch (in some traditions) and taste. Since human beings are distinguished by their use of reason, it is entirely appropriate that God should be worshipped also by the mind, and that there should be rigorous thinking about the meaning of faith. Passages of Scripture need to be expounded and interpreted for today. Prayers involve the use of the mind, so that it is employed both in the offering of worship and in the reception of grace through pondering on the Word of God contained within the Scriptures. Without intellectual rigour worship can become mere sentiment.

The eucharist

Although there are non-eucharistic forms of worship, the eucharist has always formed the heart of Christian worship. In some Christian traditions the eucharist is celebrated daily. In other traditions, it is celebrated only three or four times a year. This is not because it is regarded as unimportant: on the contrary it is so central that, according to these traditions, it requires careful preparation and it retains, as it were, its 'scarcity value'. People must work out for themselves the pattern of spirituality best suited to their individual needs. While a daily eucharist lacks the sense of 'occasion' of a weekly celebration, and can easily be taken for granted by the participants, it does provide a daily opportunity of self-offering and a daily sacramental renewal of the life in Christ. However often and in whatever way the eucharist is celebrated, it contains by long tradition both the Ministry of the Word and the Ministry of the Sacrament: the former prepares for the latter. Without the Word, worship would degenerate into superstition or magic, and without the Sacrament worship would be cold and cerebral. The appeal of sacraments is to the heart.

The eucharist has many meanings, which are shown by the many names under which it is known in different Christian traditions. The Greek word *eucharist*, as we have noted, means 'thanksgiving': the eucharist is a thanksgiving for the creation of the universe and for our whole redemption in Christ. In the Eastern Orthodox Churches it is known as the Liturgy, a word also derived from the Greek, referring to the public duty of a citizen. The Liturgy is not an optional extra, but a necessary part of Christian obedience to the command of Jesus as recorded in the biblical account of the Last Supper: 'Do this in remembrance of me.' The eucharist includes an act of corporate remembrance, in which the action of the Last Supper is represented sacramentally, and so in some traditions it is known as 'The Lord's Supper'. It is an action in which the People of God are reunited afresh with one another as well as with Christ, and for that reason it is known as the Holy Communion. It is also known as 'the Mass', from the concluding words of the old Roman Rite: *Ite, missa est*, by which the People of God were sent out into the world.

So the eucharist is not divorced from daily life: it is a corporate and personal renewal so that Christians may take part in ordinary life to the glory of God. It is sometimes thought that the setting apart of bread and wine makes it quite different in character from ordinary eating and drinking. On the contrary, 'the consecration of a part marks the destiny of the whole'.[1] Just as Christians are not set apart from the world but in the world so that the world may be sanctified, so also the bread and the wine are set apart so that all eating and drinking may be sanctified.

Here and in Chapter 9 we have considered the action and meaning of the eucharist. We must also examine its place in the Christian life as a means of grace and as a medium of spiritual renewal. Few people, when worshipping at the eucharist, think consciously of 'eucharistic sacrifice' or consider whether Christ is present by transubstantiation or trans-valuation. They join in eucharistic worship as an act of thanksgiving, as a way of renewing their life together in Christ, as a commemoration of his death and resurrection and as a means of renewing their own incorporation into this sacred mystery. In the eucharist they look back into the past at what Christ has done, and they look forward to the future to the 'Messianic banquet' at the end of time; but their focus is on the 'here and now'. They value the sacrament because its efficacy does not depend on their 'feeling in the right mood' or on the character of the presiding celebrant. They do not find themselves always concentrating on every spoken word of the service. They are stirred by sacramental imagery, and caught up in the sacramental action. Sacraments appeal primarily not to the ratiocinative intellect but to the imagination and to the 'heart', with its access to the unconscious where the life-giving images of our faith are stored.

The eucharist and symbolism

Jung has pointed out that there are two kinds of thinking. One he called 'directed thinking'. It involves thinking in words. Its material is language and verbal concepts. It is an instrument of culture, and modern education concentrates upon it, because it is vital for our modern technological society. There is another kind of thinking, which Jung calls 'fantasy thinking', when trains of images succeed one another. Verbal concepts cease, and images pile one on another. The process seems to work spontaneously and effortlessly, and without verbal forms.[2] We are conscious of this kind of thinking when we relax, and especially before we pass into unconsciousness in sleep; but to a certain extent thinking in images begins whenever we suspend concentration on directed thinking.

It would be foolish to suggest that whenever we involve ourselves in sacramental worship, fantasy thinking takes over from directed thinking. That would only happen if the participant drifted off to sleep. But it would be equally foolish to suppose that during the celebration of the sacraments we all indulge in concentrated directed thinking. That is reserved – or should be reserved – for the Ministry of the Word. Sacramental thinking is a kind of hybrid. It involves a mixture of directed and fantasy thinking. A person listens to the words that are spoken, and at the same time the eucharistic action triggers off sacramental imagery in the mind. The words of the service and the dynamic of the sacramental action ensure that fantasy thinking is sufficiently disciplined so that it does not 'take off on its own'.

Just as baptism is rich in the sacramental imagery of washing, regeneration, adoption within a family, drowning and being resurrected, and being sealed for our future destiny, so also the eucharist abounds in imagery. This is often evoked by hymns as much as by the actual words of the rite. There is the imagery of commemoration – 'That last night, at supper lying, 'mid the Twelve, his chosen band'; there is the imagery of spiritual food – 'Hail, sacred feast which Jesus makes'; there is the imagery of medicine – 'And by this food, so awful and so sweet, deliver us from every touch of ill'; the imagery of self-offering – 'One Offering, single and complete, with lips and heart we say; and what we never can repeat, he shows forth every day'; the imagery of unity – 'O may we all one Bread, one Body be, through this blessed Sacrament of unity'; the imagery of the consummation – 'O Christ, whom now beneath a veil we see, may what we thirst for soon our portion be'.

The ratiocinative processes of the conscious mind are certainly engaged by eucharistic worship, but participation goes far deeper than that. The life-giving images evoked by the eucharistic action form a bridge over which there is communication with a person's subconscious mind, with its access to the inspiration of the divine. These images are all connected with the consecrated bread and wine. So after eucharistic worship people feel renewed together in mind and soul, and the effect of the sacrament is to refresh and reinvigorate the whole person, and not only that part of it concerned with the discursive reason. People who participate in eucharistic worship have good reason to feel that they have indeed been engaging in a very real means of grace.

Charismatic worship

If Catholicism has always laid stress primarily on the given structure of the Church, and Protestantism on its given message, there has been from the beginning a third stream in Christianity where primary emphasis is on the presence and power of the Holy Spirit today.[3] Earlier in the twentieth century this tradition, in the Pentecostal churches, lay outside the mainstream of Christian life, but in the second half of the century the charismatic movement has grown greatly in both catholic and evangelistic circles.[1] The worship of charismatic congregations is characterized by exuberant joyfulness, with speaking (and even singing) in tongues, together with 'prophecies' and healings. Although the Apostle Paul claimed to speak in tongues more than most, he deprecated this in open assembly, holding that it was a gift for private edification (1 Cor 14.18–19). However in charismatic circles this often takes place (spontaneously, of course) during worship. The sincerity of such people is beyond doubt, and likewise their full-hearted faith. It may indeed be that there is a breakthrough in such worship into the subconscious areas of the personality. Whether or not a person is speaking lucidly in an unknown language or making sounds as though this were the case is difficult to establish. If the former, it is possible that connection is made with other people at a psychic and emotional level of the personality. When interpreted, charismatic messages are usually simple and doxological (e.g. 'Praise the Lord!').

The warm-heartedness of this kind of worship is in sharp contrast to the somewhat formal and cold worship that has characterized some forms of Anglican and Protestant worship in the past, and it is helpful if the charismatic movement can be kept 'mainstream' so that it can contribute warmth to the Church as a whole. However there is a tendency among some charismatics to assume that unless Christians speak in tongues, they are not really filled with the Holy Spirit of God: they are, as it were, second-rate believers. Again, it is often assumed that something is lacking to Christians if they do not always and at all times exhibit the exuberant joy of charismatics. But in fact there is something superficial about constant exuberance. Genuine Christianity has its troughs as well as its crests. Jesus himself wept on occasion, as well as on other occasions rejoiced in the Holy Spirit. The mystics write movingly of the terrible experiences of the 'dark night of the soul', when the presence of God seems to be withdrawn as a person is engulfed in spiritual darkness. Jesus himself is reported to have cried out 'My God, my God, why hast thou forsaken me?' Charismatics, for all their faith, can sometimes be sadly lacking in maturity and in the self-knowledge that is prerequisite to progress in the spiritual life.[5]

Prayer

If worship is a corporate activity, prayer is essentially individual. Two or more people may find it helpful to pray together, aloud or silently; but nonetheless prayer is a form of communion between God and one of his creatures. Prayer is the release of the Holy Spirit within an individual to enable communion with God transcendent. So far as human beings are concerned the essence of prayer is paying attention to God. 'Absolutely unmixed attention is prayer.'[6] Attention is not something that comes naturally to human beings: they need training to achieve it. It requires the ability to concentrate, and the necessary determination of the will to accomplish this. A certain tranquillity of spirit is needed, so that the mind is at rest, and not worrying about matters extraneous to the activity of prayer.

To pay attention to God is to become aware of his majesty and power, his glory and his fatherly love and concern. It is to peer into the eternal now in which God exists. The practice of the presence of God (as this paying of attention is sometimes called), which marks the beginning of prayer, results in its first words being the ascription (perhaps wordless) of praise and glory to God. Except in extreme circumstances when God's help is urgently required, genuine prayer begins with adoration. Hence the opening words of the Lord's Prayer: 'Father, hallowed be thy name.' To pay attention to God is also to become aware of our inadequacies as we bow ourselves before him; and this should lead to a deeper self-knowledge and penitence with an expression of heartfelt regret and a purpose of amendment for the future.

The question arises: if the condition of prayer is that we pay attention to God, can we be certain that God pays attention to us? Prayer depends on faith. There is no sense in talking to someone if we do not believe that he is attending to us, although in extreme situations people do find themselves crying out to a God in whom they do not believe.[7] If God is the God of love in whom we believe, we may presume that he hears such prayers with as much attention as the prayers of those of firmer faith.

Why does God hear *my* prayers? He loves all without respect of persons: each individual personality is unique, and each and all are the subject of his care and love. How does God hear prayers? We do not know. There are many many divine mysteries to which we do not and cannot know the answers. We do not know how telepathic communication can exist between two human beings separated by distance, although there is excellent evidence that it does. Similarly we do not know how our prayers reach God; but if he created the universe so that rational beings could evolve who are capable of communion with him (see p. 35), we may also assume that he evolved methods by which there could be communication between him and them. We do now know that all matter is interconnected, and we are beginning to realize that there are aspects of human personal existence which the natural sciences, because they concentrate on objectivity and repeatability, are inappropriate to investigate.

It is usually assumed that to pray means to ask God for things: indeed that is the prime meaning of the English word, defined in the dictionary as 'to make devout supplication' or 'to beseech earnestly'. However it is a very inadequate conception of Christian prayer if this is its main or even its primary meaning. Thanksgiving comes before supplication, for there is so much given by God for which to thank him before we ask him for what we do not have. God has provided us with the necessities of life; he gives us grace which we neither deserve nor always even recognize. In his providence we are surrounded by the regularities of existence which add to our feelings of security: we know that the sun will rise tomorrow as it did today (see p. 36). Above all, God has shown his love to us in the person of Christ, and his graciousness is bestowed upon us through the gift of his Holy Spirit. It is no coincidence that the central service of the Church is known as the eucharist or thanksgiving As with our public devotions, so with our private prayers.

Nonetheless we do rightly ask God for things. We do this in some critical situations when our need for help is desperate, or in times deliberately set aside for prayer. If there is a relationship of mutual love between God and us, it is only natural that we should open our hearts to him and tell him of our deepest hopes and desires, in the same way as children tell their parents. Even as we ask we are aware of the truth contained in the words of the Third Collect for Morning and Evening Prayer in the Church of England: 'Fulfil now, O Lord, the desires and petitions of thy servants as may be most expedient for them . . .' If all prayers were to be granted, life would be totally chaotic, and many prayers would conflict. If all Christian prayers were granted, life would still be chaotic. It would mean that we could no longer rely on the regularities of existence. It would result in prayer being a substitute for action, rather than the bestowal of grace to take action where the petitioner can influence the issue. In any case, our desires and God's will for us may conflict. Whatever petition and supplication may be, they are surely not intended to make God change his mind.

There are some instances where prayer in extreme situations does seem to have made a remarkable difference. This can never be definitively proved; but nonetheless circumstances are such that it seems very probable. This applies to prayers for healing (see p. 199) as well as prayers for help in some dire situation. We shall consider whether this is credible later in this chapter, when we examine the idea of providence. There are however many more instances where prayers have not been granted in the way which the petitioner requested. We may recall that Jesus' recorded prayer in Gethsemane that 'this cup pass from me' was not granted, but that he had qualified it with the words 'nevertheless not my will but thine be done'. If we believe in divine providence and grace, we shall hold that in every case there is some answer to prayer, even if it is very different from what was requested. In many cases what is given is not a change of situation, but grace to see the situation in a new light and the strength to respond to it with love and acceptance. We do not pray because we expect that God will grant our requests (in which case we would have so many disappointments that our faith would be under great stress). We pray because God within us moves us to approach God transcendent. We pray because we trust and love God, and want to tell him the secret thoughts of our heart, and because we believe that there will be an answer of some kind, even if it is not that for which we have asked. The very act of prayer aligns us with God, as we pray through Christ in the Spirit to the Father.

Meditation

In our human experience of love between two people, it is not always necessary to speak to a loved one within a relationship of love. There are other ways of deepening that relationship, including reflection upon it. The same applies to our relationship with God. Meditation may take two main forms. The first is rigorous thinking in the presence of God, whether about some short biblical text or some aspect of God's activity, deepening our understanding of the spiritual truths which underlie it and leading to an ascription of praise or some other specific response. The other main form of meditation, undertaken only by those who have a visual imagination, is to imagine some biblical scene which involves Jesus, and to immerse oneself imaginatively within the context, leading again to an ascription of praise or to some other specific response. In this form of meditation the soul passes beyond ratiocinative activity into the realm of the imagination and feelings, disciplined by the actual words of Scripture.[8]

Those who have progressed to the higher reaches of prayer have often lucidly charted their experiences, and there is a wealth of Christian mystical writings in the Catholic and Orthodox traditions; and there have been writers who have gathered together their testimony to show a general consensus about progression in the mystical way.[9] First comes purification, as the soul grows in self-knowledge leading to a deeper sense of penitence and to a more profound realization of acceptance by God which leads in turn to self acceptance. The next stage is that of illumination, when the soul is illuminated in a vision of reality which is characteristic of mystical vision, and is awakened to a new consciousness of the Absolute. This taste of transcendence is shared by some prophets, artists, poets and dreamers; but the experience is refined by the disciplines of Christian prayer so as to participate with Christ in the inner joy and beatitude which accompany this journey in love to the source of all love. And thirdly, after passing through the awfulness of the dark night of the soul, there is access to the unitive way, with experience in Christ of union with God himself.

If the whole personality is to be brought into the presence of God, it is possible to pass beyond the realm of the discursive reason, beyond the sphere of images and symbols, deeper into the ground of one's being. This is the deep level of contemplation, where the soul concentrates on God alone, and in union with God loses itself in the immensity of the divine existence. In the Eastern Orthodox tradition this is called the process of divinization.

It is sometimes supposed that for this form of prayer, which explores the depths of a person's being, and which brings an expanded consciousness of the universe, Christianity is sadly ill equipped. Those who in the latter half of the twentieth century have experienced the apparent enlargement of consciousness under the influence of drugs and other substances, and who have some knowledge and even perhaps some experience of Eastern techniques of meditation, have commonly supposed that prayer in Christian tradition is deficient because it does not open an individual to the oceanic feelings of cosmic consciousness which can be obtained through these drugs or Eastern techniques. Such a viewpoint is sadly ignorant of past Christian tradition, however much it may reflect contemporary Western Christian piety. The desert Fathers, the Christian Neo-Platonists, the monastic tradition, medieval mysticism, Counter-

Reformation piety are all rich in writings about the higher reaches of prayer, and in particular meditation.[10] The object of contemplation is well expressed in these words from the fourteenth-century *Cloud of Unknowing*:

Of all other creatures and their works, yea, and of the works of God's self, may a man through grace have fullhead of knowing, and well he can think of them; but of God himself can no man think. And therefore I would leave all that thing that I can think, and choose to my love that thing that I cannot think. For why? He may well be loved, but not thought. By love he be gotten and holden; but by thought never. And therefore, although it be good sometime to think of the kindness and worthiness of God in special, and although it be a light and a part of contemplation; nevertheless in this work it will be cast down and covered with a cloud of forgetting. And thou shalt step above it stalwartly, but listily, with a devout and a pleasing stirring of love and try to pierce that darkness above thee. And smite upon that thick cloud of unknowing with a sharp dart of longing love; and go not then for thing that befalleth.[12]

Something similar to the experiences of contemplation may be found in Eastern sources,[13] but these seem often undertaken not for the love of God, but rather for the personal experience of self-transcendence; indeed in the Buddhist tradition the whole question of God is regarded as irrelevant. There is a danger here in mistaking the technique for the goal. The danger is real, for when the soul is in touch with the psychic levels of being, there is need of expert guidance in a sphere where there are forces of evil as well as forces of good.[14] The experience of cosmic consciousness, found in the illuminative stage of the mystic way, is similar to experiences brought about through certain Eastern techniques of prayer; but cosmic consciousness, however similar to God-consciousness, is not to be confused with it.

Some people assume that these higher reaches of prayer are only available to a Christian élite, 'spiritual persons' who have mastered the long discipline of a life of prayer. But this is not so. There are techniques which can assist those as yet unversed in such ways of prayer. These include posture, the repetitive use of words or phrases (such as the 'Jesus prayer' or words from the New Testament). These act as 'mantras', stilling the mind and assisting concentration. Contemplation may come more easily for those of a simple nature rather than those of an intellectual disposition. It may be a way of prayer that comes more naturally to those who commune with nature rather than those engaged in the business and complexity of twentieth-century urban living. Certainly it needs space for its practice. It requires not so much an activist disposition as a more passive receptivity. Theologically speaking, contemplation represents the discovery of the transcendent God imminent in the ground of one's being.

The sacrament of the present moment

It may appear from a consideration of these higher reaches of prayer that they represent the proper goal of humanity in its pilgrimage through this life towards the vision of God. But contemplation is a gift given to comparatively few, even though it is, as we have seen, not something confined to an élite. There are certain people called to anticipate in this life what lies ahead in our pilgrimage after this life has ended; and certainly all are called to make time in their lives for prayer, for self-knowledge, for the practice of the presence of God. But not all are called to the higher reaches of prayer: most people are called to live active lives in the world, bringing up families, working for a living, benefiting their fellow men and women. It is not remembrance of the past or the prospect of the future that fills their lives, but the actualities of the present moment.

The opportunities of the present moment have nowhere been more finely expressed than in the writings of the eighteenth-century Jesuit J.-P. de Caussade in his work *Self-Abandonment to Divine Providence*:

The present moment is always the ambassador who declares the order of God. The heart always pronounces its fiat. The soul pours itself forth by all these means into its centre and goal; it never stops; it travels by all winds; all routes and methods advance it equally on its journey to the high sea of the Infinite. Everything is a means and instrument of holiness; everything without any exception. The 'one thing necessary' is always to be found by the soul in the present moment. There is no need to choose between prayer and silence, privacy or conversation, reading or writing, reflection or the abandonment of thought, the frequentation or the avoidance of spiritual people, abundance or famine, illness or health, life or death: the 'one thing necessary' is what each moment produces by God's design.[5]

The present moment produces both the challenge of divine providence and the grace to accept it and to use it. The present moment is the *kairos*, the moment in which God's will may be done, and eternity may be realized. The present moment is the opportunity for the establishment of the Kingdom of God within a person, the moment when the soul accepts the sovereignty of God over the small and apparently trivial details of life. One does not need to be confronted by great decisions about affairs of great moment in order to accept this sovereignty: it confronts us in the present moment in all the small decisions as well as the large ones. God is as much present spiritually in every situation of our life as he is present through the blessed sacrament: in the former case he is present by grace, and in the latter in a sacramental mode. If this indeed be the essence of spirituality, progress in prayer is no doubt an aid, provided that it is accompanied by genuine humbleness of soul and that it helps towards the acceptance of God's providence: but it is not necessary. 'The one thing necessary' is the acceptance of God's will in the present moment, and that is a possibility for everyone.

Providence, miracle and vocation

To speak of the present moment as providential requires some explanation. A distinction must be made between God's permissive providence, his directed providence and his special providence.

All things happen in this universe through the work of the Creator. He has given freedom to the universe to develop naturally under the guidance of the Holy Spirit. This permits the existence of earthquakes, hurricanes, droughts, climatic changes, plagues and other natural phenomena which take place from natural causes and which can have devastating results for human beings (see p. 134). They may cause the sickness or the death of millions. God does not actively will these disasters, but they are the inevitable result of the kind of universe that God has willed to bring into being. They exist through his permissive providence.

God has not merely given freedom to his universe, but also freedom to choose to human beings. They can make decisions which result in good or evil for their fellow human beings. Many of the evils which we suffer come from the foolish or unthinking or malicious decisions of others. God has willed that we should evolve with freedom of the will so that we may choose for or against him; and so the evil use of human freedom is also part of God's permissive providence.

In addition, there is direct providence. We have already noted, when considering the duty of thanksgiving, some instances of direct providence. God makes the sun to rise on the just and the unjust, and the rain to fall on the good and the bad. These are examples of direct providence. Bell's theorem (first demonstrated in 1966 by a theoretical physicist at CERN, the Centre for European Nuclear Research in Geneva) demonstrates that if two particles have interacted in the past, then each particle carries a memory of that interaction which can instantaneously be recalled, so subsequent measurements on the pair will always be correlated. It has been well said 'Bell's theorem tells us that there is no such thing as "separate parts". All the "parts" of the universe are connected in an intimate and immediate way previously claimed only by mystics and other scientifically objectionable people.'[16] Since all things are interconnected, there is a vast network of natural processes and personal activities through which God's providential care can operate. We have already illustrated divine immanence and transcendence by the analogy of an author who creates characters and gives them a measure of freedom to work out their role and to carry out his purpose; and this image applies to God's direct providence in the world.

There is a third category which is more difficult to discuss; that of special providence. It is impossible to prove that special providences exist. There are those who deny that they happen: 'Talk of God's activity is, then, to be understood as a way of speaking about those events within the natural order or within human history in which God's purpose finds clear expression or special opportunity. Such a view is . . . deistic in so far as it refrains from claiming any effective causation on the part of God in relation to particular occurrences.'[17] Nonetheless the concept of special providence is an ineradicable part of the Judaeo-Christian revelation, as well as testified in the lives of some individuals. It is by no means incredible in the light of modern knowledge. It may be compared to the action of an author who does intervene in his plot when it seems to be going awry.[18] Whether God does so personally we cannot tell. Although there can by the nature of the case be no proof, it is not inconceivable that there may be spiritual beings watching over us (as the doctrine of angels symbolizes) and that they may be able to help in averting disasters. But if there is sufficient grace in the present moment to meet any situation with a decision to do God's will, do we have any need of special providences providing us with special opportunities? The answer to such a question is that God may have special plans for particular people.

Special providences often do not seem to involve supersession of the natural law: they happen naturally, but it seems more than a mere coincidence that they happen at a particular time and place. In the words of a well-known commentator on the sciences:

. . . We turn to a type of phenomenon which has puzzled man since the dawn of mythology, the disruption of the humdrum chains of causal events by coincidences of an improbable nature, which are not causally related but which appear highly significant. Any theory which attempts to take such phenomena seriously must necessarily involve an even more radical break with our traditional categories of thought than the pronunciamentos of Heisenberg, Dirac or Feynman. It is certainly no coincidence that it was Wolfgang Pauli – father of the neutrino and the 'Pauli Principle', a cornerstone of modern physics – who outlined such a theory, in collaboration with C. G. Jung.[19]

Distinguished scientists who have investigated coincidence use such terms as 'synchronicity'[20] or 'seriality'[21] to describe an 'a-causal' principle existing alongside the causal principles on which the universe depends. They do not consider coincidence in relationship to divine providence but rather as a problem in its own right. The commentator cited above thinks in terms of a single irreducible evolutionary tendency towards building up more complex wholes out of more diversified parts. 'One might indeed substitute for the awkward terms "Seriality" and "Synchronicity" – with their misplaced emphasis on time alone – the non-committal expression "confluential events". Confluential events would be a-causal manifestations of the Integrative Tendency.'[22] For those who hold that the process of evolution is divinely initiated and divinely inspired, confluential events are providential, leading towards the wholeness which it is God's purpose that his universe should achieve.

Special providences do not consist exclusively of such coincidences. Some appear to signify breaches of the laws of nature. However we have learnt to think of these not so much as laws but as regularities. Life is governed by probabilities and not by clockwork. There is no longer a necessary conflict between the natural sciences and religion over providence. What seem to us to be breaches of the natural law are more likely to be the supersession of our customary physical regularities by the operation of some higher spiritual laws, especially as there is a flexibility in dynamic systems (and most processes in the world are of this kind) which makes it impossible to predict exactly what the results will be. Although it is customary to pour scorn on the occurrence of 'miracles' in some intellectual circles, these do happen very occasionally. The word 'miracle' means properly something to be marvelled at, and that is a very accurate description of it. How they happen we do not know – probably, as suggested, by the interposition of a higher spiritual law of the universe. This is an area where we can have no proofs. All that can be done is to point to some lines of possible investigation. The present state of the natural sciences is no longer so hostile to the idea of miracle and providence. There is the 'subtlety of behaviour enjoyed by complex dynamical systems'.[23] Matter is now seen not to be composed of hard irreducible structures, but until observed it is indeterminate in its micro-effects, capable of bilocation, and in its simplest forms comprising relationships between different fields of forces which spiritual forces could affect.

The concept of providence is connected with that of vocation. Vocation used to be used only of those called to Holy Orders in the Church. Luther widened the concept to include lay people as well, and this is now generally accepted. All Christians are called to serve God and their fellow men and women.[24] Some people however are called to particular functions. Many people have difficulties in deciding what their vocation should be in the secular world. They have to weigh aptitudes, personal inclinations and opportunities. Other people are conscious of a definite calling to some particular vocation, such as medicine, the ordained ministry, social work, assisting Third World peoples. Their vocation often comes to them through their awareness that they would lack personal integrity if they did not take up these particular callings. Just as with special providences God may wish to use particular people in particular ways, so with vocations he may wish to call particular people to take up a particular calling. This all forms part of his providential care for the world that he has created.

Spirituality

In thinking about spirituality we have concentrated on worship and prayer and the response of men and women to God's will in the present moment, and we have considered his providential ordering of the world, as well as our response to vocation. Spirituality is far wider than this. It includes the whole practice of religion. The earlier chapters of this book have been concerned not with practice but with theory. Their relationship is well described by a contemporary writer:

Theology and spirituality are two paths by which men seek God. On first glance they look like very different paths, but finally they converge. Spirituality proceeds by prayer, worship, discipline. By these means men have transcended themselves, their personal being has been enhanced and they have known communion with God. Theology, on the other hand, proceeds by means of intellectual enquiry. It accepts the rigour of a commitment to intellectual honesty. Yet those who pursue the way of theology find that this too is a discipline drawing themselves beyond themselves. They are drawn to a Truth which is no dead truth locked up in propositions or stored away in a book, but a living Truth, self-communicating and itself the source of all truth. A dynamic theology does not cease to be a scientific discipline, because it is inspired by the passion of an intellectual love. It cannot rest content with a knowledge *about* God and it positively abhors a chattering about God. Knowledge of God, like knowledge of friends, must ultimately be a knowledge based on communing. The knowledge of God merges finally with the love of God.[25]

Notes

1. This quotation is attributed to B.F. Westcott, by J.A.T. Robinson in *The Historic Episcopate*, p. 16; but I have been unable to trace it in his written works.

2. See C.Jung, *Symbols of Transformation* (London, 1956), pp. 7–33; also H. Montefiore, 'Symbols and the eucharist' in *Thinking about the Eucharist*, ed. I. Ramsey (London, 1972).

3. L. Newbigin, *The Household of God* (London, 1953), pp. 87–110.

4. *The Charismatic Movement in the Church of England* (London, 1981).

5. See H.A. Williams, *The True Wilderness* (London, 1965), pp. 29–34.

6. See S. Weil, *Gravity and Grace* (London, 1952), p. 107.

7. See *Peter Moen's Diary*, tr. K. Austin-Lund (London, 1951).

8. See B. Frost, *The Art of Mental Prayer* (London, 1940).

9. See E. Underhill, *Mysticism* (London, 1911).

10. K. Leech, *Soul Friend* (London, 1978), pp. 139–50.

11. See T. Leary, *The Psychedelic Experience* (New York, 1974).

12. *The Cloud of Unknowing*, ed. E. Underhill (London, 1912), pp. 77–8.

13. For a somewhat critical appraisal of Eastern mysticism, see A. Graham, *Zen Catholicism* (London, 1964). A rather more sympathetic approach can be found in H. Slade, *Exploration into Contemplative Prayer* (London, 1975); and B. Griffiths, *A New Vision of Reality* (London, 1989).

14. See A. Weisinger, *Occult Phenomena in the Light of Theology* (London, 1957).

15. J.-P. de Caussade, *Self-Abandonment to Divine Providence*, tr. A. Thorold (London, 1959), p. 33.

16. P. Seymour, *The Paranormal: Beyond Sensory Science* (London, 1992), p. 61.

17. M. Wiles, *The Remaking of Doctrine* (London, 1974), p. 38.

18. See J.V. Taylor, *The Christlike God* (London, 1992), p. 221.

19. A. Koestler, *The Roots of Coincidence* (London, 1972), p. 91.

20. C.G. Jung and W. Pauli, 'Synchronizität als ein Prinzip akaussier Zusammenhänge', *Naturerklärung und Psyche* (Zurich, 1952).

21. P. Kammerer, *Das Gesetz der Serie* (Stuttgart/Berlin, 1919).

22. A. Koestler, *op. cit.*, p. 122.

23. See J. Polkinghorne, *Science and Providence* (London, 1989). In his Templeton Lecture 1922 Polkinghorne writes 'It seems entirely possible that God also interacts with his creation through "information input" into its own physical process': *RSA Journal* CXLI (July 1993), p. 561.

24. See 'The Common Statement' in *All Are Called* (London, 1985), p. 3.

25. See J. Macquarrie, *Paths in Spirituality* (London, 1972), p. 72.

Epilogue

The provisional nature of theology

We have attempted in this book to consider Christian belief as a whole, and we have attempted as rigorously as we can the pursuit of intellectual honesty. The resultant theology is not the same as that which would have been produced two thousand years ago, a thousand years ago, or even a hundred years ago. The Christian faith is ageless because it is true; but its intellectual expression must change because thought forms alter, and the presuppositions and assumptions of one age are different from those of another. Very great care must be taken not to adapt the Christian faith to the passing fashions of a particular age, so that its message of Good News of God's Kingdom is lost; and the assumptions and presuppositions of the age need to be challenged when they can be shown to be false, and therefore inconsistent with the basic tenets of the Christian faith. On the other hand, equal care must be taken to inculturate the Christian faith into the language and thought forms of our present age *without in any way losing its core beliefs and the essential faith that these contain. That has been attempted in this book.*

The basic outline of the Christian faith remains after two thousand years of practice, commitment and criticism. Particular doctrines have to be reinterpreted in order that Christianity should be credible today. But it must not be assumed that this attempt is meant to be the last word in Christian truth. 'Every formulation of faith, whether made by an individual or the whole Church, remains imperfect, incomplete, unclear, partial and fragmentary.'[1] We can never verbalize the whole truth about eternal verities. Because we live in a particular age and culture we inevitably see certain aspects of the truth and miss others: later ages will correct our vision in those respects, but will inevitably be myopic in other ways. Yet, despite the limitations of any attempt to re-state Christian doctrine, it needs to be done for our own intellectual integrity as well as to commend the Christian faith to our contemporaries; and despite the rampant growth of secularism, the present age is a good time to attempt this.

Yet dogma cannot have a person's ultimate commitment.[2] That belongs to God and to Christ as the image of God. The mystery of God is greater than any formulation about him, and the mystery of Jesus is greater than any Christological formula. Christians are those who have obeyed the call of Christ to follow him, and who, in the words of Albert Schweitzer, 'in the toils, the conflicts, the sufferings which they pass through in his fellowship' can learn 'as an ineffable mystery' who he is.[3] All our dogmas are partial and our doctrines provisional. It is not by these, but by our prayers and our life that we make our ultimate affirmations about God, creator, redeemer and sanctifier.

It is fitting at the conclusion of this work to remind ourselves that St Thomas Aquinas, arguably the finest intellect in all the two thousand years of Christian history, had towards the end of his life a vision of divine reality in comparison with which all that he had written seemed as 'mere straw'.

As St Thomas was wont to write: *Exit in mysterium* – it vanishes into mystery; the mystery of the impenetrable splendour of the divine Being, to whom be justly due all majesty, might, dominion and praise, now and to eternity.

Notes

1. H. Küng, *The Church* (London, 1967), p. 343.

2. See essay by H. Montefiore in *Christian Believing* (London, 1976). p. 156.

3. A. Schweitzer, *The Quest of the Historical Jesus* (London, 1948), p. 401.

Index of authors cited

General index